The grace and duty of being spiritually minded : declared and practically improved

John Owen

Nabu Public Domain Reprints:

You are holding a reproduction of an original work published before 1923 that is in the public domain in the United States of America, and possibly other countries. You may freely copy and distribute this work as no entity (individual or corporate) has a copyright on the body of the work. This book may contain prior copyright references, and library stamps (as most of these works were scanned from library copies). These have been scanned and retained as part of the historical artifact.

This book may have occasional imperfections such as missing or blurred pages, poor pictures, errant marks, etc. that were either part of the original artifact, or were introduced by the scanning process. We believe this work is culturally important, and despite the imperfections, have elected to bring it back into print as part of our continuing commitment to the preservation of printed works worldwide. We appreciate your understanding of the imperfections in the preservation process, and hope you enjoy this valuable book.

THE

GRACE AND DUTY

OF BEING

SPIRITUALLY MINDED,

DECLARED AND PRACTICALLY IMPROVED.

BY JOHN OWEN, D. D.
SOMETIME VICE CHANCELLOR OF THE UNIVERSITY OF OXFORD.

CAREFULLY REPRINTED FROM THE AUTHOR'S EDITION.

"To be spiritually minded is life and peace."—Rom. viii. 6.
"Set your affections on things above."—Col. iii 2.

NEW YORK:
ROBERT CARTER, 58 CANAL-STREET.
PITTSBURG—THOMAS CARTER.

1844

THE AUTHOR'S PREFACE.

I THINK it necessary to give the reader a brief account of the nature and design of the plain ensuing discourse, which may both direct him in the reading, and be some kind of apology for myself in the publishing of it. He may therefore know, that the thoughts here communicated, were originally private meditations for my own use, in a season wherein I was every way unable to do any thing for the edification of others, and from expectation, that ever I should be so able any more in this world. Receiving, as I thought, some benefit and satisfaction in the exercise of my own meditations therein, when God was graciously pleased to restore a little strength unto me, I insisted on the same subject, in the instruction of a private congregation; and this I did partly out of a sense of the advantage I had received myself by being conversant in them, and partly from an apprehension, that the duties directed and pressed unto in the whole discourse, were seasonable from all sorts of present circumstances, to be declared and urged on the minds and consciences of professors. For leaving others to the choice of their own methods and designs, I acknowledge, that these are the two things whereby I regulate my work in the whole course of my ministry—to impart those truths, of whose power I hope I have had, in some measure, a real experience; and to press those duties, which present occasions, temptations, and other circumstances do render necessary to be attended to in a peculiar manner, are the things which I would principally apply myself to in the work of teaching others. For as in the work of the ministry in general, the whole counsel of God, concerning the salvation of the church by Jesus Christ, is to be declared—so in particular, we are not to fight uncertainly, as men beating the air, nor shoot our arrows at random, without a certain scope and design. Knowledge of the flock whereof we are overseers, with a due consideration of their wants, their graces, their temptations, their light, their strength, and weakness, are required herein. And when, in pursuance of that design, the preparation of the word to be dispensed proceeds from zeal to the glory of God, and compassion to the souls of men; when it is delivered with the demonstration of a due reverence to God, whose word it is, and of authority towards them to whom it is dispensed, with a deep sense of that great account, which both they that preach, and they that hear the word preached, must shortly give before the judgment seat of Christ, there may be a comfortable expectation of a blessed issue of the whole work. But my present design is, only to declare, in particular, the reasons why I judged the preaching and publishing of this small and plain discourse concerning the grace and duty of being spiritually minded not to be altogether unseasonable at this time, in the present circumstances of most Christians. And the first thing which I would observe to this end is, the present importunity of the world to impose itself on the minds of men, and the various ways of insinuation, whereby it possesseth and filleth them. If it attain hereto, if it can fill the minds, the thoughts and affections of men with itself, it will, to some, fortify the soul against faith and obedience, and in others, weaken all grace, and endanger eternal ruin.

For if we love the world, the love of the Father is not in us; and when the world fills our thoughts, it will entangle our affections. And first, the present state of public affairs in it, with an apprehended concernment of private persons therein, continually exerciseth the thoughts of many, and is almost the only subject of their mutual converse. For the world is at present in a mighty hurry, and being in many places cast off from all foundations of steadfastness, it makes the minds of men giddy with its revolutions, or disorderly in the expectations of them.

Thoughts about these things are both allowable and unavoidable, if they take not the mind out of its own power, by their multiplicity, vehemency, and urgency, until it be unframed as to spiritual things, retaining neither room nor time for their entertainment.

Hence, men walk and talk, as if the world were all, when comparatively it is nothing.

And when men come with their warmed affections reeking with the thoughts of these thngs, to the performance of, or attendance to, any spiritual duty, it is very difficult for them, if not impossible, to stir up any grace to a due and vigorous exercise. Unless this plausible advantage which the world hath obtained, of insinuating itself and its occasions into the minds of men, so as to fill them and possess them, be watched against and obviated, so far, at least, as that it may not transform the mind into its own image and likeness, this grace of being spiritually minded, which is life and peace, cannot be attained nor kept to its due exercise.

Nor can we be any of us delivered from this snare

at this season, proceeding from the prevalent abhorrence of our affections to things spiritual and heavenly, without a watchful endeavor to keep and preserve our minds in the constant contemplation of them, as will appear in the ensuing discourse.

Again, there are so great and pregnant evidences of the prevalency of an earthly, worldly frame of spirit, in many who make profession of religion, that it is high time they were called to a due consideration, how unanswerable they are therein, to the power and spirituality of that religion which they do profess. There is no way whereby such a frame may be evinced to prevail in many, yea, in the generality of such professors, that is not manifest to all. In their habits, attires, and vestments, in their usual converse and misspence of time, in their over liberal entertainment of themselves and others, to the borders of excess, and sundry other things of a like nature; there is in many such a conformity to the world, (a thing severely forbidden,) that it is hard to make a distinction between them. And these things do manifest such a predominancy of carnal affections in the minds of men, as, whatever may be pretended to the contrary, it is inconsistent with spiritual peace. To call men off from this evil frame of heart and mind, to discover the sin and danger of it, to direct them to the ways and means whereby it may be effected, to supply their thoughts and affections with better objects, to discover and press that exercise of them which is indispensably required of all believers, if they desire life and peace, is some part of the work of the ensuing discourse. It may be, it will be judged but a weak attempt as to the attaining of that end: but it cannot be denied to have these two advantages—first, that it is seasonable—and secondly, that it is sincerely intended. And if it have this only success, that it may occasion others, who have more ability and opportunity than I have, to bring in their assistance for an opposition to the vehement and importunate insinuations of the world in these things, to have an entertainment in the minds of professors, this labor will not be lost. But things are come to that pass amongst us, that unless a more than ordinary vigorous exercise of the ministry of the word, with other means appointed to the same end, be engaged in, to recall professors to that strict mortification, that separation from the ways of the world, that heavenly mindedness, that delight in the contemplation of spiritual things, which the gospel, and the whole nature of the Christian religion do require; we shall lose the glory of our profession, and leave it very uncertain what will be our eternal condition. The same may be spoken concerning love of the world, as to the advantages and emoluments which men trust to attain to themselves thereby. This is that which renders men earthly minded, and most remote from having their conversations above. In the pursuit of this corrupt affection do many professors of religion grow withering, useless, sapless; giving no evidence that the love of God abideth in them. On these and many other accounts, do many Christians evidence themselves to be strangers to spiritual mindedness, from a life of meditation and holy contemplation on things above: yet unless we are found in these things in some good measure, no grace will thrive or flourish in us; no duty will be rightly performed by us; no condition sanctified or improved: nor are we prepared in a due manner, or made meet for the inheritance of the saints in light. Wherefore, as was said, to direct and provoke men to that which is the only remedy of all these evils, which alone is the means of giving them a view into, and a foretaste of, eternal glory; especially to such who are in my own condition, namely, in a very near approach to a departure out of this world; is the design and scope of the ensuing discourse, which is recommended to the grace of God, for the benefit of the reader.

ROMANS VIII. VI.

BUT TO BE SPIRITUALLY MINDED IS LIFE AND PEACE.

CHAPTER I.

The words of the Text explained.

The expression in our translation sounds differently from that in the original. To be spiritually minded, say we. In the original it is phronema tou pneumatos as that in the former part of the verse is phronema tes sarkos; which we render to be carnally minded. In the margin we read, the minding of the flesh and the minding of the spirit. And there is great variety in the rendering of the words in all translations, both ancient and modern. Prudentia, Sapientia, Intelligentia, Mens, Cogitatio, Discretio, id quod Spiritus sapit; the Wisdom, the Understanding, the mind, the Thought or Contrivance, the Discretion of the Spirit, that which the spirit savoreth, are used to express it. All our English translations, from Tindal's the first of them, have constantly used, to be spiritually minded. Neither do I know any words whereby the emphasis of the original, considering the design of the apostle in the place, can be better expressed. But the meaning of the Holy Ghost in them must be further inquired into.

In the whole verse there are two entire propositions,

containing a double antithesis, the one in their subjects, the other in their predicates. And this opposition is the highest and greatest, that is, between eternal blessedness, and eternal ruin.

The opposite subjects, are the minding of the flesh, and the minding of the spirit; or the being carnally minded, and spiritually minded. And these two do constitute two states of mankind, unto the one of which every individual person in the world doth belong. And it is of the highest concernment unto the souls of men, to know unto which of them they appertain. As unto the qualities expressed by the flesh and the spirit, there may be a mixture of them in the same persons at the same time; there is so in all that are regenerate. For in them the flesh lusteth against the spirit, and the spirit lusteth against the flesh, and these are contrary. Gal. v. 17. Thus different contrary actings in the same subject constitute not distinct states. But where either of them is predominant, or hath a prevalent rule in the soul, there it makes a different state. This distinction of states, the apostle expresseth, v. 9. 'But ye are not in the flesh, but in the spirit.' Some are in the flesh, and cannot please God, v. 8. They are after the flesh v. 5. they walk after the flesh, v. 1. they live after the flesh v. 13.—This is one state. Others are in the spirit, v. 9. after the spirit, v. 5. walk after the spirit, v. 1. This is the other state. The first sort are carnally minded, the other are spiritually minded. Unto one of these, doth every living man belong; he is under the ruling conduct of the flesh, or of the spirit; there is no middle state; though there are different degress in each of these as to good and evil.

The difference between these two states is great,

and the distance in a manner infinite, because an eternity, in blessedness or misery doth depend upon it.—And this at present is evidenced by the different fruits and effects of the principles and their operations, which constitute these different states; which is expressed in the opposition that is between the predicates of the proposition; for the minding of the flesh is death; but the minding of the spirit is life and peace.

1. To be carnally minded is death. Death, as it is absolutely penal, is either spiritual, or eternal. The first of these it is formally, the other meritoriously. It is formally death spiritual; for they that are carnally minded, are dead in trespasses and sins, Eph. ii. 1. For those who fulfil the desires of the flesh and of the mind, are by nature children of wrath, v. 3. are penally under the power of spiritual death. They are dead in sins and the uncircumcision of the flesh, Coll. ii. 13.'

And it is death eternal, meritoriously. 'For if ye live after the flesh ye shall die, Rom. viii. 13. as the wages of sin is death, chap. vi. 23.'

The reason why the apostle denounces so woful a doom, so dreadful a sentence, on the carnal mind, he declares in the two next verses: 'for the carnal mind is enmity against God; for it is not subject unto the law of God, nor indeed can be; so then they that are in the flesh cannot please God. If it be thus with the carnal mind, it is no wonder that to be carnally minded is death; it is not meet it should be any thing else. That which is enmity against God, is under the curse of God.

In opposition hereunto it is affirmed, that to be spiritually minded, or the minding of the spirit, is life and peace. And these are the things which we are particularly to inquire into; namely, What is this minding of the spirit; and then, How it is life and peace.

1. The *spirit*, in this context, is evidently used in a double sense, as is usual where both the Holy Spirit himself, and his work on the souls of men, are related unto—1. The person of the Spirit of God himself, or the Holy Ghost, is intended by it, v. 9. If so be that the Spirit of God dwelleth in you. And so also v. 11. The spirit of him that raised up Jesus from the dead. He is spoken of as the principal efficient cause of all the spiritual mercies and benefits here and afterwards insisted on. 2. It is used for the principle of spiritual life wrought in all that are regenerate by the Holy Ghost.—'For that which is born of the Spirit is Spirit,' John iii. 6.

It is most probable that the name spirit is here used in the latter sense, not for the spirit himself, but for that which is born of the spirit, the principle of spiritual life in them that are born of God. For it is in its nature, actings, inclinations, and operations, opposed unto the flesh, v. 1. 4, 5; but the flesh here intended is that inherent corrupt principle of depraved nature, whence all evil actions do proceed, and wherewith the actions of all evil men are vitiated. The opposition between them is the same with that mentioned and declared by the apostle, Gal. v. 17, 18, &c. Wherefore the spirit in this place is the 'holy vital principle of new obedience wrought in the souls of believers by the Holy Ghost, enabling them to live unto God.'

2. Unto the spirit there is phronema ascribed, which, as we have intimated, is translated with great variety. Phronesis, is the principal power and act of the mind. It is its light, wisdom, prudence, knowledge, understanding, and discretion. It is not so with respect unto

speculation, or ratiocination merely; which is danoia, or sunesis. But this phronesis is its power as it is practical, including the habitual frame and inclination of the affections also. It is its faculty to conceive of things with a delight in them and adherence unto them from that suitableness which it finds in them, unto all its affections. Hence we translate phonein sometimes to think, that is, to conceive and judge, Rom. xii. 3. Sometimes to set the affections, Col. iii. 3. to have such an apprehension of things as to cleave unto them with our affections. Sometimes to mind; to mind earthly things, Phil iii. 19, which includeth that relish and savor which the mind finds in the things it is fixed on. No where doth it design a notional conception of things only; but principally the engagement of the affections unto the things which the mind apprehends.

Phronema, the word here used, expresseth the actual exercise tes phroneseos, of the power of the mind before described. Wherefore the minding of the spirit is the actual exercise of the mind as renewed by the Holy Ghost, as furnished with a principle of spiritual life and light in its conception of spiritual things, and the setting of its affection of them, as finding that relish and savor in them, wherewith it is pleased and satisfied.

And something we must yet further observe, to give light unto this description on the minding of the Spirit, as it is here spoken of.

1. It is not spoken of absolutely as unto what it is in itself, but with respect unto its power and prevalency in us; significantly rendered to be spiritually minded; that is, to have the mind changed and renewed by a principle of spiritual life and light, so as to be continually

acted and influenced thereby unto thoughts and meditations of spiritual things, from the affections cleaving unto them with delight and satisfaction. So on the contrary it is when men mind earthly things. From a principle of love unto them, arising from their suitableness unto their corrupt affections, their thoughts, meditations, and desires, are continually engaged about them. Wherefore,

2. Three things may be distinguished in the great duty of being spiritually minded, under which notion it is here recommended unto us.

1. The actual exercise of the mind in its thoughts, meditations, and desires about things spiritual and heavenly. So it is expressed in the verse foregoing. They that are after the flesh do mind the things of the flesh; they think on them, their contrivances about them, and their desires after them. But they that are after the spirit, the things of the spirit. They mind them by fixing their thoughts and meditations upon them.

2. The inclination, disposition, and frame of the mind, in all its affections, whereby it adheres and cleaves unto spiritual things. This minding of the spirit resides habitually in the affections. Wherefore the phronema of the spirit, or the mind, as renewed and acted by a spiritual principle of light and life, is the exercise of its thoughts, meditations, and desires, on spiritual things, proceeding from the love and delight of its affections in them, and engagement unto them.

3. A complacency of mind from that gust, relish, and savor, which it finds in spiritual things, from their suitableness unto its constitution, inclinations, and desires. There is a *salt* in spiritual things, whereby they are condited and made *savory* unto a renewed mind: though to others they are as the *white of an egg*,

that hath no taste or savor in it. In this *gust and relish* lies the sweetness and satisfaction of spiritual life. Speculative notions about spiritual things, when they are alone, are dry, sapless, and barren. In this *gust* we taste by experience that God is gracious, and that the love of Christ is better than wine, or whatever else hath the most grateful relish unto a sensual appetite. This is the proper foundation of that joy which is unspeakable and full of glory.

All these things do concur in the minding of the spirit, or to constitute any person spiritually minded. And although the foundation of the whole duty included in it, lies in the *affections*, and their immediate adherence unto spiritual things, whence the thoughts and meditations of the mind about them do proceed, yet I shall treat of the distinct parts of this duty in the order laid down, beginning with the exercise of our thoughts and meditations about them. For they being the first genuine actings of the mind, according unto the prevalency of affections in it, they will make the best and most evident discovery of what nature the spring is from whence they do arise. And I shall not need to speak distinctly unto what is mentioned in the third place, concerning the *complacency* of the mind in what its affections are fixed on, for it will fall in with sundry other things that are to be spoken unto.

But before we do proceed, it is not amiss, as I suppose, to put a remark upon those important truths, which are directly contained in the words proposed as the foundation of the present discourse. As,

1. To be spiritually minded is the great distinguishing character of true believers from all unregenerate persons. As such is it here asserted by the Apostle. All those who are carnally minded, who are in the flesh,

they are unregenerate, they are not born of God, they please him not, nor can do so, but must perish for ever. But those who are spiritually minded, are born of God, do live unto him, and shall come to the enjoyment of him. Hereon depends the trial and determination of what state we do belong unto.

2. Where any are spiritually minded, there, and there alone, is life and peace. What these are, wherein they do consist, what is their excellency and pre-eminence above all things in this world, how they are the *effects* and consequents of our being spiritually minded, shall be afterwards declared.

There is neither of these considerations, but is sufficient to demonstrate of how great concernment unto us it is to be spiritually minded, and diligently to inquire whether we are so or not.

It will therefore be no small advantage unto us, to have our souls and consciences always affected with, and in due subjection unto, the power of this truth; namely, that to be spiritually minded is life and peace; whence it will follow, that whatever we may think otherwise, if we are not so, we have neither of them, neither life nor peace. It will, I say, be of use unto us, if we are affected with the power of it. For many greatly deceive themselves in hearing the word. They admit of sacred truths in their understanding, and assent unto them; but take not in the power of them on their consciences, nor strictly judge of their state and condition by them, which proves their ruin. For hereby they seem to themselves to believe that, whereof in truth they believe not one *syllable* as they ought. They hear it, they understand it in the notion of it, they assent unto it, at least they do not contradict it; yea, they commend it oftentimes, and approve of it; but yet they believe it not; for if they did, they would judge themselves by it, and reckon it, that it will be with them at the last day, according as things are determined therein.

Or such persons are, as the apostle *James* declares, like a man beholding his natural face in a glass; 'for he beholdeth himself, and goeth his way, and straightway forgetteth what manner of man he was, Jam. i. 23, 24.' There is a representation made of them, their state and condition unto them in the word they behold it, and conclude that it is even so with them, as the word doth declare. But immediately their minds are filled with other thoughts, acted by other affections, taken up with other occasions, and they forget in a moment the representation made of themselves and their condition.—Wherefore all that I have to offer on this subject will be utterly lost, unless a firm persuasion hereof be fixed on our minds, unless we are under the power of it, that to be spiritually minded is life and peace; so that whatever our light and profession be, our knowledge or our duty, without this we have indeed no real interest in life and peace.

These things being premised, I shall more practically open the nature of this duty, and what is required unto this frame of spirit. To be spiritually minded may be considered either as unto the *nature* and *essence* of it, or as unto its *degrees;* for one may be so more than another, or the same person may be more so at one time than another. In the first way it is opposed unto being carnally minded; in the other, unto being earthly minded.

To be carnally minded is, as the Apostle speaks, *death;* it is so every way; and they who are so, are dead in trespasses and sins. This is opposed unto being spiritually minded as unto its nature or essence. Where a man, as unto the substance and being of the grace and duty intended, is not spiritually minded, he is carnally minded; that is, under the power of death, spiritual, and obnoxious unto death eternal. This is the principal foundation we proceed upon; whence we demonstrate the indispensable necessity of the frame of mind inquired after.

There are two ways wherein men are *earthly minded*. The one is absolute, when the love of earthly things is wholly predominant in the mind. This is not formally and properly to be carnally minded, which is of a larger extent. The one denomination is from the root and principle, namely, the flesh; the other from the object, or the things of the earth. The latter is a branch from the former, as its root. To be earthly minded, is an operation and effect of the carnal mind in one especial way and instance. And it is exclusive of life and salvation, as the carnal mind itself, Phil. 3. 19. 1 John 2. 16. This therefore is opposed unto the being of spiritual mindedness, no less than to be carnally minded is. When there is in any love of earthly things that is predominant, whence a person may be rightly denominated earthly minded, he is not, nor can be, spiritually minded at all; he hath no interest in the frame of heart and spirit intended thereby. And thus it is evidently with the greatest part of them who are called Christians in the world, let them pretend what they will to the contrary.

Again; there is a being earthly minded, which consists in an inordinate affection unto the things of this world.—It is that which is sinful, which ought to be mortified, yet is it not absolutely inconsistent with the substance and being of the grace inquired after. Some who are really and truly spiritually minded, may yet, for a time at least, be under such an inordinate affection unto, and care about, earthly things, that if not absolutely, yet comparatively, as unto what they ought to be and might be, they may be justly said to be earthly minded. They are so in respect of those degrees in being spiritually minded, which they ought to aim at, and may attain unto. And where it is thus, this grace can never thrive or flourish, it can never advance unto any eminent degree.

This is the Zoar of many professors; that little one wherein they would be spared. Such an earthly mindedness as is wholly inconsistent with being spiritually minded, as unto the state and condition, which depends thereon, they would avoid. For this they know would be absolutely exclusive of life and peace: they cannot but know that such a frame is as inconsistent with salvation, as living in the vilest sin that any man can contract the guilt of. There are more ways of spiritual and eternal death than one, as well as of natural. All that die, have not the plague; and all that perish eternally, are not guilty of the same profligate sins. The covetous are excluded from the kingdom of God, no less severely than fornicators, idolaters, adulterers, and thieves,' 1 Cor. 6, 9, 10. But there is a degree in being earthly minded, which they suppose their interest, advantages, relations, and occasions of life, do call for, which they would be a little indulged in: they may abide in such a frame without a disparagement of their profession; and the truth, is, they have too many companions to fear an especial reflection on themselves. The multitude of the guilty takes away the sense and shame of the guilt. But besides, they hope that it is not inconsistent absolutely with being *spiritually minded;* only they cannot well deny but that it is contrary unto such degrees in that grace, such thriving in that duty, as is recommended unto them. They think well of others who are spiritually minded in an eminent degree. At least they do so as unto the thing itself in general; for when they come unto particular instances of this or that man, for the most part, they esteem what is beyond their own measure to be little better than pretence. But in general, to be spiritually minded in an eminent degree, they cannot but esteem it a thing excellent and desirable. But it is for them who are more at leisure than they are; their circumstances and occasions require them to satisfy themselves with an inferior measure.

To obviate such pretences, I shall insist on nothing in the declaration of this duty, and the necessity of it, but what is incumbent on all that believe, and without which they have no grounds to assure their conscience before God. And at present in general I shall say, 'Whoever he be, who doth not sincerely aim at the highest degree of being spiritually minded, which the means he enjoyeth would lead him unto, and which the light he hath received doth call for; who judgeth it necessary unto his present advantages, occasions, and circumstances, to rest in such measures or degrees of it, as he cannot but know that they come short of what he ought to aim at, and so doth not endeavor after completeness in the will of God herein, can have no satisfaction in his own mind; hath no unfailing grounds, whereon to believe that he hath any thing at all of the reality of this grace in him.' Such a person possibly may have life which accompanies the essence of this grace, but he cannot have peace, which follows on its degree in a due improvement.

And it is to be feared, that far the greatest number of them who satisfy themselves in this apprehension, willingly neglecting an endeavor after the further degrees of this grace, and growth in this duty, which their light or convictions, and the means they enjoy, do suggest unto them, are indeed carnally minded, and every way obnoxious unto death.

CHAPTER II.

A particular account of the nature of this grace and duty of being spiritually minded. How it is stated in, and evidenced by, our thoughts.

Having stated the general concernments of that frame of mind which is here recommended unto us, we may proceed to inquire more particularly into the nature of it, according unto the description before given, in distinct propositions. And we shall carry on both these intentions together; first, to show what it is, and wherein it doth consist; and then how it doth evidence itself, so as that we may frame a right judgment whether it be in us or not. And we shall have no regard unto them who either neglect or despise these things, on any pretence whatever. For this is the word according unto which we shall all shortly be judged: To be carnally minded is death; but to be spiritually minded, is life and peace.

Thoughts and meditations, as proceeding from spiritual affections, are the first things wherein this spiritual mindedness doth consist, and whereby it doth evidence itself. Our thoughts are like the blossoms on a tree in the spring. You may see a tree in the spring all covered with blossoms, that nothing else of it appears. Multitudes of them fall off and come to nothing. Oft-times where there are most blossoms, there is least fruit. But yet there is no fruit, be it of what sort it will, good or bad but it comes in and from some of those blossoms. The mind of man is covered with thoughts, as a tree with blossoms. Most of them fall off, vanish, and come to nothing, end in vanity; and sometimes where the mind doth most abound with them, there is the least fruit; the *sap* of the mind is wasted and consumed in them. Howbeit there is no fruit which actually we bring forth, be it good or bad, but it proceeds from some of these thoughts.—Wherefore ordinarily these give the best and surest measure of the frame of men's minds. 'As a man thinketh in his heart, so is he,' Prov. xxiii. 7. In case of strong or violent temptations, the real frame of a man's heart is not to be judged by the multiplicity of thoughts about any object. For whether they are from Satan's suggestions, or from inward darkness, trouble, and horror, they will impose such a continual sense of themselves on the mind, as shall engage all its thoughts about them.—As when a man is in a storm at sea, the current of his thoughts runs quite another way, than when he is in safety about his occasions. But ordinarily, voluntary thoughts are the best measure and indication of the frame of our minds. As the nature of the soil is judged by the grass which it brings forth: so may the disposition of the heart by the predominancy of voluntary thoughts. They are the original acting of the soul; the way whereby the heart puts forth and empties the treasure that is in it; the waters that first rise and flow from that fountain. Every man's heart is his treasury; and the treasure that is in it, is either good or evil; as our Saviour tells us. There is a good and bad treasure of the heart; but whatever a man hath, be it good or evil, there it is. This treasure is opening, emptying, and spending itself continually; though it can never be exhausted. For it hath a fountain in nature or grace, which no expense can diminish; yea, it increaseth and getteth strength by it. <u>The more you spend of the treasure of your hearts in any kind, the more will you abound in treasure of the same kind.</u> Whether it be good or evil, it grows by expense and exercise; and the principal way whereby it puts forth itself, is by the thoughts of the mind. If the heart be evil, they are for the most part vain, filthy, corrupt, wicked, foolish; if it be under the power of a principle of grace, and so have a good treasure in it, it puts forth itself by thoughts suitable unto its nature, and complaint with its inclinations.

Wherefore, these thoughts give the best masure of the frame of our minds and hearts. I mean such as are voluntary, such as the mind of its own accord is apt for, incilines, and ordinarily betakes itself unto. Men may have a multitude of thoughts about the affairs of their callings and the occasions of life, which yet may give no due measure of the inward frame of their hearts. So men whose calling and work it is to study the *scriptures*, or the things revealed therein, and to preach them unto others; cannot but have many thoughts about spiritual things; and yet may be, and oftentimes are, most remote from being spiritually minded. They may be forced by their work and calling, to think of them early and late, evening and morning; and yet their minds be no way rendered or proved spiritual thereby. It were well if all of us who are preachers, would diligently examine ourselves herein. So is it with them who oblige themselves to read the scripture, it may be so many chapters every day; not withstanding the diligent performance of their task, they may be most remote from being spiritually minded. See Ezek. 33, 31. But there is a certain *track* and *course* of thoughts, that men ordinarily betake themselves unto, when not affected with present occasions. If these be vain, foolish, proud, ambitious sensual, or filthy; such is the mind and its frame. If they be holy, spiritual, and heavenly, such may the frame of the mind be judged to be. But these things must be more fully explained.

It is the great character and description of the frame of men's minds in an unregenerate condition, or before the renovation of their natures, that every imagination of the thoughts of their hearts are only evil continually. Gen. 6. 5. They are continually coining figments and imaginations in their hearts, stamping them into thoughts that are vain, foolish, and wicked. All other thoughts in them are occasional; these are the natural, genuine product of their hearts. Hence the clearest, and sometimes first, discovery of the bottomless evil treasure of filth, folly, and wickedness, that is in the heart of man by nature, is from the innumerable multitude of evil imaginations, which are there coined and thrust forth every day. So the wicked are said to be like the troubled sea when it cannot rest, whose waters cast up mire and dirt, Isa. 57, 20. There is a fulness of evil in their hearts, like that of water in the sea. This fulness is troubled, or put into continual motion, by their lusts, and impetuous desires. Hence the mire and dirt of evil thoughts are continually cast up in them.

It is therefore evident, that the predominancy of voluntary thoughts, is the best and most sure indication of the inward frame and state of the mind. For if it be so on the one side as unto the carnal mind, it is so on the other as unto the spiritual. Wherefore, to be spiritually minded in the first place is, to have the course and stream of those thoughts which we ordinarily retreat unto, we approve of as suited unto our affections, to be about spiritual things. Therein consists the minding of the spirit.

But, because all men, unless horribly profligate, have thoughts about spiritual things, yet we know that all men are not spiritually minded, we must consider, what is required unto such thoughts, to render them a certain indication of the state of our minds. And there are these three things required hereunto.

1. That they be natural, arising from ourselves, and not from outward occasions. The Psalmist mentions the inward thoughts of men. Psal. 49, 11, and 64, 6. But, whereas all thoughts are the inward acts of the mind, it should seem that this expression makes no distinction of the especial kind of thoughts intended, from those of another sort. But the difference is not in the formal nature of them, but in the causes, springs, and occasions. Inward thoughts are such as arise merely and solely from men's inward principles, dispositions, and inclinations, that are not suggested or excited by any outward objects. Such, in wicked men, are those actings of their lusts, whereby they 'entice and seduce themselves. Jam. 1, 14. Their lusts stir up thoughts, leading and encouraging them to make provision for the flesh. These are their inward thoughts. Of the same nature are those thoughts which are the minding of the spirit. They are the first natural egress, and genuine acting of the habitual disposition of the mind and soul.

Thus in covetous men there are two sorts of thoughts, whereby their covetousness acts itself. First, such as are occasioned by outward objects and opportunities. So it was with Achan, Josh. vii. 21. When, saith he, 'I saw among the spoils a goodly Babylonish garment, and two hundred shekels of silver, and a wedge of gold, then I coveted them. His sight of them, with an opportunity of possessing himself of them, excited covetous thoughts and desires in him. So it is with others every day, whose occasions call them to converse with the objects of their lusts. And some by such objects may be surprised into thoughts, that their minds are not habitually inclined unto. And therefore when they are known, it is our duty to avoid them. But the same sort of persons have thoughts of this nature arising from themselves only, their own dispositions and inclinations, without any outward provocations. 'The vile person will speak villany, and his heart will work iniquity, Isa. xxxii. 6.' 'And this he doth as the liberal deviseth liberal things,' v. 8, from his own disposition and inclination, he is contriving in his thoughts how to act according to them. So the unclean person hath two sorts of thoughts with respect unto the satisfaction of his lusts. First, such as are occasioned in his mind by the external objects of it. Hereunto stage-plays, revellings, dancings, with the society of bold persons, persons of corrupt communication, do contribute their wicked service. For the avoidance of this snare, Job made a covenant with his eyes, chap. xxx. 1. And our Saviour gives that holy declaration of the evil of it, Mat. v. 28. But he hath an habitual spring of these thoughts in himself constantly inclining and disposing him thereunto. Hence the apostle Peter tells us, that such persons have eyes full of an adulteress, that cannot cease from sin, ii. Eph. 2, 14. Their own affections make them restless in their thoughts and contrivances about sin. So is it with them who are given to excess in wine or strong drink. They have pleasing thoughts raised in them from the object of their lust represented unto them. Hence Solomon gives that advice against the occasion of them, Prov. xxiii. 31. But it is their own habitual disposition which carries them unto pleasing thoughts of the satisfaction of their lusts, which he describes, v. 34, 35. So is it in other cases. The thoughts of this latter sort, are men's inward thoughts: and such must these be of spiritual things, wherever we may be esteemed spiritually minded.

Psalm 45, 1. Saith the Psalmist, 'My heart is inditing a good matter; I speak of the things which I have made touching the King. He was meditating on spiritual things; on the things of the person and kingdom of Christ. Hence his heart bubbled up (as it is in the original) a good matter. It is an allusion taken from a quick spring of living waters; from its own life and fulness it bubbles up the water that runs and flows from it. So is it with these thoughts, in them that are spiritually minded. There is a living fulness of spiritual things in their mind and affections, that springeth up into holy thoughts about them.

From hence doth our Saviour give us the great description of spiritual life. It is a well of living water, springing up into everlasting life.' John iv. 12. The spirit, with his graces, residing in the heart of a believer, is a well of living water. Nor is it such a well as, content with its own fulness, doth not of its own accord, without any instrument or pains in drawing, send out its refreshing waters, as it is with most *wells*, though of living water. For this is spoken by our Saviour in answer and opposition unto that objection of the woman, upon this mention of giving living water, v. 10. Sir, saith she, 'thou hast nothing to draw with, and the well is deep, whence wilt thou have this water?' v. 11. True, saith he, such is the nature of this well and water—dead earthly things. They are of no use, unless we have instruments, lines, and buckets, to draw withal. But the living water which I shall give is of another nature. It is not water to be kept in a pit or cistern without us, whence it must be drawn; but it is within us; and that not dead and useless, <u>but continually springing up unto the use and refreshment of them that have it. For so is it with the principle of the new creature, of the new nature, the spirit and his graces in the hearts of them that do believe.</u> It doth of itself, and from itself, without any external influence on it, incline and dispose the whole soul unto spiritual actings that tend unto eternal life. Such are the thoughts of them that are spiritually minded; they arise from the inward principle, inclination, and disposition of the soul, are the bubblings of this well of living water; they are <u>the mindings of the spirit.</u>

So our Saviour describes them, Matt. xii. 35. A good man out of the good treasure of the heart, bringeth forth good things. First, the man is good; as he said before, make the tree good, or the fruit cannot be good, v. 33. He is made so by grace in the change and renovation of his nature; for in ourselves we are every way evil. This good man hath a treasure in his heart. So all men have, as the next words are; the evil man out of the evil treasure of the heart. And this is the great difference that is between men in this world

Every man hath a treasure in his heart; that is, a prevailing inexhaustible principle of all his actings and operations: but in some this treasure is good; in others it is evil; that is, the prevailing principle in the heart, which carries along with it its dispositions and inclinations, is in some good and gracious, in others it is evil. Out of this good treasure, a good man bringeth forth good things. The first opening of it, the first bringing of it forth, is by these thoughts. The thoughts that arise out of the heart, are of the same nature with the treasure that is in it. If the thoughts that naturally arise and spring up in us, are for the most part vain, foolish, sensual, earthly, selfish, such is the treasure that is in our hearts, and such are we. But where the thoughts that thus naturally proceed from the treasure that is in the heart, are spiritual and holy, it is an argument that we are spiritually minded.

Where it is not thus with our thoughts, they give no such evidence as that inquired after. Men may have thoughts of spiritual things, and that many of them, and that frequently, which do not arise from this principle, but may be resolved into two other causes:—1. Inward force; 2. Outward occasions.

1. Inward force, as it may be called. This is by convictions. Convictions put a kind of force upon the mind; or an impression, that causeth it to act contrary unto its own habitual disposition and inclination. It is in the nature of water to descend: but apply an instrument unto it, that shall make a compression of it, and force it unto a vent, it will fly upwards vehemently, as if that were its natural motion; but so soon as the force of the impression ceaseth, it returns immediately unto its own proper tendency, descending

towards its centre. So is it with men's thoughts ofttimes. They are earthly; their natural course and motion is downwards unto the earth, and the things thereof: but when any efficacious conviction presseth on the mind, it forceth the egress of its thoughts upwards towards heavenly things; it will think much and frequently of them, as if that were their proper motion and course; but so soon as the power of the conviction decays or wears off, that the mind is no more sensible of its force and impression, the thoughts of it return again unto their old course and track, as the water tends downwards.

This state and frame is graphically described, Psal. lxxviii. 34—37. 'When he slew them, then they sought him, and they returned, and inquired early after God. And they remembered that God was their rock, and the high God their Redeemer. Nevertheless, they did but flatter him with their mouths, and they lied unto him with their tongues; for their heart was not right with him, neither were they steadfast in his covenant.' Men in troubles, dangers, sickness, fears of death, or under effectual conviction of sin, from the preaching of the word, will endeavor to think and meditate on spiritual things: yea, they will be greatly troubled that they cannot think of them more than they do, and esteem it their folly that they think of any thing else. But as freedom and deliverance approach, so these thoughts decay and disappear; the mind will not be compelled to give place unto them any more. The Prophet give the reason of it, Jer. xiii. 23. 'Can the Ethiopian change his skin, or the leopard his spots? then may ye also do good, that are accustomed to do evil.' They have had another haunt; been taught another cause; the habit and inclination of the mind lies another way; and they will no longer tend towards spiritual things, than an impression is on them from their convictions.

And it is an argument of very mean attainments, of a low and weak degree in this frame of heart, or in our being spiritually minded, when our thoughts of spiritual things do rise or fall, according to renewed occasional convictions. If when we are under rebukes from God in our persons or relations, in fears of death, and the like, and withal, have some renewed convictions of sin, in commission, or omission of duties, and thereon do endeavor to be more spiritually minded, in the constant exercise of our thoughts on spiritual things, which we fail in; and these thoughts decay, as our convictions with the causes of them wear off, or are removed; we have attained a very low degree in this grace, if we have any interest in it at all.

Water that ariseth and floweth from a living spring, runneth equally and constantly, unless it be obstructed or diverted by some violent opposition; but that which is from thunder-showers runs furiously for a season, but is quickly dried up. So are those spirited thoughts which arise from a prevalent internal principle of grace in the heart; they are even and constant, unless an interruption be put upon them for a season by temptations; but those which are excited by the thunder of convictions, however their streams may be filled for a season, quickly dry up, and utterly decay.

2. Such thoughts may arise in the minds of men not spiritually minded, from outward means and occasions. Such I intend as are indeed useful; yea, appointed of God for this end among others, that they may engenerate and stir up holy thoughts and affections in us;

but there is a difference in their use and operation. In some, they excite the inward principle of the mind to act in holy thoughts, according unto its own sanctified disposition and prevalent affections: this is their proper end and use. In others they occasionally suggest such thoughts unto the minds of men, which spring only from the notions of things proposed unto them. With respect unto this end also, they are of singular use unto the souls of men, howbeit such thoughts do not prove men to be spiritually minded. Where you *till* and *manure* your land, if it brings forth plentiful crops of corn, it is an evidence that *soil* itself is good and fertile; the dressing of it only gives occasion and advantage to put forth its own fruit-bearing virtue: but if in the tilling of the land, you lay much dung upon it, and it brings forth here and there an handful where the dung lay, you will say the soil itself is barren; it brings forth nothing of itself. These means that we shall treat of, are as the *tilling* of a *fruitful soil*, which help it in bringing forth its fruit, by exciting its own virtue and power. They stir up holy affections unto holy thoughts and desires; but in others, whose hearts are barren, they only serve, as it were, some of them here and there, to stir up spiritual thoughts, which gives no evidence of a gracious heart or spirit.—But because this is a matter of great importance, it shall be handled distinctly by itself.

CHAPTER III.

Outward means and occasions of thoughts of such spiritual things, which do not prove men to be spiritually minded. Preaching of the word. Exercise of gifts. Prayer. How we may know whether our thoughts of spiritual things in Prayer, are truly spiritual thoughts, proving us to be spiritually minded.

1. Such a means is the preaching of the word itself. It is observed concerning many in the Gospel, that they heard it willingly, received it with joy, and did many things gladly, upon the preaching of it; and we see the same things exemplified in multitudes every day. But none of these things can be without many thoughts in the minds of such persons about the spiritual things of the Word; for they are the effects of such thoughts, and being wrought in the minds of men, will produce more of the same nature: yet were they all hypocrites concerning whom these things were spoken, and were never spiritually minded.

The cause of this miscarriage is given us by our Saviour, Matt. xiii. 20, 21. 'He that received the seed into stony places, the same is he that heareth the word, and anon receiveth it with joy; yet hath he not root in himself, but dureth for a while.' The good thoughts they have, proceed not from any principle in themselves. Neither their affections nor their thoughts of these things, have any internal root whereon they should grow. So is it with many who live under the present dispensation of the Gospel. They have thoughts of spiritual things continually suggested unto them: and they do abide with them more or less, according as they are affected: for I speak not of them who are either despisers of what they hear, or wayside hearers, who understand nothing of what they hear, and immediately lose all sense of it, and all thoughts about it; but 1 speak of them who attend with some dilligence, and receive the word with some *joy.* These insensibly grow in knowledge and understanding, and therefore cannot be without some thoughts of spiritual things: howbeit for the most part, they are, as was said, but like unto waters that run after a shower of rain. They pour out themselves as if they proceeded from some strong living spring, whereas indeed they have none at all. When once the waters of the shower are spent, their channel is dry; there is nothing in it but stones and dirt. When the doctrine of the word falls on such persons as showers of rain, it gives a course, sometimes greater, sometimes less, unto their thoughts towards spiritual things: but they have not a well of water in them springing up into everlasting life. Wherefore after a while their minds are dried up from such thoughts; nothing remains in them but *earth,* and that perhaps *foul* and *dirty.*

It must be observed, that the best of men, the most holy and spiritually minded, may have, nay, ought to have, their thoughts of spiritual things excited, multiplied, and confirmed by the preaching of the word. It is one end of its dispensation, one principal use of it in them by whom it is received. And it hath this effect two ways. 1. As it is the spiritual food of the soul, whereby its principle of life and grace is maintained and strengthened. The more this is done, the more shall we thrive in being spiritually minded. 2. As it administereth occasion unto the exercise of grace. For proposing the proper object of faith, love, fear, trust, reverence unto the soul, it draws forth all those graces into exercise. Wherefore, although the vigorous actings of spiritual thoughts be occasional from the word, be more under and after the preaching of it, than at other times, it is no more but what ariseth from the nature and use of the ordinance, by God's own appointment; nor is it any evidence that those with whom it is so, are not spiritually minded; but on the contrary, that they are. Yet, where men have no other thoughts of this matter but what are occasioned by the outward dispensation of the word, such thoughts do not prove them to be spiritually minded. Their endeavors in them are like those of men in a dream. Under some oppression of their spirits, their imagination fixeth on something or other, that is most earnestly to be desired or avoided. Herein they seem to themselves to strive with all their might, to endeavor to go, run, or contend, but all in vain; every thing fails them, and they are not relieved until they are awaked. So such persons, in impressions they receive from the word, seem to strive and contend in their thoughts and resolutions to comply with what is proposed unto them; but their strength fails; they find no success, for want of a *principle* of spiritual life; and after a time give over their endeavors, until they are occasionally renewed again. Now the thoughts which in the dispensation of the word do proceed from an inward principle of grace excited unto its due exercise, are distinguishable from those which are only occasionally suggested unto the mind by the word outwardly preached. For, 1. They are especial actings of faith and love towards the things themselves that are preached. They belong unto our receiving the truth in the love thereof. And love respects the goodness of the things themselves, and not merely the truth of the propositions wherein they are expressed. The other thoughts are only the sense of the mind, as affected with light and truth, without any cordial love unto the things themselves. 2. They are accompanied with complacency of soul, arising from love, experience, more or less, of the power of them, and their suitableness unto the new nature or principle of grace in them. For when our minds find that so indeed it is in us, as it is in the word; that this is that which we would be more conformable unto; it gives a secret complacency with satisfaction unto the soul. The other thoughts, which are only occasional, have none of these concomitants or effects, but are dry and barren, unless it be in a few words or transient discourse. 3. The former are means of spiritual growth. So some say the natural growth of vegetables is not by insensible motion, but by gusts and sensible eruptions of increase. There are both in spiritual growth, and the latter consists much in those thoughts which the principle of the new nature is excited unto by the word in the latter.

2. The duty of *prayer* is another means of the like nature. 'One principal end of it is to excite, stir up, and draw forth, the principle of grace, of faith and love in the heart, unto a due exercise in holy thoughts of God and spiritual things, with affections suitable unto them. Those who design not this end in prayer, know not at all what it is to pray. Now all sorts of persons have frequent occasion to join with others in prayer, and many are under the conviction that it is their own duty to pray every day, it may be, in their families and otherwise. And it is hard to conceive how men can constantly join with others in prayer,

much more how they can pray themselves, but that they must have thoughts of spiritual things every day; howbeit it is possible that they may have no root, or living spring, of them in themselves, but they are only occasional impressions on their minds from the outward performance of the duty. I shall give some instances of the grounds hereof, which, for many reasons require our diligent consideration.

Spiritual thoughts may be raised in a person in his own duty, by the exercise of his gifts, when there is no acting of grace in them at all; for they lead and guide the mind unto such things as are the matter of prayer; that is, spiritual things. Gifts are nothing but a spiritual improvement of our natural faculties or abilities. And a man cannot speak or utter any thing but what proceeds from his rational faculties by invention or memory, or both, managed in and by his thoughts, unless he speak by rote, and that which is not rational. What therefore proceeds from a man's rational faculty, in and by the exercise of his gifts, that his thoughts must be exercised about.

A man may read a long prayer that expresseth spiritual things, and yet never have one spiritual thought arise in his mind about them. For there is no exercise of any faculty of his mind required unto such reading, but only to attend unto the words that are to be read. This I say may be so; I do not say that it is so, or that it must be so. But, as was said in the exercise of gifts, it is impossible but there must be an exercise of reason, by invention, judgment, and memory; and consequently, thoughts of spiritual things. Yet may they all be merely occasional, from the present external performance of the duty, without any living spring or exercise of grace. In such a course, may men of tolerable gifts continue all their days, unto the satisfaction of themselves and others, deceiving both them and their own souls.

This being evident from the scripture and experience, an inquiry may be made thereon, as unto our own concernment in these things; especially of those who have received spiritual gifts of their own, and of them also in some degree, who usually enjoy the gifts of others in this duty. For it may be asked, how we shall know whether the thoughts which we have of spiritual things in and upon prayer, arise from gifts only, those of our own or other men's giving occasion unto them, or are influenced from a living principle and spring of grace in our hearts? A case this is (however by some it may be apprehended) of great importance, and which would require much time fully to resolve. For there is nothing whereby the refined sort of hypocrites more deceive themselves and others, nothing whereby some men give themselves more countenance in an indulgence unto their lusts, than by this part of the form of godliness, when they deny the power thereof. And besides, it is that wherein the best of believers ought to keep a diligent watch over themselves, in every particular instance of the performance of this duty. With respect hereunto, in an especial manner, are they to watch unto prayer. If they are at any time negligent herein, they may rest in a bare exercise of gifts, when on a due examination and trial they have no evidence of the acting of grace in what they have done. I shall therefore, with what brevity I can, give a resolution unto this inqury. And to this end observe,

1. It is an ancient complaint, that spiritual things are filled with great obscurity and difficulty; and it is true.

Not that there is any such thing in themselves, for they all come forth from the Father of lights, and are full of light, order, beauty and wisdom; and light and order are the only means whereby any thing makes a discovery of itself. But the ground of all darkness and difficulty in these things lies in ourselves. We can more clearly and steadily see and behold the moon and the stars, than we can see the sun, when it shines in its greatest lustre. It is not because there is more light in the moon and stars than in the sun, but because the light of the sun is greater than our visive faculty can directly bear and behold. So we can more clearly discover the truth and distinct nature of things moral, and natural, than we can of things that are heavenly and spiritual. See John iii. 14. Not that there is more substance or reality in them, but because the ability of our understanding is more suited unto the comprehension of them. The other are above us. We know but in part, and our minds are liable to be hindered and disordered in their apprehension of things heavenly and spiritual, by ignorance, temptations, and prejudices of all sorts. In nothing more are men subject unto mistakes, than in the application of things unto themselves, and a judgment of their interest in them. Fear, self-love, with the prevalency of temptations and corruptions, do all engage their powers to darken the light of the mind, and to pervert its judgment. In no case doth the deceitfulness of the heart, or of sin, which is all one, more act itself. Hence multitudes say peace to themselves, to whom God doth not speak peace; and some who are children of light, do yet walk in darkness. Hence is that fervent prayer of the Apostle, for help in this case, Ephes. i. 16, 17, 18, 19. There is also a great similitude between temporary faith, and that which is saving and durable; and between gifts and grace, in their operations, which is that now under consideration. It is acknowledged, therefore, that without the especial light and conduct of the spirit of God, no man can make such a judgment of his state and his actions, as shall be a stable foundation of giving glory to God, and of obtaining peace unto his own soul: and therefore the greatest part of mankind do constantly deceive themselves in these things.

But ordinarily, under this blessed conduct in the search of ourselves and the concernments of our duty, we may come to a satisfaction whether they are influenced by faith, and have grace exercised in them, especially this duty of prayer, or whether it derive from the power of our natural faculties, raised by light and spiritual gifts only; and so whether our spiritual thoughts therein spring from a vital principle of grace, or whether they come from occasional impressions on the mind, by the performance of the duty itself.

If men are willing to deceive themselves, or to hide themselves from themselves, to walk with God at all peradventures, to leave all things at hazard, to put off all trials unto that at the last day, and so never call themselves to an account, as to the nature of their duties in any particular instance; it is no wonder, if they neither do, nor can, make any distinction in this matter; as to the true nature of their thoughts in spiritual duties. Two things are required hereunto.

1. That we impartially and severally examine and try the frames and actings of our minds in holy duties, by the word of truth; and thereon not be afraid to speak that plainly to our souls, which the word speaks unto us. This diligent search ought to respect

our principles, aims, ends, actings, with the whole deportment of our souls in every duty. See 2 Cor. 13, 5. If a man receiveth much money, and look only on the outward form and superscription, when he supposeth that he hath great store of current coin in gold and silver, he may have only heaps of lead or copper by him. But he that trades in it, as the comfort and support of his natural life and condition, he will try what he receives, both by the balance and the touchstone, as the occasion requires, especially if it be in a time when much adulterated coin is passing in the world. And if a man reckons on his duties by tale and number, he may be utterly deceived, and be spiritually poor and a bankrupt, when he esteems himself rich, increased in goods, and wanting nothing.—Some duties may appearingly hold in the balance as to weight, which will not hold it at the touch-stone, as to worth. Both means are to be used, if we would not be mistaken in our accounts. Thus God himself, in the midst of a multitude of duties, calls the people to try and examine themselves, whether or not they are such as have faith and grace in them, and so like to have acceptance with him. Isa. lviii. 2—5.

2. We must add unto our own diligent inquiry, fervent prayers unto God, that he would search and try us, as to our sincerity, and discover unto us the true frame of our hearts. Hereof we have an express example, Psalm cxxxix. 23, 24. 'Search me, O God, and know my heart; try me, and know my thoughts; and see if there be any wicked way in me, and lead me in the way everlasting.' This is the only way whereby we may have the spirit of God witnessing unto our sincerity, with our own spirits. There is need of calling in divine assistance in this matter, both from the im-

portance of it, and from its difficulty; God alone knowing fully and perfectly what is the hearts of men.

I no way doubt, but that in the impartial use of these means, a man may come to assured satisfaction in his own mind, such as wherein he shall not be deceived, whether he doth animate and quicken his thoughts of spiritual things in duties, with inward vital grace, or whether they are impressions on his mind, by the occasion of the duty.

A duty this is of great importance and necessity, now hypocrisy hath made so great an inroad on profession, and gifts have deflowered grace in its principal operations. No persons are in greater danger of walking at hazard with God, than those who live in the exercise of spiritual gifts in duties, unto their own satisfaction and others. For they may countenance themselves with an appearance of every thing that should be in them in reality and power, when there is nothing of it in them. And so it hath fallen out. We have seen many earnest in the exercise of this gift, who have turned vile and debauched apostates. Some have been known to live in sin, and an indulgence of their lusts, and yet to abide constant in their duties, Isa. i. 15. And we may hear prayers sometimes that openly discover themselves unto spiritual sense, to be the labor of the brain, by the help of gifts in memory and invention, without an evidence of any mixture of humility, reverence, or godly fear; without any acting of faith and love. They flow as wine, yet smell and taste of the unsavory cask from whence they proceed. It is necessary, therefore, that we should put ourselves on the severest trial, lest we should be found not to be spiritually minded in spiritual duties.

Gifts are gracious vouchsafements of Christ, to

make *grace* useful unto ourselves and others; yea, they may be made useful unto the grace of others, who have no grace in themselves. But as unto our own souls, they are of no other advantage or benefit, but to stir up grace unto its proper exercise; and to be a vehicle to carry it on, in its proper use. If we do not always regard this in their exercise, we had better be without them. If instead hereof, they once begin to impose themselves practically upon us, so as that we rest in spiritual light, acting our inventions, memories and judgments with a ready utterance, or such as it is, there is no form of prayer can be more prejudicial unto our souls. As wine, if taken moderately and seasonably, helps the stomach in digestion, and quickens the natural spirits, enabling the powers of nature unto their duty, is useful and helpful unto it; but if it be taken in excess, it doth not help nature, but oppress it, and takes on itself to do what nature should be assisted unto; it fills men's bodies with diseases, as well as their souls with sin. So whilst spiritual gifts are used and employed only to excite, aid, and assist grace in its operations, they are unutterably useful: but if they put themselves in the room thereof, to do all that grace should do; they are hurtful and pernicious. We have need, therefore, to be very diligent in this inquiry, whether our spiritual thoughts, even in our prayers, be not rather occasioned from the duty, than springing from a gracious principle in our hearts, or are the actings of real sovereign grace.

2. Where thoughts of spiritual things in prayer are occasional only, in the way before described, such prayers will not be a means of spiritual growth to the soul. They will not make the soul humble, holy, watchful, and diligent in universal obedience. Grace

will not thrive under the greatest constancy in such duties. It is an astonishing thing to see how, under frequency of prayer, and a seeming fervency therein, many of us are at a stand as to visible thriving in the *fruits* of grace; and it is to be feared, without any increase of strength in the *root* of it. God's hand is not shortened that he cannot save, nor his ear deafened that he cannot hear. He is the same as in the days of old, when our fathers cried unto him and were delivered, when they trusted in him, and were not confounded. Jesus Christ is the same yesterday, and to day, and forever; prayer is the same that it was and shall lose nothing of its prevalency whilst this world endureth. Whence is it then, that there is so much prayer amongst us, and so little success? I speak not with respect to the outward dispensation of divine providence in afflictions or persecutions, wherein God always acts in a way of sovereignty, and ofttimes gives the most useful answer unto our prayers by denying our requests: I intend that only whereof the Psalmist giveth us his experience, Psalm, cxxxviii. 3. 'In the day when I cried, thou answeredst me, and strengthenedst me with strength in my soul.' Where prayers are effectual, they will bring in spiritual strength. But the prayers of many seem to be very spiritual, and to express all conceivable supplies of grace; and they are persisted in with constancy; and God forbid we should judge them to be hypocritical and wholly insincere. Yet is there a defect somewhere, which should be inquired after: for they are not so answered, as that they who pray them, are strengthened with strength in their souls: there is not that spiritual thriving, that growth in grace, which might be expected to accompany such supplications.

I know that a man may pray often, pray sincerely and frequently for an especial mercy, grace, or deliverance from a particular temptation; and yet no spiritual supply of strength unto his own experience come in thereby. So Paul prayed thrice for the removal of his temptation, and yet had the exercise of it continued. In such a case there may be no defect in prayer, and yet the grace in particular aimed at not be attained. For God hath other holy ends to accomplish hereby on the soul. But how persons should continue in prayer, in general, according to the mind of God, so far as can be outwardly discovered, and yet thrive not at all, as unto spiritual strength in their souls, is hard to be understood.

And which is yet more astonishing, men abide in the duty of prayer, and that in constancy, in their families, and otherwise, and yet live in known sins. Whatever spiritual thoughts such men have, in and by their prayers, they are not spiritually minded. Shall we now say, that all such persons are gross hypocrites; such as know they do but mock God and man; know that they have not desires nor aims after the things which they mention in their own prayers; but do these things either for some corrupt end, or at best to satisfy their convictions? Could we thus resolve, the whole difficulty of the case were taken off. 'For such double minded men have no reason to think that they shall receive any thing of the Lord,' as James speaks, chap. i. 7. Indeed, they do not. They never act faith reference unto their own prayers. But it is not so with all of this sort; some judge themselves sincere, and in good earnest in their prayers, not without some hopes and expectations of success. I will not say of all such persons, that they are among the number of them concerning whom the wisdom of God says, 'Because I called unto them, and they refused; they shall call on me, but I will not answer; they shall seek me early, and shall not find me,' Prov. i. 18—21. And although we may say unto such persons in general, either leave your sinning, or leave your praying, from Psalm l. 16, 17, and that with respect unto present scandal, and certain miscarriage in the end, if both be continued in; yet in particular I would not advise any such person to leave off his praying, until he had left his sin. This were to advise a sick man to use no remedies until he were well cured. Who knows but that the Holy Spirit, who works when and how he pleaseth, may take a time to animate these lifeless prayers, and make them a means of deliverance from the power of this sin. In the mean time, the fault and guilt is wholly their own, who have effected a consistency between a way of sinning and a course in praying; and it ariseth from hence, that they have never labored to fill up their requests with grace. What there hath been of earnestness or diligence in them, hath been from a force put upon them by their convictions and fears. For no man was ever absolutely prevailed on by sin, who prayed for deliverance, according to the mind of God. Every praying man that perisheth, was an hypocrite. The faithfulness of God in his promises will not allow us to judge otherwise. Wherefore the thoughts that such persons have of spiritual things, even in their duties, do not arise from within, nor are a natural emanation of the frames of their hearts and affections.

3. Earnestness and apparent fervency in prayer, as to the outward delivery of the words of it, yea, though the mind be so affected as to contribute much thereunto, will not of themselves prove, that the thoughts

of men therein do arise from an internal spring of grace. There is a fervency of spirit in prayer, that is one of the best properties of it, being an earnest acting of love, faith, and desire: But there is a fervency wherewith the mind itself may be affected, that may arise from other causes.

1. It may do so from the engagement of natural affections unto the object of their prayer, or the things prayed for. Men may be mighty earnest and intent in their minds, in praying for a dear relation, or for deliverence from imminent troubles, or imminent dangers; and yet all this fervour arise from the vehement actings of natural affections about the things prayed for, excited in an especial manner by the present duty. Hence God calls the earnest cries of some for temporal things not a crying unto him, but an howling, Hosea, vii. 14. That is, the cry of hungry ravenous beasts, that would be satisfied.

2. Sometimes it ariseth from the sharpness of convictions, which will make men even roar in their prayers for disquietment of heart. And this may be, where there is no true grace as yet received, nor, it may be, ever will be so. For the perplexing work of conviction goes before real conversion; and as it produceth many other effects and changes in the mind, so it may do this of great fervency in vocal prayers, especially if it be accompanied with outward afflictions, pains, or troubles. Psalm lxxviii, 34, 35.

3. Oft-times the mind and affections are very little concerned in that fervor and earnestness which appear in the outward performance of the duty; but in the exercise of gifts, and through their own utterance, men put their natural affections into such an agitation as shall carry them out into a great vehemency in

their expressions. It hath been so with sundry persons who have been discovered to be rotten hypocrites, and have afterwards turned cursed apostates. Wherefore all these things may be, where there is no gracious spring, or vital principle, acting itself from within in spiritual thoughts.

Some, it may be, will design an advantage by their conceptions, unto the interest of profaneness and scoffing; for if there be these evils under the exercise of the gift of prayer, both in constancy, and with fervency—if there may be a total want of the exercise of all true grace with it and under it; then it may be, all that is pretended of this gift, and its use, is but hypocrisy and talk. But, I say, 1, It may be as well pretended, that because the sun shining on a dunghill doth occasion offensive and noisome steams; therefore all that is pretended of its influence on spices and flowers, causing them to give out their fragrancy, is utterly false. No man ever thought that spiritual gifts did change, or renew the minds and natures of men; where they are alone, they only help and assist unto the useful exercise of natural faculties and powers; and, therefore, where the heart is not savingly renewed, no gifts can stir up a saving exercise of faith; but, where it is so, they are a means to cause the savor of it to flow forth. 2. Be it so, that there may be some evils found under the exercise of the gift of prayer, what remedy for them may be proposed? Is it that men should renounce their use of it, and betake themselves unto the reading of prayers only? 1. The same may be said of all spiritual gifts whatever; for they are all of them liable to abuse. And shall we reject all the powers of the world to come, the whole complex of gospel gifts for the communication whereof the Lord Christ hath promised to continue his spirit with his church unto the end of the world, because by some they are abused? 2. Not only the same, but far greater evils may be found in and under the reading of prayers, which needs no further demonstration than what it gives of itself every day. 3. It is hard to understand, how any benefit at all can accrue to any by this relief, when the advantages of the other way are evident.

Wherefore the inquiry remains, 'how we may know to our own satisfaction, that the thoughts we have of spiritual things in the duty of prayer, are from an internal fountain of grace,' and so are an evidence that we are spiritually minded, whereunto all these things do tend. Some few things I shall offer towards satisfaction herein.

1. I take it for granted on the evidence before given, that persons who have any spiritual light, and will diligently examine and try their own hearts, will be able to discern what real actings of faith, of love, and delight in God, there are in their duties; and consequently what is the spring of their spiritual thoughts. In general we are assured, that 'he that believeth, hath the witness in himself.' 1 John, 5. 10. Sincere faith will be its own evidence: and where there are sincere actings of faith, they will evidence themselves, if we try all things impartially by the word. But if men do, as for the most part they do, content themselves with the performance of any duty, without an examination of their principles, frames, and actings of grace in them, it is no wonder if they walk in all uncertainty.

2. When the soul finds a sweet spiritual complacency in and after its duties, it is an evidence that

grace hath been acted in its spiritual thoughts and desires, Jer. 31. The prophet receiveth a long gracious message from God, filled up with excellent promises and pathetical exhortations to the church. The whole is as it were summed up in the close of it, v. 24. 'For I have satiated the weary soul, and I have replenished every sorrowful soul.' Whereon the prophet adds, 'upon this I awaked, and beheld, and my sleep was sweet unto me.' God's gracious message had so composed his spirits, and freed his mind from trouble, that he was at quiet repose in himself, like a man asleep. But after the end of it, he stirs up himself to a review and consideration of what had been spoken unto him: I awaked and beheld, or I stirred up myself, and considered what had been delivered unto me; and saith he, my sleep was sweet unto me; I found a gracious complacency in, and refreshment unto my soul, from what I had heard and received. So is it oft-times with a soul that hath had real communion with God in the duty of prayer. It finds itself both in it, and afterwards, when it is awakened unto the consideration of it spiritually refreshed; it is sweet unto him.

This holy complacency, this rest and sweet repose of mind, is the foundation of the delight of believers in this duty. They do not pray only because it is their duty so to do, nor yet because they stand in need of it, so as that they cannot live without it, but they have delight in it; and to keep them from it, is all one as to keep them from their daily food and refreshment. Now we can have no delight in any thing but what we have found some sweetness, rest, and complacency in. Without any such experience, we may do or use any thing, but cannot do it with delight.

And it ariseth, 1, from the approach that is made unto God therein. It is in its own nature an access unto God on a throne of grace. Eph. ii. 18. Heb. x. 19, 20. And when this access is animated by the actings of grace, the soul hath a spiritual experience of a nearness in that approach. Now, God is the fountain and centre of all spiritual refreshment, rest and complacency; and in such an access unto him, there is a refreshing taste of them communicated unto the soul: Psal. xxxvi. 7—9. 'How excellent is thy loving kindness, O God! therefore the children of men put their trust under the shadow of thy wings. They shall be abundantly satisfied with the fatness of thine house: and thou shalt make them drink of the river of thy pleasures. For with thee is the fountain of life: in thy light we shall see light.' God is proposed in the excellency of his loving kindness, which is comprehensive of his goodness, grace, and mercy. And so is he also as the spring of life and light, all spiritual powers and joys. Those that believe, are better described by their trust under the shadow of his wings. In his worship, the fatness of his house, they make their approaches unto him. And the fruit hereof is, that he makes them to drink of the river of his pleasures, the satisfying refreshing streams of his grace and goodness; they approach unto him as unto the fountain of life, so as to drink of that fountain, in renewed communications of life and grace; and in the light of God, the light of his countenance, to see light in satisfying joy. In these things doth consist, and from them doth arise, that spiritual complacency which the souls of believers find in their duties. 2. From the due exercise of faith, love, and delight, the graces wherein the life of the new creature doth principally consist. There is a suitableness to our natural constitution, and a secret complacency of our natures, in the proper actings of life natural, for its own preservation and increase: there is so in our spiritual constitution, in the proper actings of the powers of our spiritual life, unto its preservation and increase. These graces, in their due exercise, compose and refresh the mind, as those which are perfective of its state, which quell and cast out whatever troubles it: thence a blessed satisfaction and complacency befalls the soul; herein he that believeth hath the witness in himself. Besides, faith and love are never really acted on Christ, but they prepare and make meet the soul to receive the communications of love and grace from him, which it never faileth of, although it be not always sensible thereof. 3. From the testimony of conscience, bearing witness to our sincerity, in aims, ends, and performances of the duty. Hence a gracious repose of mind, and great satisfactoriness, ensue.

If we have no experience of these things, it is evident that we walk at random in the best of our duties; for they are among the principal things that we do, or ought to pray for; and if we have not experience of the effects of our prayers on our hearts, we neither have advantage by them, nor give glory to God in them.

But yet here, as in most other spiritual things, one of the worst of vices is ready to impose itself in the room and place of the best of our graces: and this is, self-pleasing in the performance of the duty. This, instead of a grace steeped in humility, as all true grace is, is a vile effect of spiritual pride, or the offering of a sacrifice to our own net and drag: it is a glorying in the flesh; for whatever of self any doth glory in, it is but flesh. When men have had enlargements in their expressions, and especially when they apprehend that others are satisfied or affected therewith, they are apt to have a secret self-pleasing in what they have done, which, before they are aware, turns into pride, and a noxious elation of mind. The same may befall men in their most secret duties, performed outwardly by the aid of spiritual gifts: but this is most remote from, and contrary to, that spiritual complacency in duty, which we speak of, which yet it will pretend to, until it be diligently examined. The language of this spiritual complacency is, 'I will go in the strength of the Lord God; I will make mention of thy righteousness, even of thine only.' Ps. lxxi. 16. That of spiritual pride is, God, I thank thee that I have done thus and thus, as it was expressed by the Pharisee. That is, in God alone; this is in self: that draws forth the savor of all graces; this immediately covers and buries them all, if there be any in the soul: that fills the soul eminently with humility and self-abasement; this with a lifting up of the mind and proud self-conceit: that casts out all remembrance of what we have done ourselves, retaining only a sense of what we have received from God, of the impressions of his love and grace; this blots out all remembrance of what we have freely received from God, and retains only what we have done ourselves. Wherever it is, there is no due sense either of the greatness or goodness of God.

Some, it may be, will say, that if it be so, they for their parts, are cut off. They have no experience of any such spiritual rest and complacency in God, in or after their prayers; at the best, they begin them with tears, and end them in sorrow; and sometimes they know not what is become of them, but fear that God is not glorified by them, nor their own souls bettered.

I answer, 1. There is great spiritual refreshment in that godly sorrow which is at work in our prayers.—Where the Holy Ghost is a spirit of grace and supplication, he causeth mourning, and in that mourning there is joy. 2. The secret encouragement which we receive by praying, to adhere unto God constantly in prayer, ariseth from some experience of this holy complacency, though we have not a sensible evidence of it. 3. Perhaps some of them who make this complaint, if they would awaken and consider, would find that their souls, at least sometimes, had been thus refreshed, and brought unto an holy rest in God. 4. Then shall you know the Lord, if you follow on to know him. Abide in seeking after this complacency, and satisfaction in God, and you shall attain it.

3. It is a sure evidence that our thoughts of spiritual things in our supplications are from an internal spring of grace, and are not merely occasioned by the duty itself, when we find the daily fruit and advantage of them; especially in the preservation of our souls in an holy, humble, watchful frame.

Innumerable are the advantages, benefits, and effects of prayer, which are commonly spoken unto; growth in grace and consolation is the substance of them. Where there is continuance in prayer, there will be spiritual growth in some proportion. For men to be earnest in prayer, and thriftless in grace, is a certain indication of prevalent corruptions, and want of being spiritually minded in prayer itself. If a man eats his daily food, let him eat never so much, or so often, if he be not nourished by it, his body is under the power of prevalent distempers; and so is his spirtual constitution, who thriveth not in the use of the food of the new creature. But that which I fix upon with respect unto the present inquiry, is, the frame that it preserves the soul in; it will keep it humble, and upon a diligent watch, as unto its dispositions and actings. He who prays as he ought, will endeavor to live as he prays. This none can do who doth not with diligence keep his heart unto things he hath prayed about. To pray earnestly and live carelessly, is to proclaim that a man is not spiritually minded in his prayer. Hereby then, we shall know what is the spring of those spiritual thoughts, which our minds are exercised withal in our supplications. If they are influenced unto a constant daily watch for the perservation of that frame of spirit, those dispositions and inclinations unto spiritual things which we pray for, they are from an internal spring of grace. If there be generally an unsuitableness in our minds unto what we seem to contend for in our prayers, the gift may be in exercise, but the grace is wanting. If a man be every day on the Exchange, and there talk diligently and earnestly about merchandise, and the affairs of trade; but when he comes home thinks no more of them, because indeed he hath nothing to do, no interest in them, he may be a very poor man, notwithstanding his pretences: and he may be spiritually very poor, who is on occasions fervent in prayer, if, when he retires unto himself, he is not careful and diligent about the matter of it.

4. When spiritual affections, and due preparation of heart unto the duty, excite and animate the gift of prayer, and not the gift make impressions on the affections; then are we spiritually minded therein. Gifts are servants, not rulers, in the mind; are bestowed on us to be serviceable unto grace; not to lead it, but to

follow it, and to be ready with their assistance on its exercise; for the most part, where they lead all, they are all alone. This is the natural order of these things. Grace habitually inclineth and disposeth the heart unto this duty. Providence and rule give the occasions for its exercise; sense of duty calls for prepartion; grace coming into actual exercise, gifts come in with their assistance; if they lead all, all is out of order. It may be otherwise sometimes: a person indisposed and lifeless, engaging into prayer in a way of obedience, upon conviction of duty, may, in and by the gift, have his affections excited, and graces engaged unto its proper work. It may be so, I say; but let men take heed how they trust to this order and method: for where it is so, there may be little or nothing of the exercise of true grace in all their fervor and commotion of affections; but when the genuine actings of faith, love, holy reverence, and gracious desires, stir up the gift unto its exercise, calling in its assistance to the expression of themselves, then are the heart and mind in their proper order.

5. It is so when other duties of religion are equally regarded and attended to with prayer itself. He, all whose religion lies in prayer and hearing, hath none at all. God hath an equal respect to all other duties, and so must we have also. So is it expressed as to the religion herein, because there is none without it, Jam. i. 27. I shall not value his prayers at all, be he never so earnest and frequent in them, who gives not alms according to his ability: and this in an especial manner is required of us who are ministers; that we be not like an hand set up in cross ways, directing others which way to go but staying behind itself.

This digression about the rise and spring of spiritual thoughts in prayer, I judged not unnecessary, in such a time and season, wherein we ought to be very jealous, lest gifts impose themselves in the room of grace; and be careful that they are employed only to their proper end, which is to be serviceable to grace in its exercise, and not otherwise.

3. There is another occasion of thoughts of spiritual things, when they do not spring from a living principle within, and so are no evidence of being spiritually minded. And this is the discourse of others. They that fear the Lord will be speaking one to another, of the things wherein his glory is concerned, Mal. iii. 16. To declare the righteousness, the glory of God, is the delight of his saints. Psalm. cxlv. 3—8. 'Great is the Lord, and greatly to be praised, and his greatness is unsearchable. One generation shall praise thy works to another, and shall declare thy mighty works. I will speak of the glorious honor of thy majesty, and of thy wondrous works. And men shall speak of the might of thy terrible acts; and I will declare thy greatness. They shall abundantly utter the memory of thy great goodness, and shall sing of thy righteousness. The Lord is gracious and full of compassion, slow to anger, and of great mercy;' and, accordingly, there are some who are ready on all occasions to be speaking, or making mention, of things divine, spiritual, and holy; and it is to be wished that there were more of them. All the flagitious sins that the world is filled withal, are not a greater evidence of the degeneracy of christian religion, than this is, that it is grown unusual, yea, a shame or scorn, for men to speak together of the things of God. It was not so when religion was in its primitive power and glory; nor is it so with them who really fear God, and are sensible

of their duty. Some I say there are, who embrace all occasions of spiritual communication. Those with whom they converse, if they are not profligate, if they have any spiritual light, cannot but so far comply with what they say, as to think of the things spoken which are spiritual. Oft-times the track and course of men's thoughts lie so out of the way, are so contrary unto such things, that they seem strange to them; they give them no entertaiment. You do but cross their way with such discourses, whereon they stand still a little, and so pass on. Even the countenances of some men will change hereon, and they betake themselves to an unsatisfied silence, until they can divert unto other things. Some will make such replies of empty words, as shall evidence their hearts to be far enough estranged from the things proposed unto them. But with others, such occasional discourses will make such impressions on their minds, as to stir up present thoughts of spiritual things. But though frequent occasions hereof may be renewed, yet will such thoughts give no evidence that any man is spiritually minded. For they are not genuine, from an internal spring of grace.

From these causes it is, that the thoughts of spiritual things are with many, as guests that come into an inn, and not like children that dwell in the house. They enter occasionally, and then there is a great stir about them, to provide meet entertainment for them. In a while they are disposed of, and so depart, being neither looked nor inquired after any more. Things of another nature are attended to; new occasions bring in new guests, for a season. Children are owned in the house, are missed if they are out of the way, and have their daily provision constantly made for them. So is it with these occasional thoughts about spiritual things. By one means or other they enter into the mind, and there are entertained for a season. On a sudden they depart, and men hear of them no more. But those that are natural and genuine, arising from a living spring of grace in the heart, disposing the mind unto them, are as the children of the house; they are expected in their places, and at their seasons. If they are missing, they are inquired after. The heart calls itself to an account, whence it is that it hath been so long without them, and calls them over into its wonted converse with them.

CHAPTER IV.

Other evidences of thoughts about spiritual things, arising from an internal principle of grace, whereby they are an evidence of our being spiritually minded. The abounding of these thoughts, how far, and wherein such an evidence.

II. The second evidence that our thoughts of spiritual things proceed from an internal fountain of sanctified light and affections, or that they are acts or fruits of our being spiritually minded, is, that they abound in us, that our minds are filled with them. We may say of them, as the Apostle doth of other graces; if these things are in you and abound, you shall not be barren. It is well indeed, when our minds are like the land of Egypt in the years of plenty, when it brought forth by handfuls; when they flow from the well of living water in us, with a full stream and current. But there is a measure of abounding, which is necessary to evidence our being spiritually minded in them.

There is a double effect ascribed here to this frame of spirit; first life, and then peace. The nature and being of this grace depends on the former consideration of it, namely, its procedure from an internal principle of grace, the effect and consequence whereof is life. But that it is peace also, depends on the degree and measure of the actings of this part of it in our spiritual thoughts; and this we must consider.

It is the character of all men in the state of depraved nature and apostacy from God, 'that every imagination of the thoughts of their hearts, is only evil continually,' Gen. vi. 5. All persons in that condition are not swearers, blasphemers, drunkards, adulterers, idolaters, or the like. These are the vices of particular persons, the effects of particular constitutions and temptations. But thus it is with them, all and every one of them, 'all the imaginations of the thoughts of their hearts are evil, and that continually.' Some as to the matter of them, some as unto their end, all as to their principle; for out of the evil treasure of the heart can proceed nothing but what is evil. That infinite multitude of open sins which is in the world, gives a clear prospect or representation of the nature and effects of our apostacy from God. But he that can consider the numberless number of thoughts which pass through the mind of every individual person every day, all evil and that continually, he will have a further comprehension of it.

We can therefore have no greater evidence of a change in us from this state and condition, than a change wrought in the course of our thoughts. A relinquishment of this or that particular sin, is not an evidence of a translation from this state. For as was said, such particular sins proceed from particular lusts and temptations, and are not the immediate, universal consequence of that depravation of nature which is equal in all. Such alone is the vanity and wickedness of the thoughts and imaginations of the heart. A change herein is a blessed evidence of a change of state. He who is cured of a dropsy, is not immediately healthy, because he may have the prevailing seeds and matter of other diseases in him, and the next day die of a lethargy: but he who, from a state of sickness, is restored in the temperature of the mass of blood and the animal spirits, and all the principles of life and health, unto a good crasis and temperature, his state of body is changed. The cure of a particular sin may leave behind it the seeds of eternal death, which they may quickly effect; but he who hath obtained a change in this character, which belongs essentially unto the state of depraved nature, is spiritually recovered. And the more the stream of our thoughts is turned, the more our minds are filled with those of a contrary nature, the greater and more firm is our evidence of a translation out of that depraved state and condition.

There is nothing so unaccountable as the multiplicity of thoughts of the minds of men; they fall from them like the leaves of trees, when they are shaken with the wind in autumn. To have all these thoughts, all the several figments of the heart, all the conceptions that are framed and agitated in the mind, to be evil and that continually, what an hell of horror and confusion must it needs be! A deliverance from this loathsome, hateful state, is more to be valued than the whole world. Without it neither life, nor peace, nor immortality, nor glory, can ever be attained.

The design of conviction is to put a stop to these

thoughts, to take off from their number, and thereby to lessen their guilt. It deserves not the name of conviction of sin, which respects only outward actions, and regards not the inward actings of the mind. And this alone will for a season make a great change in the thoughts, especially it will do so when assisted by superstition, directing them unto other objects. These two in conjunction are the rise of all that devotional religion which is in the papacy. Conviction labors to put some stop and bounds to thoughts absolutely evil and corrupt; and superstition suggests other objects for them, which they readily embrace; but it is a vain attempt. The minds and hearts of men are continually minting and coining new thoughts and imaginations; the cogitative faculty is always at work. As the streams of a mighty river running into the ocean, so are the thoughts of a natural man, and through self they run into hell. It is a fond thing to set a dam before such a river, to curb its streams. For a little space there may be a stop made, but it will quickly break down all obstacles, or overflow all its bounds. There is no way to divert its course, but only by providing other channels for its waters, and turning them thereinto; the mighty stream of the evil thoughts of men will admit of no bounds or dams to put a stop unto them. There are but two ways of relief from them; the one, respecting their moral evil, the other their natural abundance. The first, by throwing salt into the spring, as Elisha cured the waters of Jericho; that is, to get the heart and mind seasoned with grace; for the tree must be made good before the fruit will be so. The other is, to turn their streams into new channels, putting new aims and ends upon them, fixing them on new objects; so shall we abound in spiritual thoughts; for abound in thoughts we shall, whether we will or not.

To this purpose is the advice of the Apostle, Eph. v. 18, 19. 'And be not drunk with wine, wherein is excess, but be filled with the spirit, speaking to yourselves in Psalms and Hymns and Spiritual Songs.' When men are drunk with wine unto an excess, they make it quickly evident, what vain, foolish, ridiculous imaginations it filleth their minds with. In opposition hereunto, the Apostle adviseth believers to be filled with the Spirit, to labor for such a participation of him as may fill their minds and hearts, as others fill themselves with wine. To what end, unto what purpose, should they desire such a participation of him, to be so filled with him? It is unto this end, namely, that he by his grace may fill them with holy spiritual thoughts, as on the contrary, men drunk unto an excess, are filled with those that are foolish, vain, and wicked. So the words of ver. 19 do declare, for he adviseth us to express our abounding thoughts in such duties as will give an especial vent to them.

Wherefore, when we are spiritually minded, we shall abound in spiritual thoughts, or thoughts of spiritual things. That we have such thoughts, will not sufficiently evidence that we are so, unless we abound in them. And this leads us to the principal inquiry on this head; namely, what measure we ought to assign hereof, how we may know when we abound in spiritual thoughts, so as that they may be an evidence of our being spiritually minded.

I answer in general, among other scriptures, read over Psalm, cxix. with understanding. Consider therein what David expresseth of himself, as to his constant delight in, and continual thoughts of the law of God, which was the only means of divine revelation at that season. Try yourselves by that pattern; examine yourselves whether you can truly speak the same words with him; at least, if not in the same degree of zeal, yet with the same sincerity of grace. You will say, that was David. It is not for us, it is not our duty to be like him, at least not to be equal with him. But as far as I know, we must be like him, if ever we intend to come to the place where he is. It will ruin our souls, if, when we read in the scripture how the saints of God express their experience in faith, love, delight in God and constant meditations on him, we grant that it was so with them; that they were good and holy men, but it is not necessary that it should be so with us. These things are not written in the scripture to show what they were, but what we ought to be. All things concerning them were written for our admonition. 1 Cor. 10, 11. And if we have not the same delight in God as they had, the same spiritual mindedness in thoughts and meditations of heavenly things, we can have no evidence that we please God as they did, or shall go to that place whither they are gone. Profession of the life of God passeth with many at a very low and easy rate. Their thoughts are for the most part vain and earthly, their communication unsavory, and sometimes corrupt, their lives at best uneven and uncertain, as unto the rule of obedience; yet all is well, all is life and peace. The holy men of old, who obtained this testimony that they pleased God, did not so walk before him. They meditated continually in the law; thought of God in the night seasons; spake of his ways, his works, his praise; their whole delight was in him, and in all things they followed hard after him. It is the example of David in particular, that I have proposed. And it is a promise of the grace to be administered by the Gospel, that he who is feeble shall be as David. Zech. xii. 12—18. And if we are not so in his being spiritually minded, it is to be feared we are not partakers of the promise. But that we may the better judge of ourselves therein, I shall add some few rules to this direction by example.

1. Consider, what proportion your thoughts of spiritual things bear, with those about other things. Our principal interest and concern, as we profess, lie in things spiritual, heavenly and eternal. Is it not then a foolish thing to suppose, that our thoughts about these things should not hold some proportion with those about other things; nay, that they should not exceed them? No man is so vain in earthly things, as to pretend that his principal concern lieth in that whereof he thinks very seldom in comparison of other things. It is not so with men, in reference to their families, their trades, their occasions of life. It is a truth, not only consecrated by the testimony of him who is truth, but evident also in the light or reason, that where our treasure is, there will our hearts be also. And the affections of our hearts do act themselves by the thoughts of our minds. Wherefore, if our principal treasure be as we profess, in things spiritual and heavenly, and wo unto us if it be not so! on them will our affections, and consequently our desires and thoughts, be principally fixed.

That we may the better examine ourselves by this rule, we must consider of what sort men's other thoughts are; and as unto our present purpose, they may be reduced to these heads.

1. There are such as are exercised about their call-

ings and lawful occasions. These are numberless and endless; especially among a sort of men who rise early and go to bed late, and eat the bread of carefulness, or are particularly industrious and diligent in their ways. These thoughts men approve themselves in, and judge them their duty, as they are in their proper place and measure. But no heart can conceive the multitude of these thoughts, which, partly in contrivances, partly in converse, are engaged and spent about these things. And the more men are immersed in them, the more do themselves and others esteem them diligent and praiseworthy. And there are some who have neither necessity nor occasion to be engaged much in the duties of any especial calling, who yet by their words and actions declare themselves to be confined almost in their thoughts to themselves, their relations, their children, and their self concerns; which, though most of them are very impertinent, yet they justify themselves in them. All sorts may do well to examine what proportion their thoughts of spiritual things bear to those of other things. I fear with most, it will be found to be very small, with many, next to none at all. What evidence then can they have that are spiritually minded, that their principal interest lies in things above? Perhaps it will be asked, whether it be necessary that men should think as much and as often about things spiritual and heavenly, as they do about the lawful affairs of their callings. I say more, and more often, if we are what we profess ourselves to be. Generally, it is the best sort of men, as to the things of God and man, who are busied in their callings, some of one sort, some of another. But even among the best of these, many will continually spend the strength of their minds and vigor of their spirits, about their affairs all the day long; and, so they can pray in the morning and evening, with some thoughts sometimes of spiritual things, occasionally administered, suppose they acquit themselves very well. As if a man should pretend that his great design is, to prepare himself for a voyage to a far country, where is his patrimony and his inheritance! but all his thoughts and contrivances are about some few trifles, which, if indeed he intend his voyage, he must leave behind him; and of his main design he scarce thinketh at all. We all profess that we are bound for heaven, immortality, and glory: but is it any evidence we really design it, if all our thoughts are consumed about the trifles of this world, which we must leave behind us, and have only occasional thoughts of things above? I shall elsewhere show, if God will, how men may be spiritually minded in their earthly affairs. If some relief may not be thence obtained, I cannot tell what to say or answer for them, whose thoughts of spiritual things do not hold proportion with, yea, exceed them, which they lay out about their callings.

This whole rule is grounded on that of our Saviour, Mat. vi. 31—34. 'Take no thought, saying, what shall we eat, or what shall we drink? or wherewith we shall be clothed? But seek first the kingdom of God and his righteousness, and all these things shall be added unto you. Take therefore no thought for the 'morrow.' When we have done all we can, when we have made the best of them we are able, all earthly things, as unto our interest in them, amount to no more, but what we eat, what we drink, and wherewith we are clothed. About these things our Saviour forbids us to take any thought, not absolutely, but with a double limitation. As first, that we take no such thought about them, as should carry along with it a disquietment of mind, through a distrust of the fatherly care and providence of God. This is the design of the context. Secondly, no thought that for constancy and intenseness of spirit, should be like unto those which we ought to have about spiritual things. Seek first the kingdom of God and his righteousness. Let that be the chief and principal thing in your thoughts and consciences. We may therefore conclude, that at least they must hold an exceeding proportion with them.

Let a man, industriously engaged in the way of his calling, try himself by this rule every evening. Let him consider what have been his thoughts about his earthly occasions, and what about spiritual things; and thereon ask of himself whether he be spiritually minded or not. Be not deceived; as a man thinketh, so is he. And if we account it a strange thing, that our thoughts should be more exercised about spiritual things, than about the affairs of our callings, we must not think it strange, if, when we come to the trial, we cannot find that we have either life or peace.

Moreover, it is known, how often, when we are engaged in spiritual duties, other thoughts will interpose, and impose themselves on our minds. Those which are about men's secular concernments will do so. The world will frequently make an inroad on the ways to heaven, to disturb the passengers and wayfaring men. There is nothing more frequently complained of, by such as are awake unto their duty, and sensible of their weakness. Call to mind, therefore, how often, on the other hand, spiritual thoughts do interpose, and as it were impose themselves on your minds, whilst you are engaged in your earthly affairs. Sometimes, no doubt, with all that are true believers it is so. 'Or ever I was aware, saith the spouse, my soul made me as the chariots of Aminadab.' Cant. vi. 12. Grace in her own soul surprised her into a ready willing frame for spiritual communion with Christ, when she was intent on other occasions. But if these thoughts of heavenly things so arising in us, bear no proportion with the other sort, it is an evidence what frame and principle is predominant in us.

2. There are a multitude of thoughts in the minds of men, which are vain, useless, and altogeher unprofitable. These ordinarily, through a dangerous mistake, are looked on as not sinful, because, as it is supposed, the matter of them is not so; and therefore men rather shake them off for their folly, and their guilt. But they arise from a corrupt fountain, and wofully pollute both the mind and conscience. Wherever there are vain thoughts, there is sin. Jerem. iv. 14. Such are those numberless imaginations, whereby men fancy themselves 'to be what they are not, to do what they do not, to enjoy what they enjoy not, to dispose of themselves and others,' at their pleasure. That our nature is liable to such a pernicious folly, which some of tenacious fancies have turned into madness, we are beholden alone to our cursed apostacy from God, and the vainity that possessed our minds thereon. Hence the prince of Tyrus thought 'he was a God, and sat in the seat of God.' Ezek. xxviii. 2. So it hath been with others; and in those, in whom such imaginations are kept within some better order and bounds, yet being traced to their original, they will be found to spring, some of them, immediately from pride, some from sensual lusts, some from the love of the world,

all from self, and the old ambition to be as God, to dispose of all things as we think meet. I know no greater misery or punishment in this world, than the debasing of our nature to such vain imaginations; and a perfect freedom from them is a part of the blessedness of heaven. It is not my present work to show how sinful they are; let them be esteemed only fruitless, foolish, vain and ludicrous. But let men examine themselves, what number of these vain, useless thoughts, night and day, do rove up and down in their minds. If now it be apprehended too severe, that men's thoughts of spiritual things should exceed them that are employed about their lawful callings, let them consider what proportion they bear to those which are altogether vain and useless. Do not many give more time to them, than they do to holy meditations, without an endeavor to mortify the one, or to stir up and enliven the other. Are they not more wonted to their seasons, than holy thoughts are? And shall we suppose that those with whom it is so, are spiritually minded?

3. There are thoughts that are formally evil; they are so in their nature, being corrupt contrivances to fulfil the desires of the flesh in the lusts thereof. These also will attempt the minds of believers. But they are always looked on as professed enemies to the soul, and are watched against. I shall not therefore make any comparison between them and spiritual thoughts, for they abound only in them that are carnally minded.

2. The second rule to this purpose is, that we would consider, whether thoughts of spiritual things do constantly take possession of their proper seasons. There are some times and seasons in the course of men's lives, wherein they retire themselves unto their own

thoughts. The most busied men in the world have some times of thinking unto themselves. And those who design no such thing, as being afraid of coming to be wiser or better than they are, do yet spend time therein, whether they will or not. But they who are wise will be at home as much as they can, and have as many seasons for such their retirements, as is possible for them to attain. If that man be foolish, who busieth himself so much abroad in the concerns of others, that he hath no time to consider the state of his own house and family; much more is he so, who spendeth all his thoughts about other things, and never makes use of them in an inquiry, how it is with himself and his own soul. However, men can hardly avoid, but that they must have some seasons, partly stated, partly occasional, wherein they entertain themselves with their own thoughts. The evening and the morning, the times of waking on the bed, those of the necessary cessation of all ordinary affairs, of walking, journeying, and the like, are such seasons.

If we are spiritually minded, if thoughts of spiritual things abound in us, they will ordinarily, and that with constancy, possess these seasons, look upon them as those which are their due, which belong to them. For they are expressly assigned unto them in the way of rule, expressed in examples and commands. See Psalm xvi. 7, 8. and xcii. 2. Deut. 6, 7. If they are usually given up unto other ends and occasions, are possessed with thoughts of another nature, it is an open evidence that spiritual thoughts have but little interest in our minds, little prevalency in the conduct of our souls. It is our duty to afford to them stated times taken away from other affairs that call for them. But if instead thereof we rob them of what is, as it were, their own, which no other things or business can lay any just claim to, how dwelleth the love of spiritual things in us? Most professors are convinced that it is their duty to pray morning and evening, and it is to be wished that they were all found in the practice of it. But if ordinarily they judge themselves, in the performance of that duty, to be discharged from any further exercise of spiritual thoughts, applying them to things worldly, useless, or vain, they can make no pretence to be spiritually minded.

And it must be observed, which will be found to be true, that if the seasons which are, as it were, due unto such meditations, be taken from them, they will be the worst employed of all the minutes of our lives. Vain and foolish thoughts, corrupt imaginations, will make a common haunt to the minds of men in them, and habituate themselves to an expectation of entertainment; whence they will grow importunate for admission.—Hence, with many, those precious moments of time, which might greatly influence their souls unto life and peace, if they were indeed spiritually minded, make the greatest provision for their trouble, sorrow, and confusion. For the vain and evil thoughts which some persons accustom themselves to in such seasons, are, or ought to be, a burden upon their consciences more than they can bear. That which providence tenders to their good, is turned into a snare; and God doth righteously leave them to the fruits of their own folly, who so despise his gracious provision for their good. If we cannot afford unto God our spare time, it is evident that indeed we can afford nothing at all. Micah ii. 1. They devise iniquity upon their beds. The seasons proper for holy contemplation, they make use of to fill their minds with wicked imaginations, and when the morning is light, they practise it; walking all day, on all occasions, suitably unto their devices and imaginations of the night. Many will have cause to complain to eternity, of those leisure times which might have been improved for their advantage to eternal blessedness.

If we intend therefore to maintain a title to this grace of being spiritually minded, if we would have any evidence of it in ourselves, without which we can have none of life or peace, and what we pretend thereof is but an effect of security, we must endeavor to preserve the claim and right of spiritual thoughts to such seasons, and actually put them in possession of them.

3. Consider how we are affected with our disappointments about these seasons. Have we by negligence, by temptations; have we by occasional diversions or affairs of life, been taken off from thoughts of God, of Christ, of heavenly things, when we ought to have been engaged in them; how are we affected with a review hereof? A carnal mind is well enough satisfied with the omission of any duty, so it have the pretence of a necessary occasion. If it hath lost a temporal advantage, through attendance to a spiritual duty, it will deeply reflect on itself, and it may be, like the duty, the worse afterwards. But a gracious soul, one that is truly spiritually minded, will mourn under a review of such omissions, and by every one of them is stirred up to more watchfulness for the future. Alas, will it say, how little have I been with Christ this day! How much time hath passed me without a thought of him! How foolish was I, to be wanting to such or such an opportunity! I am in arrears to myself, and have no rest until I be satisfied.

I say, if indeed we are spiritually minded, we will

duly and carefully call over the consideration of those times and seasons, wherein we ought to have exercised ourselves in spiritual thoughts; and if we have lost them, or any of them, mourn over our own negligence. But if we can omit and lose such seasons or oppotunities from time to time, without regret or self-reflections, it is to be feared that we wax worse and worse. Way will be made hereby for further omissions, until we grow wholly cold about them.

And indeed that woful loss of time that is found amongst many professors, is greatly to be bewailed.—Some lose it on themselves, by a continual track of fruitless impertinent thoughts about their own concerns.—Some in vain converse with others, wherein for the most part they edify one another only unto vanity. How much of this time might, nay, ought to be redeemed for holy mediations? The good Lord make all professors sensible of their loss of former seasons, that they may be the more watchful for the future, in this great concern of their souls. Little do some think what light, what assurance, what joy, what readiness for the cross or for heaven, they might have attained, had they laid hold on all just seasons of exercising their thoughts about spiritual things which they have enjoyed, who now are at a loss in all, and surprised with every fear or difficulty that doth befal them.

This is the first thing that belongs unto our being spiritually minded; for although it doth not absolutely or essentially consist therein, yet is it inseparable from it, and the most undeceiving indication of it. And thus of abounding and abiding in thoughts about spiritual things, such as arise and spring naturally from a living principle, a spiritual frame and disposition of heart within.

CHAPTER V.

The objects of spiritual thoughts, or what they are conversant about, evidencing them in whom they are, to be spiritually minded. Rules directing unto steadiness in the contemplation of heavenly things. Motives to fix our thoughts with steadiness in them.

BEFORE I proceed to the next general head, and which is the principal thing, the foundation of the grace and duty inquired after, some things must be spoken, to render what hath been already insisted on, yet more particularly useful. And this is, to inquire what are, or what ought to be, the special objects of those thoughts, which, under the qualifications laid down, are the evidences of our being spiritually minded. And it may be, we may be useful to many herein, by helping them to fix their minds which are apt to rove into all uncertainty. For this is befallen us through the disorder and weakness of the faculties of our souls, that sometimes what the mind guides, leads, and directs unto, in things spiritual and heavenly, our wills and affections, through their depravity and corruption, will not comply withal, and so the good designings of the mind are lost. Sometimes what the will and affections are inclined to and ready for, the mind, through its weakness and inconstancy, cannot lead them to the accomplishment of; so to will is present with us, but how to perform that will we know not. So, many are barren in this duty, because they know not what to fix upon, nor how to exercise their thoughts, when they have chosen subject for their meditations. Hence they spend their time in fruitless desires that they could use their thoughts to more purpose, rather than making any progress in the duty itself. They tire themselves, not because they are not willing to go, but because they cannot find their way. Wherefore both these things shall be spoken to; both what are the proper objects of our spiritual thoughts, and how we may be steady in our contemplations of them. And I shall to this purpose, first give some general rules, and then some particular instances, in way of direction.

1. Observe the especial calls of Providence, and apply your minds to thoughts of the duties required in them, and by them. There is a voice in all signal dispensations of Providence. 'The voice of the Lord crieth unto the city, the men of wisdom shall see thy name; hear ye the rod, and who hath appointed it.' Mic. vi. 9. There is a call, a cry in every rod of God, in every chastening providence; and therein makes a declaration of his name, his holiness, his power, his greatness. This every wise, substantial man will labor to discern, and so comply with the call. God is greatly provoked when it is otherwise. 'Lord, when thy hand is lifted up, they will not see, but they shall see and be ashamed.' Isa. xxvi. 11. If therefore we would apply ourselves to our present duty, we are wisely to consider what is the voice of God, in his present providential dispensations in the world.— Hearken not unto any who would give another interpretation of them, but that they are plain declarations of his displeasure and indignation against the sins of men. Is not his wrath in them revealed from heaven against the ungodliness of men, especially such as detain the truth in unrighteousness, or false hypocritical professors of the gospel? Doth he not also signally declare the uncertainty and instability of earthly enjoyments, from life itself to a shoe-latchet?

As also, how vain and foolish it is to adhere inordinately unto them. The fingers that appeared writing on the wall the doom of Belshazzar, did it in characters that none could read, and words that none could understand but Daniel. But the present call of God in these things, is made plain upon tables, that he may run who readeth it. If the heavens gather blackness with clouds, and it thunder over us; if any that are on their journey will not believe that there is a storm coming, they must bear the severity of it.

Suppose then this to be the voice of providence; suppose there be in these, indications of the mind and will of God, what are the duties that we are called to thereby? They may be referred unto two heads.

1. A diligent search into ourselves, and an holy watch over ourselves, with respect to those ways and sins which the displeasure of God is declared against. That present providences are indications of God's anger and displeasure, we take for granted. But when this is done, the most are apt to cast the causes of them on others, and to excuse themselves so long as they see others more wicked and profligate than themselves, openly guilty of such crimes, as they abhor the thoughts of; they cast all the wrath on them, and fear nothing, but that they shall suffer with them. But, alas! when the storm came on the ship at sea, wherein there was but one person who feared God; upon an inquiry for whose sake it came, the lot fell on him. John i. 7. The cause of the present storm may as well be the secret sins of professors, as the open provocations of ungodly men. God will punish severely those whom he hath known. Amos iii. 2. It is therefore certainly our duty to search diligently, that nothing be found resting in us, against which God

is declaring his displeasure. Take heed of negligence and security herein. When our Saviour foretold his disciples that one of them should betray him, he who alone was guilty, was the last that said, Master, is it I? Let no ground of hopes you have of your spiritual condition and acceptance with God, no sense of your sincerity in any of your duties, no visible difference between you and others in the world, impose themselves on your minds to divert them from diligence in this duty. The voice of the Lord crieth unto the city, and the man of wisdom will see his name.

2. A diligent endeavor to 'live in an holy resignation of our persons, our lives, our families, all our enjoyments, unto the sovereign will and wisdom of God;' so as that we may be in a readiness to part with all things upon his call without repining. This also is plainly declared in the voice of present providences. God is making wings for men's riches; he is shaking their habitations, taking away the visible defences of their lives; proclaiming the instability and uncertainty of all things here below: and if we are not minded to contend with him, we have nothing left to give us rest and peace for a moment, but an holy resignation of all unto his sovereign pleasure.

Would you now know what you should fix and exercise your thoughts upon, so as that they may be evidences of your being spiritually minded? I say, be frequently conversant in them about these things. They lie before you, they call upon you, and will find you a just employment. Count them part of your business, allow them some part of your time, cease not until you have the testimony of your consciences, that you have in sincerity stated both these duties in your minds; which will never be done without many thoughts about them. Unless it be so with you, God will be greatly displeased at the neglect of his coming and call, now it is so plain and articulate. Fear the woful dooms recorded, Prov. i. 25—28. Isa. lvi. 12. Chap. 66. 4. to this purpose. And if any calamity, public or private, do overtake you under a neglect of these duties, you will be wofully surprised, and not know which way to turn for relief. This therefore is the time and season wherein you may have an especial trial and experiment whether you be spiritually minded or not. It is the wisdom of faith to excite and draw forth grace into exercise according to present occasions. If this grace be habitually resident in you, it will put itself forth in many thoughts about these present duties.

But, alas! for the most part, men are apt to walk contrary to God in these things, as the wisdom of the flesh is contrary to him in all things. A great instance we have with respect to these duties, especially the latter of them. For, 1, who almost makes a dilligent search into, and trial of, his heart and ways, with respect to the procuring causes of the displeasure and judgments of God? Generally, when the tokens and evidences of them most abound, the world is full of outrageous provoking sins. These visibly proclaim themselves to be the causes of 'the coming of the wrath of God on the children of disobedience.' Hence most men are apt to cast the whole reason of present judgments upon them, and put it wholly from themselves. Hence commonly there is never less of self-examination, than when it is called for in a peculiar manner. But, as I will not deny, but that open daring sins of the world are the procuring causes of the wrath of God against it in temporal judgments; so the wisest course for us, is to refer them to the great judgments of the last day. This the Apostle directs us to. 2 Thess. i. 6—10. Our duty is to consider on what accounts judgment begins at the house of God, and to examine ourselves with respect thereunto.

Again, the other part of our present duty in compliance with the voice of providence, is an humble resignation of ourselves and all our concernments unto the will of God, sitting loose in our affections from all earthly temporal enjoyments. This we neither do, nor can do, let us profess what we will, unless our thoughts are greatly exercised about the reasons of it and motives to it. For this is the way whereby faith puts forth its efficacy, to the mortification of self and all earthly enjoyments. Wherefore without this we can make no resignation of ourselves to the will of God. But, alas, how many at present openly walk contrary unto God herein! The ways, the countenances, the discourses of men, give evidence hereto. Their love to present things, their contrivances for their increase and continuance, grow and thrive under the calls of God to the contrary. So it was of old; they did eat, they drank, they married, and gave in marriage, until the day that Noah entered into the ark. Can the generality of professors at this day give testimony to the exercise of their thoughts upon such things as should dispose them to this holy resignation; that they meditate on the calls of God, and thence make themselves ready to part with all at his time and pleasure! How can persons pretend to be spiritually minded, the current of whose thoughts lies in direct contrariety to the mind of God?

Here lies the ground of their self-deceivings; they are the professors of the Gospel in a peculiar manner; they judge themselves believers; they hope they shall be saved, and have many evidences for it. But one negative evidence, will render an hundred that are positive, useless. All these things have I done, saith the young man; yet one thing thou wantest, saith our Saviour; and the want of that one, rendered his all things of no avail to him. Many things you have done, many things you do, many grounds of hope abide with you; neither yourselves nor others doubt of your condition; but are you spiritually minded? If this one thing be wanting, all the rest will not avail you; you have indeed neither life nor peace. And what grounds have you to judge that you are so, if the current of your thoughts lie in direct contrariety to the present calls of God? If at such a time as this is, your love to the world be such as ever it was, and perhaps be increased; if your desires are strong to secure the things of this life to you and yours; if the daily contrivance of your minds be, not how you may attain a constant resignation of yourselves and your all unto the will of God, which will not be done without much thoughtfulness and meditation on the reasons of it and motives to it, I cannot understand how you can judge yourselves to be spiritually minded.

If any therefore shall say, that they would abound more in spiritual thoughts, only they know not what to fix them upon; I propose this, in the first place, as that which will lead them to the due performance of present duties.

Secondly. The special trials and temptations of men, call for the exercise of their thoughts in a peculiar manner, with respect to them. If a man hath a bodily disease, pain, or distemper, it will cause him to think much of it, whether he will or not; at least if he be wise, he will do so; nor will he always be complaining of their smart, but inquire into their causes, and seek their removal. Yet are there some distempers, as lethargies, which in their own nature take away all sense and thoughts of themselves; and some are of such a slow, secret progress, as hectic fevers, that they are not taken notice of. But both these are mortal. And shall men be more negligent about the spiritual distempers of their souls; so as to have multiplied temptations, the cause of all spiritual diseases, and take no thought about them? Is it not to be feared, that where it is so, they are such as either in their own nature have deprived them of spiritual sense, or by their deceitfulness are leading on insensibly to death eternal? Not to have our minds exercised about these things, is to be stupidly secure. Prov. xxxiii. 34, 35.

There is, I confess, some difficulty in this matter, how to exercise our thoughts aright about our temptations; for the great way of the prevalency of temptation, is by stirring up multiplied thoughts about their objects, or what they lead to. And this is done or occasioned several ways. (1). From the previous power of lust in the affections. This will fill the mind with thoughts. The heart will coin imaginations, in compliance therewith. They are the way and means whereby lust draws away the heart from duty, and enticeth unto sin: Jam. i. 14, the means at least whereby men come to have eyes full of adultery, 2 Pet. 2, 14, or live in constant contemplation of the pleasures of sin. (2.) They arise and are occasioned by renewed representations of the object of sin; and this is two-fold. (1.) That which is real, as Achan saw the wedge of gold, and coveted it. Josh. vii. 21. Prov. xxii. 31. Against this is the prayer of the Psalmist, turn away mine eyes from beholding vanity; and the covenant of Job, chap. xxxi 1. (2.) Imaginary, when the imagination, being tinted or infected by lust, continually represents the pleasures of sin and the actings of it unto the mind. 'Herein do men make provision for the flesh, to fulfil the lust thereof.' Rom. xiii. 14. (3.) From the suggestions of satan, who useth all his wiles and artifices to stir up thoughts about that sin whereunto the temptation leads; and temptation seldom fails of its end, when it can stir up a multitude of unprofitable thoughts about its object. For when temptations multiply thoughts about sin, proceeding from some or all of these causes, and the mind hath wonted itself to give them entertainment, those in whom they are, want nothing but opportunities and occasions, taking off the power of outward restraints, for the commission of actual sin. When men have devised mischief, they practise it when it is in the power of their hand. Mic. ii. 1. It is no way safe to advise such persons to have many thoughts about their temptations; they will all turn to their disadvantage.

I speak to them only, unto whom their temptations are their affliction and their burden. And such persons also must be very careful how they suffer their thoughts to be exercised about the matter of their temptation, lest it be a snare, and be too hard for them. Men may begin their thoughts of any object with abhorrence and detestation, and if it be in case of temptation, end them in complacency and approbation. The deceitfulness of sin lays hold on something or other that lusts in the mind, stays upon with delectation, and so corrupts the whole frame of spirit which began the duty. There have been instances wherein persons have entered with a resolution to punish sin, and have been ensnared by the occasion, to the commission of the sin they thought to punish.—Wherefore, it is seldom that the mind of any one, exercised with an actual temptation, is able safely to conflict with it, if it entertain abiding thoughts of the matter of it, or of the sin whereunto it leads. For sin hath *mille nocendi artes*, and is able to transfuse its poison into the affections from every thing it hath once made a bait of, especially if it hath already defiled the mind with pleasing contemplations of it. Yea, oftentimes a man that hath some spiritual strength, and therein engageth to the performance of duties, if in the midst of them the matter of his temptation is so presented to him, as to take hold of his thoughts; in a moment, as if he had seen, (as they say,) Medusa's head, he is turned into a stone; his spirits are all frozen, his strength is gone, all actings of grace cease, his armour falls from him, and he gives up himself a prey to his temptation. It must be a new supply of grace that can give him any deliverance. Wherefore, whilst persons are exercised with any temptation, I do not advise them to be conversant in their thoughts about the matter of it. For sometimes remembrances of former satisfaction of their lusts; sometimes present surprisals, with the suitableness of it to corruption not yet mortified; sometimes the craft of satan, fixing their imagination on it, will be too hard for them, and carry them to a fresh compliance with that sin, which they would be delivered from.

But this season calls, in an especial manner, for the exercise of the thoughts of men, about the ways and means of deliverance from the snare wherein they are taken, or the danger they find themselves exposed to. Think of the guilt of sin, that you may be humbled. Think of the power of sin, that you may seek strength against it. Think not of the matter of sin, the things that are in the world suited to the lusts of the flesh, the lust of the eye, and the pride of life, lest you be more and more entangled. But the present direction is, think much of the ways of relief from the power of your own temptation leading to sin: but this men, unless they are spiritually minded, are very loth to come to. I speak not of them that love their shackles, that glory in their yoke, that like their temptations well enough, as those which give the most satisfactory entertainment to their minds. Such men know not well what to do, unless they may in their minds converse with the objects of their lusts, and multiply thoughts about them continually. The apostle calls it making provision for the flesh, to fulfil the lusts thereof. Their principal trouble is, that they cannot comply with them to the utmost, by reason of some outward restraints: these dwell near to those fools who make a mock of sin, and will ere long take up their habitation among them.

But I speak, as I said before, of them only, whose temptations are their afflictions, and who groan for deliverance from them. Acquaint such persons with the great, indeed, only way of relief in this distress, as it is expressed, Heb. ii. 17, 18. 'He is a merciful and faithful High Priest in things appertaining unto God; for in that he himself hath suffered, being tempted, he is able to succor them that are tempted. And chap. iv. 15, 16. 'For we have not an High Priest that cannot be touched with the feelings of our infirmities, but was in all points tempted like as we are, yet without sin. Let us therefore come boldly to the throne of grace, that we may obtain mercy, and find grace to help in time of need.' Let them know that the only way for their deliverance is by acting faith on thoughts on Christ, his power to succor them that are tempted, with the ways whereby he administereth a sufficiency of grace unto that end; retreating for relief to him on the urgency of temptations, they can hardly be brought to a compliance therewithal. They are ready to say, are not Abana and Pharpar, rivers of Damascus, better than all the waters of Israel? Is it not better to betake ourselves, and to trust to our own promises, resolutions, and endeavors, with such other ways of escape, as are in our own power? I shall speak nothing against any of them in their proper place, so far as they are warranted by scripture rule. But this I say, none shall ever be delivered from perplexing temptations unto the glory of God and their own spiritual advantage, but by the acting and exercising of faith on Christ Jesus, and the sufficiency of his grace for our deliverance. But when men are not spiritually minded, they cannot fix their thoughts on spiritual things: therefore do men daily pine away under their temptations; they get ground upon them, until their breach grow great like the sea, and there be no healing of it.

I mention this, only to show the weight and necessity of the duty proposed. For when men under the power of conviction, are pressed with temptation, they will do any thing rather than betake themselves to the only efficacious relief. Some will groan and cry out under their vexation from the torture they are put to, in the conflict between their temptations and convictions. Some will betake themselves to the pretended relief that any false religion tenders to them. But to apply themselves in thoughts of faith unto Jesus Christ, whose grace alone is sufficient for all, that they will not be persuaded to.

We are all of us liable to temptations. Those who are not sensible of it, are under the power of what the temptation leads to; and they are of two sorts. First, such as are extraordinary, when the hand of God is on them in a peculiar manner for our rebuke. It is true, God tempts none, as temptation formally leads unto sin; but he orders temptations, so far forth as they are afflictive and chastisements. Thus it is when he suffers an especial corruption within, to fall in conjunction with an especial temptation without, and to obtain a prevalency thereby. Of these there is no doubt but any man, not judicially hardened, may know both his disease and the remedy. But that ordinary course of temptations which we are exercised withal, needs a diligent attendance for their discovery, as well as for our deliverance from them; and it is to be feared that many are kept in spiritual weakness, useless, and in darkness all their days, through the power of their temptations, yet never know what they are, or wherein they consist; these gray hairs are sprinkled on them, yet they know it not; some approve themselves in those very things and ways which are their temptations. Yet in the exercise of due watchfulness, diligence, and prudence, men may know both the plague of their own hearts, in their prevailing corruptions, and the ways whereby it is excited through temptation, with the occasions it makes use of, and the advantages it takes. For instance; one may have an eminency in gifts, and usefulness or success in his labors, which gives him great acceptance with others;

such an one shall hardly avoid a double temptation: first of spiritual pride, and self-exaltation. Hence the apostle will not admit a novice, one inexperienced in the ways of grace, and deceits of sin, into the office of the ministry, lest he should be lifted up with pride, and fall into the condemnation of the Devil. 1 Tim. iii. 6. He himself was not without danger hereof. 2 Cor. xii. 17. The best of men can hardly fortify their minds against the secret workings of pride, upon successes and applause, unless they keep them constantly balanced with thoughts of their own vileness in the sight of God. And, secondly, remissness unto exact universal mortification, which they countenance themselves against, by their acceptance and success above others in the ministry. It were much to be desired, that all who are ministers, would be careful in these things; for although some of us may not much please others, yet we may so far please ourselves, as to expose our souls to these snares; and the effects of negligence herein do openly appear unto the disadvantage of the gospel. Others are much conversant in the world and the affairs of it. Negligence, as to a spiritual watch, vanity in converse, love of earthly things, with conformity to the world, will on all occasions impose themselves upon them. If they understand not their temptations herein, spiritual mindedness will be impaired in them continually. Those that are rich, have their especial temptations, which, for the most part, are many, plausible, and effectual: and those that are poor, have their's also. The snares of some lie in their constitutions, of others, in their society, of most, in the various circumstances of life. Those who are upon their watch in any due measure, who exercise any wisdom or observation concerning themselves, may know wherein their temptations lie, what are the advantages whereby they perplex their minds, and endanger their souls.

In these cases generally, men are taught what are the ways and means of their deliverance and preservation. Wherefore there are three things required to this duty, and spiritual wisdom to them all. 1. To know what are the especial temptations from whence you suffer, and whereby the life of God is obstructed in you. If this be neglected, if it be disregarded, no man can maintain either life or peace, or is spiritually minded. 2. Know your remedy, your relief, wherein alone it doth consist. Many duties are required of us to this end, and are useful thereunto; but know assuredly, that no one of them, not all of them in conjunction, will bring in relief unto the glory of God and your own peace, without application by faith to him who is able to succour them that are tempted. Wherefore, (3.) herein lies your great duty with respect to your temptations, namely, in a constant exercise of your thoughts on the love, care, compassion, and tenderness of Christ, with his ability to help, succour, and save them that do believe; so to strengthen your faith and trust in him, which will prove assuredly successful and victorious.

The same duty is incumbent on us with respect to any urgent, prevalent, general temptation There are seasons wherein an hour of temptation comes on the earth to try them that dwell therein. What if a man should judge that now it is such an hour, and that the power of darkness is put forth therein? what if he should be persuaded that a general security, coldness, deadness, and decay in grace, especially as to the vigorous actings of zeal, love, and delight in God, with an indifference to holy duties, are the effects of this hour of temptation? I do not say determinately, that so it is; let others judge as they see cause; but if any one do so judge, undoubtedly it is his duty to be exercised in his thoughts, how he may escape in this day of trial, and be counted worthy to stand before the Son of Man. He will find it his concernment to be conversant in his mind with the reasons and motives to watchfulness, and how he may obtain such supplies of grace as may effectually preserve him from such decays.

3. All things in religion, both in faith and practice, are to be the objects of such thoughts. As they are proposed or occur to our minds in great variety on all sorts of occasions, so we ought to give them entertainment in our meditations. To hear things, to have them proposed to us, it may be, in the way of a divine ordinance, and to let them slip out, or flow from us, as water that is poured into a leaking vessel, is the ruin of many souls. I shall therefore choose out some instances, as was before proposed, of those things which I judge, that they who would be spiritually minded, ought to abide and abound in thoughts concerning them.

1. It is our duty greatly to mind the things that are above, eternal things, both as to their reality, their present state, and our future enjoyment of them; herein consists the life of this grace and duty. To be heavenly minded, that is, to mind the things of heaven, and to be spiritually minded, is all one; or it is the effect of being spiritually minded as unto its original and essence, or the first proper actings of it; it is the cause of it, as to its growth and degrees; and it is the evidence of it, in experience. Nor do I understand how it is possible for a man to place his chief interest

in things above, and not have many thoughts of them. It is the great advice of the apostle, on a supposition of our interest in Christ, and conformity to him. Col. iii. 1, 2. If ye then be risen with Christ, seek those things that are above, where Christ sitteth at the right hand of God. Set your affections, (or your thoughts;) mind much the things that are above. It becomes those who, through the virtue of the resurrection of Christ, are raised unto newness of life, to have their thoughts exercised on the state of things above; with respect to the presence of Christ among them, and the singular use of our prospect into these things, or our meditations on them, he instructs us in 2 Cor. iv. 16—18. 'For which cause we faint not; but though our outward man perish, yet the inward man is renewed day by day. For our light affliction, which is but for a moment, worketh for us a far more exceeding and eternal weight of glory. Whilst we look not at the things which are seen, but at the things which are not seen; for the things which are seen are temporal, but the things which are not seen are eternal.' Not to faint under the daily decays of our outward man, and the approaches of death thereby; to bear afflictions as things light and momentary; to thrive under all in the inward man, are unspeakable mercies and privileges. Can you attain a better frame? Is there any thing that you would more desire, if you are believers? Is it not better to have such a mind in us, than to enjoy all the peace and security that the world can afford? One principal means whereby we are made partakers of these things, is a due meditation on things unseen and eternal. These are the things that are within the vail, whereon we ought to cast the anchor of our hope, in all the storms we meet with, (Heb. vi. 19, 20.) whereof we shall speak more afterwards.

Without doubt, the generality of Christians are greatly defective in this duty, partly for want of light in them, partly for want of delight in them; they think little of an eternal country. Wherever men are, they do not use to neglect thoughts of that country wherein their inheritance lies. If they are absent from it for a season, yet will they labor to acquaint themselves with the principal concernments of it. But this heavenly country, wherein lies our eternal inheritance, is not regarded. Men do not as they ought, exercise themselves unto thoughts of things eternal and invisible: it were impossible if they did so, that their minds should be so earthly, and their affections cleave so as they do to present things. He that looks steadily on the sun, although he cannot bear the lustre of his beams fully, yet his sight is so affected with it, that when he calls off his eyes from it, he can see nothing, as it were, of the things about him; they are all dark to him: and he who looks steadily in his contemplations on things above, eternal things, though he cannot comprehend their glory, yet a vail will be cast by it on all the desirable beauties of earthly things, and take off his affections from them.

Men live and act under the power of a conviction, that there is a state of immortality and glory to come; with a persuasion hereof they much relieve themselves in their sorrows, sufferings, and temptations; yet with many it is only a reserve, when they can be here no more; but as to daily contemplation of the nature and causes of it, or as unto any entrance into it by faith and hope, the most are strangers thereto. If we are spiritually minded, nothing will be more natural to us, than to have many thoughts of eternal things, as those wherein all our own principal concerns do lie, as well as those which are excellent and glorious in themselves. The direction thereon is, that we would make heavenly things, the things of the future state of blessedness and glory, a principal object of our thoughts; that we would think much about them; that we would meditate much upon them. Many are discouraged herein by their ignorance and darkness, by their want of due conceptions, and steady apprehensions of invisible things. Hence one of these two things befal them, when they would meditate on things above: 1. The glory of them, the glory of God in them, being essentially infinite and incomprehensible, doth immediately overwhelm them and, as it were, in a moment put them to an utter loss, that they cannot frame one thought in their minds about them : or, 2, they want skill and ability to conceive aright of invisible things, and to dispose of them in such order in their minds, as that they may sedately exercise their thoughts about them. Both these shall be afterwards spoken unto : at present I shall only say that,

Whosoever shall sincerely engage in this duty, according to what he hath, and shall abide constant therein, will make such a refreshing progress in his apprehension of heavenly things, as he will be greatly satisfied with. We are kept in darkness, ignorance, and unsteadiness of meditations about them, not from the nature of the things themselves, but from our own sloth, negligence, and readiness to be turned aside by apprehensions of difficulties, of the lion in the way; wherefore I shall consider two things : 1. What are the principal motives to this duty of fixing our thoughts on the things that are above, and the advantages which we receive thereby : 2. Give some directions how, and on what in particular, we may exercise our thoughts on those things above.

1. Faith will be increased and strengthened by it. Invisible things are the proper objects of faith: it is the evidence of things not seen.—Heb. xi. 1. Wherefore in our thoughts of them, faith is in its proper exercise, which is the principal means of its growth and increase. And hereon two things will ensue:

1. The soul will come unto a more satisfactory abiding sense of the reality of them. Things of imagination, which maintain a value of themselves by darkness, will not bear a diligent search into them; they lose of their reputation on every serious inquiry. If rational men would but give themselves the liberty of free inquiry by their own thoughts, it would quickly cashier the fool's paradise of Mahomet, the purgatory of the Papists, and all such creatures of imagination and superstition. But where things are real and substantial, the more they are inquired into, the more they evidence their being and subsistence. It is not, therefore, every profession of a faith of a future state of blessedness, that will realize it in our minds: and therefore, for the most part, it is rather a notion that men have of heavenly things, which they do not contradict, than any solid satisfaction in, or spiritual sense of, their reality; for these are things that eye hath not seen nor ear heard, nor will enter into the heart of man to conceive; whose existence, nature, and real state, are not easily comprehended; but through the continual exercise of holy thoughts about them, the soul obtains an entrance into the midst of them, finding in them both durable substance and riches. There is no way, therefore, to strengthen faith to any degree, but by a daily contemplation on

the things themselves. They who do not think of them frequently, shall never believe them sincerely. They admit not of any collateral evidence, where they do not evidence themselves unto our souls. Faith, as we said, thus exercised, will give them a subsistence, not in themselves, which they have antecedent thereto; but in us, in our hearts, in the minds of them that believe. Imagination creates its own object: faith finds it prepared beforehand. It will not leave a bare notion of them in the understanding, but give them a spiritual subsistence in the heart; as Christ himself dwells in our hearts by faith. And there are two things that will discover this subsistence of them in us:—1. When we find them in a continual readiness to rise up in our minds on all occasions wherein the thoughts and remembrance of them are needful and useful to us. There are many seasons, some whereof shall be immediately spoken to; and many duties, wherein and whereto the faith and thoughts of things invisible and eternal are needful to us, so as that we cannot fill up those seasons, nor perform those duties, in a due manner without them. If on all such occasions they do, from the inward frame of our minds, present themselves to us, or through our acquaintance and familiarity with them, we recur in our thoughts to them, they seem to have a real subsistence given to them in our souls: but if on such occasions, wherein alone they will yield us help and relief, we accustom ourselves to other thoughts, if those concerning them are, as it were, out of the way, and arise not in our minds of their own accord, we are yet strangers to this effect of faith. 2. They are realized to us, they have a subsistence in us, when the soul continually longeth to be in them: when they have given such a relish to our hearts, as the first fruits of glory, that we cannot but desire, on all opportune occasions, to be in the full enjoyment of them, faith seems to have had its effeatual work herein upon us. For want of these things, many among us walk in disconsolation all their days.

2. It will gradually give the heart an acquaintance with the especial nature and use of these things. General thoughts and notions of heaven and glory do but fluctuate up and down in the mind, and very little influence it to other duties; but assiduous contemplation, will give the mind such distinct apprehensions of heavenly things, as shall duly affect it with the glory of them. The more we discern of the glory and excellency of them in their own nature, of their suitableness unto ours, as our only proper rest and blessedness, as the perfection and complement of what is already begun in us by grace, of the restless tendency of all gracious dispositions and inclinations of our hearts towards their enjoyment, the more will faith be established in its cleaving unto them; so in the contemplation of these things consist the principal food of faith, whereby it is nourished and strengthened: and we are not to expect much work where there is not provision of proper food for them that labor. No wonder if we find faith faint and weak in the work it hath to do, which oft-times is great and weighty, if we neglect to guide it daily to that which should administer strength to it.

(2.) It will give life and exercise to the grace of hope. Hope is a glorious grace, whereunto blessed effects are ascribed in the Scripture, and an effectual operation to the support and consolation of believers; by it are we purified, sanctified, saved; and, to sum up the whole of its excellency and efficacy, it is a principal way of the working of Christ as inhabiting in us; Col. i. 27. Christ in you the hope of glory. Where Christ evidenceth his presence with us, he gives us an infallible hope of glory; he gives us an assured pledge of it, and worketh our souls to an expectation of it. Hope in general is but an uncertain expectation of a future good which we desire; but as it is a gospel-grace, all uncertainty is removed from it, which would hinder us of the advantage intended in it. It is an earnest expectation, proceeding from faith, trust, and confidence, accompanied with longing desires of en-enjoyment. From a mistake of its nature it is that few Christians labor after it, exercise themselves to it, or have the benefit of it; for to live by hope, they suppose infers a state not only beneath the life of faith, and all assurance in believing, but also exclusive of them. They think to hope to be saved is a condition of men who have no grounds of faith or assurance. But this is to turn a blessed fruit of the spirit into a common affection of nature. Gospel hope is a fruit of faith, trust, and confidence; yea, the height of the actings of all grace issues in a well grounded hope, nor can it rise any higher. Rom. v. 2—5.

Now the reason why men have no more use of, no more benefit by, this excellent grace, is because they do not abide in the thoughts and contemplaiton of the things hoped for. The especial object of hope is eternal glory. Col. i. 27. Rom. v. 2. The peculiar use of it, is to support, comfort, and refresh the soul in all trials, under all weariness and despondences, with a firm expectation of a speedy entrance into that glory, with an earnest desire after it. Wherefore, unless we acquaint ourselves, by continual meditation, with the reality and nature of this glory, it is impossible it should be the object of a vigorous, active hope, such as whereby the apostle says we are saved. Without this we can neither have that evidence of eternal things, nor that valuation of them, nor that preparedness in our minds for them, as should keep us in the exercise of gracious hope about them.

Suppose sundry persons engaged in a voyage to a most remote country, wherein all of them have an apprehension that there is a place of rest, and an inheritance provided for them. Under this apprehension they all put themselves upon their voyage, to possess what is so prepared. Howbeit some of them have only a general notion of these things, they know nothing distinctly concerning them, and are so busied about other affairs, that they have no leisure to inquire into them, or suppose that they cannot come to any satisfactory knowledge of them in particular, and so are content to go on with general hopes and expectations. Others there are, who by all possible means acquaint themselves particularly with the nature of the climate whither they are going, with the excellency of the inheritance, and provision that is made for them. Their voyage proves long and wearisome, their difficulties many, and their dangers great, and they have nothing to relieve and encourage themselves, but the hope and expectation of the country whither they are going. Those of the first sort will be very apt to despond and faint; their general hopes will not be able to relieve them. But those who have a distinct notion and apprehension of the state of things whither they are going, and of their incomparable excellency, have always in a readiness wherewith to cheer their minds and support themselves.

In that journey or pilgrimage wherein we are engaged towards an heavenly country, we are sure to meet with all kinds of dangers, difficulties and perils. It is not a general notion of blessedness that will excite and work in us a spiritual refreshing hope. But when we think and meditate on future glory as we ought, that grace which is neglected for the most part as to its benefit, and dead as to its exercise, will of all others be most vigorous and active, putting itself forth on all occasions. This therefore is an inestimable benefit of the duty exhorted unto, and which they find the advantage of, who are really spiritual minded.

3. This alone will make us ready for the cross, for all sorts of sufferings that we may be exposed unto.

There is nothing more necessary to believers at this season, than to have their minds furnished with provision of such things as may prepare them for the cross and sufferings. Various intimations of the mind of God, circumstances of Providence, the present state of things in the world, with the instant peril of the latter days, all call them hereto. If it be otherwise with them, they will at one time or other be wofully surprised, and think strange of their trials, as if some strange thing did befal them. Nothing is more useful to this end, than constant thoughts and contemplations of eternal things and future glory. From thence alone can the soul have in readiness what to lay in the balance against all sorts of sufferings. When a storm begins to arise at sea, the mariners bestir themselves in the management of the tackling of the ship, and other applications of their art for their safety: but if the storm increase and come to extremity, they are forced to forego all other means, and betake themselves unto a sheet anchor to hold their ship steady against its violence. So when a storm of persecution and trouble begins to arise, men have various ways and considerations for their relief. But if it once comes to extremity, if sword, nakedness, famine, and death, are inevitably coming upon them, they have nothing to betake themselves to, that will yield them solid relief, but the consideration and faith of things invisible and eternal.

So the apostle declares this state of things 2 Cor. iv. 16—18, the words before insisted on. 'For which cause we faint not, but though our outward man perish, yet the inward is renewed day by day. For our light affliction, which is but for a moment, worketh for us a far more exceeding and eternal weight of glory; while we look not at the things which are seen, but at the things which are not seen; for the things which are seen are temporal, but the things which are not seen are eternal." He lays all sorts of afflictions in one scale, and on the consideration of them, declares them to be light, and but for a moment. Then he lays glory in the other scale, and finds it to be ponderous, weighty, and eternal; an exceeding weight of glory. In the one, is sorrow for a little while, in the other, eternal joy. In the one, pain for a few moments, in the other, everlasting rest; in the one, is the loss of some few temporary things; in the other, the full fruition of God in Christ, who is all in all.

Hence the same apostle casts up the account of these things, and gives us his judgment concerning them. Rom. viii. 18. For I reckon that the sufferings of this present time are not worthy to be compared to the glory that shall be revealed in us; there is no comparison between them, as if one had as much evil and misery in them, as the other hath of good and blessedness; as though his state was any way to be complained of, who must undergo the one, whilst he hath an interest in the other; or as though to escape the one, he hazard the enjoyment of the other.

It is inseparable from our nature to have a fear of, and aversion from, great distressing sufferings, that are above the power of nature to bear. Even our Lord Jesus himself, having taken on him all the sinless properties of our natures, had a fear and aversation, though holy and gracious with respect to his own. Those who, through a stout heartedness, do contemn them before their approach, boasting in themselves of their abilities to undergo them, censuring such as will not unadvisedly engage in them, are such as seldom glorify God when they are really to conflict with them. Peter alone trusted to himself that he would not forsake his master, and seemed to take the warning ill that they should all do so; and he alone denied him. All church histories are filled with instances of such as, having borne themselves high before the approach of trials, have shamefully miscarried when their trials have come. Wherefore it is moreover allowed unto us, to use all lawful means for the avoiding of them. Both rules and examples of the scripture give sufficient warranty for it. But there are times and seasons wherein, without any tergiversation, they are to be undergone unto the glory of God, and in the discharge of our duty, confessing Christ before men, as we would be owned by him before his Father in heaven. All things do now call us to prepare for such a season, to be martyrs in resolution, though we should never really lose our lives by violence. Nothing will give us this preparation, but to have our minds exercised in the contemplation of heavenly things, of things that are invisible and eternal. He who is thus spiritual minded, who hath his thoughts and affections set on things above, will have always in a readiness what to oppose unto any circumstance of his sufferings.

Those views which such an one hath had by faith, of the uncreated glories above, of the things in heavenly places, where Christ sits at the right hand of God, of the glory within the vail, whereby they have been realised and made present to his soul, will now visit him every moment, abide with him continually, and put forth their efficacy to his support and refreshment. Alas! what will become of many of us, who are grovelling continually on the earth, whose bellies cleave to the dust, who are strangers to the thoughts of heavenly things, when distressing troubles shall befal us? Why, shall we think that refreshing thoughts of things above will then visit our souls, when we resisted their admittance in days of peace? Do you come to me in your distress, saith Jeptha, when in the time of your peace you drove me from you? When we would thus think of heavenly things to our refreshment, we shall hardly get them to make an abode with us. I know God can come in by the mighty power of his spirit and grace, to support and comfort the souls of them who are called, and even surprised into the greatest of sufferings. Yet do I know also, that it is our duty not to tempt him, in the neglect of the ways and means which he hath appointed for the communication of his grace to us.

Our Lord Jesus Christ himself, as the author and finisher of our faith, for the joy that was set before him, endured the cross and despised the shame. Heb.

xii. 2. His mediatory glory in the salvation of the church, was the matter of the joy set before him. This he took the view and prospect of, in all his sufferings, to his refreshment and support. And his example, as the author and finisher of our faith, is more efficaciously instructive than any other rule or precept. Eternal glory is set before us also; it is the design of God's wisdom and grace, that by the contemplation of it we should relieve ourselves in all our sufferings, yea, and rejoice with joy unspeakable and full of glory. How many of those blessed souls now in the enjoyment of God and glory, who passed through fiery trials and great tribulations, were enabled to sing and rejoice in the flames by a prepossession of this glory in their minds through believing? Yea, some have been so filled with them, as to take off all sense of pain under the most exquisite tortures. When Stephen was to be stoned, to encourage him in his sufferings and comfort him in it, the heavens were opened, and he saw Jesus standing at the right hand of God. Who can conceive what contempt of all the rage and madness of the Jews, what a neglect of all the pains of death, this view raised his holy soul unto? To obtain therefore, such views frequently by faith, as they do who are truly spiritually minded, is the most effectual way to encourage us unto all our sufferings. The apostle gives us the force of this encouragement, in a comparison with earthly things. 1 Cor. ix. 25. 'Every man who striveth for the mastery, is temperate in all things; now they do it to obtain a corruptible crown, but we an incorruptible.' If men, when a corruptible crown of vain honor and applause is proposed to them, will do and endure all that is needful for the attainment of it, and relieve themselves in their hardships with thoughts and imaginations of attaining it, grounded on uncertain hopes; shall not we, who have a crown immortal and invisible proposed to us, and that with the highest assurance of the enjoyment of it, cheerfully undergo, endure, and suffer, what we are to go through in the way to it.

4. This is the most effectual means to wean the hearts and affections from things here below; to keep the mind to an undervaluation, yea, a contempt of them, as occasion shall require. For there is a season wherein there is such a contempt required in us of all relations and enjoyments, as our Saviour calleth, the hating of them; that is, not absolutely, but comparatively, in comparison of him and the Gospel, with the duties which belong to our profession. Luke xiv. 26.

'If any man come to me, and hate not father and mother, and wife and children, and brethren and sisters, yea, and his own life also, he cannot be my disciple.' Some, I fear, if they did but consider it, would be apt to say, This is a hard saying, who can bear it? and others cry out with the disciples in another case, Lord, who then can be saved? But it is the word whereby we must be judged, nor can we be the disciples of Christ on any other terms. But here, in an especial manner, lie the wound and weakness of faith and profession in these our days. The bellies of men cleave unto the dust, or their affections to earthly things.

I speak not of those who, by rapine, deceit, and oppression, strive to enrich themselves; nor of those who design nothing more than the attainment of greatness and promotion in the world, though not by ways of open wickedness; least of all, of them who make religion, and perhaps their ministry therein, a means for the attaining secular ends and preferments. No wise man can suppose such persons, any of them, to be spiritually minded, and it is most easy to disprove all their pretences. But I intend only those at present, whose ways and means of attaining riches are lawful, honest, and unblameable; who use them with some moderation, and do profess that their portion lies in better things; so as it is hard to fasten a conviction on them, in matters of their conversation. Whatever may seem to reflect upon them, they esteem it to be that, whose omission would make them foolish in their affairs, or negligent in their duty. But even among these also, there is oft-times that inordinate love unto present things, that esteem and valuation of them, that concernment in them, as are not consistent with their being spiritually minded. With some, their relations, with some, their enjoyments, with most, both in conjunction, are an idol which they set up in their hearts, and secretly bow down unto. About these are their hopes and fears exercised; on them is their love, in them is their delight. They are wholly taken up with their own concerns, count all lost that is not spent on them., and all time mispent that is not engaged about them. Yet the things which they do, they judge to be good in themselves; their hearts do not condemn them as to the matter of them. The valuation they have of their relations and enjoyments they suppose to be lawful, within the bounds which they have assigned to it. Their care about them is, in their own minds, but their duty. It is no easy matter, it requires much spiritual wisdom to fix right boundaries to our affections, and their actings about earthly things. But let men plead and pretend what they please, I shall offer one rule in this case which will not fail. And this is, that when men are so confident in the good state and measure of their affection and their actings towards earthly things, as that they will oppose their engagements in them to known duties of religion, piety and charity, they are gone into a sinful excess. Is there a state of the poor that requires their liberality and bounty? you must excuse them, they have families to provide for; when what is expected from them signifies nothing at all, as unto a due provision for their families, nor is what would lessen their inheritances or portions one penny in the issue. Are they called to an attendance on seasons of religious duties; they are so full of business, that it is impossible for them to have leisure for any such occasions; so by all ways declaring that they are under the power of a prevalent predominant affection to earthly things. This fills all places with lifeless, sapless, useless professors, who approve themselves in their condition, whilst it is visibly unspiritual and withering.

The heart will have something whereon in a way of pre-eminence, it will fix itself and its affections. This in all its perpetual motions it seeks for rest and satisfaction in; and every man hath an edge, the edge of his affections is set in one way or other, though it be more keen in some than others. And whereas, all sorts of things, that the heart can fix upon or turn the edge of its affections unto, are distributed by the Apostle into things above and things beneath, things heavenly and things earthly, if we have not such a view and prospect of heavenly things as to cause our hearts to cleave to them and delight in them, let us pretend what we will, it is impossible but that we shall be under the power of a predominant affection unto the things of this world.

Herein lies the great danger of multitudes at this present season; for let men profess what they will, under the power of this frame, their eternal state is in hazard every moment; and persons are engaged in it in great variety of degrees; we may cast them under two heads.

1. Some do not at all understand that things are amiss with them, or that they are much to be blamed. They plead, as was before observed, that they are all lawful things which their hearts cleave to, and which it is their duty to take care of and regard. May they not delight in their own relations, especially at such a time, when others break and cancel all duties and bonds of relation in the service of, and provision they make for, their lusts? May they not be careful in good and honest ways of diligence about the things of the world, when they most either lavish their time away in the pursuit of bestial lusts, or heap them up by deceit and oppression? May they not contrive for the promotion of their children in the world, to add the other hundred or thousand pounds to their advancement, that they may be in as good condition as others, seeing he is worse than an infidel who provides not for his own family? By such reasonings and secret thoughts do many justify themselves in their earthly mindedness. And so fixed are they in the approbation of themselves, that if you urge them to their duty, you shall lose their acquaintance, if they do not become your enemies for telling them the truth. Yea, they will avoid one duty that lieth not against their earthly interest, because it leads to another. They will not engage in religious assemblies, or be constant to their duty in them, for fear duties of charity should be required of them, or expected from them. On what

grounds such persons can satisfy themselves that they are sptritually minded, I know not. I shall leave only one rule with persons that are thus minded. 'Where our love to the world hath prevailed, by its reasonings, pleas, and pretences, to take away our fear and jealousy over our own hearts, lest we should inordinately love it, there it is assuredly predominant in us.'

2. Others are sensible of the evil of their hearts, at least are jealous and afraid lest it should be found that their hearts do cleave inordinately to these things. Hence they endeavor to contend against this evil, sometimes by forcing themselves unto such acts of piety or charity as are contrary to that frame, and sometimes by laboring a change of the frame itself: especially they will do so when God is pleased to awaken them by trials and afflictions, such as write vanity and emptiness on all earthly enjoyments. But for the most part, they strive not lawfully, and obtain not what they seem to aim at.

This disease with many is mortal; and will not be thoroughly cured in any but by the due exercise of this part of spiritual mindedness. There are other duties required also to the same end, namely, of the mortification of our desires and affections unto earthly things, whereof I have treated elsewhere. But without this, or a fixed contemplation on the desirableness, beauty, and glory of heavenly things, it will not be attained. Further to evidence the truth hereof, we may observe these two things. First, If by any means a man seem to have taken off his heart from the love of present things, and be not at the same time taken up with the love of things that are heavenly, his seeming mortification is of no advantage unto him. So persons frequently through discontent, disappointments, or dissatisfaction with relations, or mere natural weariness, have left the world, the affairs and cares of it, as unto their wonted conversations in it, and have betaken themselves to monasteries, convents, or other retirements suiting their principles, without any advantage to their souls. Secondly, God is no such severe lord and master, as to require us to take off our affections from, and mortify them under, those things which the law of our nature makes dear to us, as wives, children, houses, lands, and possessions, and not propose to us somewhat that is incomparably more excellent to fix them upon. So he invites the elect of the Gentiles to Christ, Psal. xlv. 10. 'Hearken, O daughter, and consider, and incline thine ear, forget also thine own people, and thy father's house;' that is, come into the faith of Abraham, who forsook his country and his father's house, to follow God wheresoever he pleased. But he proposeth this for their encouragement, ver. 11. 'So shall the King greatly desire thy beauty, for he is thy Lord, and worship thou him.' The love of the Great King, is an abundant satisfactory recompense for parting with all things in this world. So when Abraham's servant was sent to take Rebecca for a wife unto Isaac, he required that she should immediately leave father and mother, brothers, and all enjoyments, and go along with him; but withal, that she might know herself to be no loser thereby, he not only assured her of the greatness of his master, but also a present gave her jewels of silver, and jewels of gold, and raiment. Gen. xxiv. 53. And when our Saviour requires that we should part with all for his sake and the gospel, he promiseth an hundred fold in lieu of them, even in this life; namely, an interest in things spiritual and heavenly. Wherefore without an assidnous meditation on heavenly things, as a better, more noble and suitable object for our affections to be fixed on, we can never be freed in a due manner from an inordinate love of things here below.

It is sad to see some professors, who will keep up spiritual duties in churches and in their families, who will speak and discourse of spiritual things, and keep themselves from the open excesses of the world; yet when they come to be tried by such duties as entrench on their love and adherence to earthly things, quickly manifest how remote they are from being spiritually minded in a due manner. Were they to be tried, as our Saviour tried the young man who made such a profession of his conscientious and religious conversation; Go sell what thou hast, give to the poor, and follow me; something might be pleaded in excuse for their tergiversation. But, alas! they will decline their duty when they are not touched to the hundredth part of their enjoyments.

I bless God, I speak not thus of many, of my own knowledge; and may say with the apostle to the most to whom I usually speak in this manner; 'But, beloved, we are persuaded better things of you, and things that accompany salvation, though we thus speak.'— Heb. vi. 9. Yea, the same testimony may be given of many in this city, which the same apostle gives to the churches of Macedonia, 2 Cor. viii. 1—3. 'Understand the grace of God bestowed on the churches of Macedonia, how that, in a great trial of affliction, the abundance of their joy and their poverty abounded unto the riches of their liberality; for to their power, and beyond their power, they were willing of themselves.' There hath been nothing done amongst us, that may or can be boasted of; yet, considering all circumstances, it may be, there have not been more instances of true evangelical charity, in any age or place, for these many years. For them who have been but useful and helpful therein, the Lord remember them for good, and spare them according to the multitude of his mercies. It is true, they have not, many of them, founded colleges, built hospitals, or raised works of state and magnificence: for very many of them are such, as whose 'deep poverty comparatively hath abounded unto the riches of their liberality.' The backs and bellies of multitudes of poor and needy servants of Christ, have been warmed and refreshed by them, blessing God for them. Thanks be to God, saith the apostle in this case, for his unspeakable gift. 2 Cor. ix. 15. Blessed be God, who hath not left the gospel without this glory, nor the profession of it without this evidence of its power and efficacy. Yea, God hath exalted the glory of persecutions and afflictions; for many, since they have lost much of their enjoyments by them, and have their all endangered continually, have abounded in duties of charity beyond what they did in the days of their fulness and prosperity. So out of the eater there hath come forth meat. And if the world did but know what fruits, in a way of charity and bounty, unto the praise of God and glory of the gospel, have been occasioned by their making many poor, it would abate of their satisfaction in their successes.

But with many it is not so: their minds are so full of earthly things, they so cleave to them in their affections, that no sense of their duty, no example of others, no concernment of the glory of God or the gospel, can make any impression on them. If there be yet in them so much light and life of grace as to design a deliverance from this woful condition, the means insisted on must be made use of.

Especially this advice is needful to those who are rich, who have large possessions, or abound in the goods of this world. The poor, the afflicted, the sorrowful, are prompted, from their outward circumstances, as well as excited by inward grace, frequently to remember and to think of the things above, wherein lies their only reserve and relief against the trouble and urgency of their present condition. But the enjoyment of these things in abundance, is accompanied with a two-fold evil, lying directly contrary to this duty.

1. A desire of increase and adding thereunto. Earthly enjoyments enlarge men's earthly desires; and the love of them grows with their income. A moderate stock of waters, sufficient for our use, may be kept within ordinary banks. But if a flood be turned into them, they know no bounds, but overflow all about them.—The increase of wealth and riches enlargeth the desires of men after them, beyond all bounds of wisdom, sobriety, or safety. He that labors hard for his daily bread, hath seldom such earnest vehement desires of an addition to what he hath, as many have, who already have more than they know how to use, or almost what to do with. Thus they must have more, and the last advantage serves for nothing but to stir them up to look out for another. And yet such men would, on other accounts, be esteemed good Christians, and spiritually minded, as all good Christians are.

2. They draw the heart to value and esteem them, as those which bring in their satisfaction, and make them to differ from those whom they see to be poor

and miserable. Now these things are contrary to, and where they are habitually prevalent, utterly inconsistent with being spiritually minded. Nor is it possible, that any who in the least degree are under their power, can ever attain deliverance, unless their thoughts are fixed, and their minds thereby possessed with due apprehensions of invisible things and eternal glory.

These are some few of the many advantages which we may obtain by fixing our thoughts and meditations, and thereby our affections, on the things that are above. And there are some things which make me willing to give a few directions for the practice of this duty. For whatever else we are and do, we neither are nor can be, truly spiritually minded, whereon life and peace depend, unless we really exercise our thoughts unto meditations of things above. Without it, all our religion is but vain: and as I fear men are generally wanting and defective herein, in point of practice; so I do also, that many, through the darkness of their minds, the weakness of their intellectuals, and ignorance of the nature of all things unseen, do seldom set themselves unto the contemplation of them, I shall, therefore, give some few directions for the practice of this duty.

CHAPTER VI.

Directions unto the exercise of our thoughts on things above; things future, invisible, and eternal; on God himself, with the difficulties of it, and oppositions unto it, and the way of their removal. Right notions of future Glory stated.

WE have treated in general, before, of the proper objects of our spiritual thoughts as to our present duty. That which we were last engaged in, is an especial instance in heavenly things; things future and invisible, with a fountain and spring of them all in Christ and God himself. And because men generally are unskilled herein, and great difficulties arise in the way of the discharge of this part of the duty in hand, I shall give some especial directions concerning it.

1. Possess your minds with right notions and apprehensions of things above, and of the state of future glory. We are in this duty to look at the things which are not seen. 2 Cor. iv. 16. It is faith only whereby we have a prospect of them; for we walk by faith, and not by sight. And faith can give us no interest in them, unless we have due apprehensions of them; for it doth but assent and cleave to the truth of what is proposed unto it. And the greatest part of mankind both deceive themselves, and feed on ashes, in this matter: they fancy a future state, which hath no foundation but in their own imaginations. Wherefore the apostle, directing us to seek and mind the things that are above, adds, for the guidance of our thoughts, the consideration of the principal concernment of them where Christ sitteth at the right hand of God. Col. iii. 1, 2. He would lead us to distinct apprehensions of

those heavenly things, especially of the presence of Christ in his exaltation and glory. Wherefore the true notion of these things which we are to possess our minds withal, may here be considered.

All that have an apprehension of a future state of happiness, agree in this matter, that it contains in it, or is accompanied with, a deliverance and freedom from all that is evil. But in what it is so, they are not agreed. Many esteem only those things that are grievous, troublesome, wasting, and destructive to nature, to be so; that is, what is penal, in pain, sickness, sorrow, loss, poverty, with all kinds of outward troubles, and death itself, are evils. Wherefore, they suppose that the future state of blessedness will free them from all these things, if they can attain to it. This they will lay in the balance against the troubles of life, and sometimes it may be against the pleasures of it, which they must forego. Yea, persons profane and profligate will, in words at least, profess, that heaven will give them rest from all their troubles. But it is no place of rest for such persons.

Unto all others also, to believers themselves, these things are evil, such as they expect a deliverance from in heaven and glory: and there is no doubt, but it is lawful for us, and meet, that we should contemplate on them, as those which will give us a deliverance from all outward troubles, death itself, and all that leads thereto. Heaven is promised as rest to them that are troubled. 2 Thes. i. 7. It is our duty, under all our sufferings, reproaches, persecutions, troubles, and sorrows, to raise up our minds to the contemplation of that state, wherein we shall be freed from them all. It is a blessed notion of heaven, that God shall therein wipe away all tears from our eyes. Rev. vii. 17, or remove far from us all causes of sorrow; and it would be to our advantage, if we accustomed our minds more to this kind of relief than we do; if, upon the incursion of fears, dangers, sorrows, we did more readily retreat to thoughts of that state wherein we shall be freed from them all; even this most inferior consideration of it, would render the thoughts of it more familiar, and the thing itself more useful to us. Much better it were, than on such occasions to be exercised with heartless complaints, uncertain hopes, and fruitless contrivances.

But there is that, which, to them who are truly spirtually minded, hath more evil in it than all these things together, and that is, sin. Heaven is a state of deliverance from sin, from all sin, in all the causes, concomitants, and effects of it. He is no true believer, to whom sin is not the greatest burden, sorrow, and trouble. Other things, as the loss of our dear relations, or extraordinary pains, may make deeper impressions on the mind, by its natural affections, at some seasons, than ever our sins did at any one time, in any one instance. So a man may have a greater trouble in sense of pain, by a fit of the toothache, which will be gone in an hour, than in an hectic fever or consumption, which will assuredly take away his life. But take in the whole course of our lives, and all the actings of our souls in spiritual judgment as well as natural affection, and I do not understand how a man can be a sincere believer, to whom sin is not the greatest burden and sorrow.

Wherefore, in the first place, it belongs to the true notion of heaven, that it is a state wherein we shall be eternally freed from sin, and all the concernments of it, but only the exaltation of the glory of God's grace in Christ, by the pardon of it. He that truly hates sin and abhors it, whose principal desire and design of life is to be freed from it, as far as it is possible; who walks in self-abasement, through a sense of his many disappointments, when he hoped it should act in him no more, cannot, as I judge, but frequently betake himself for refreshment to thoughts of that state wherein he shall be freed from it, and triumph over it to eternity. This is a notion of heaven that is easily apprehended and fixed on the mind, which we may dwell upon, to the great advantage and satisfaction of our souls.

Frequent thoughts and meditations of heaven, under this notion, argue a man to be spiritually minded. For it is a convincing evidence that sin is a burden to him, that he longs to be delivered from it and all its consequents; that no thoughts are more welcome to him, than those of that state wherein sin shall be no more. And although men are troubled about their sins, and would desirously be freed from them, so far as they perplex their minds, and make their consciences uneasy; yet if they are not much in the prospect of this relief, if they find not refreshment in it, I fear their trouble is not such as it ought to be. Wherefore, when men can so wrangle and wrestle with their convictions of sin, and yet take up the best of their relief in hopes that it will be better with them, at some time or other, in this world, without longing desires after that state wherein sin shall be no more; they can give no evidence that they are spiritually minded.

It is quite otherwise with sincere believers in the exercise of this duty. The considerations of the grace and love of God, of the blood of Christ, of the purity and holiness of that good spirit that dwelleth in them, of the light, grace, and mercy, which they have attained through the promises of the gospel, are those which make the remainders of sin most grievous and burdensome to them. This is that which even breaks their hearts, and makes some of them go mourning all the day long, namely, that any thing of that which alone God hates, should be found in them, or be remaining with them. It is, in this condition, an evidence that they are spiritually minded, if, together with watchful endeavors for the universal mortification of sin, and utter excision of it, both root and branch, they constantly add these thoughts of that blessed state, wherein they shall be absolutely and eternally freed from all sin, with refreshment, delight, and complacency.

These things belong to our direction for the fixing of our thoughts and meditations on things above. This the meanest and weakest person, who hath the least spark of sincerity and grace, is capable of apprehending, and able to practice: and it is that which the sense they have of the evil of sin will put them on every day, if they shut not their eyes against the light of the refreshment that is in it. Let them who cannot arise in their minds to fixed and stable thoughts of any other notion of these invisible things, dwell on this consideration of them, wherein they will find no small spiritual advantage and refreshment to their souls.

2. As to the positive part of this glorious future state, the thoughts and apprehensions of men are very various. And that we may know as well what to avoid, as what to embrace, we shall a little reflect on some of them.

1. Many are able to entertain no rational conceptions about a future state of blessedness and glory, no notions wherein either faith or reason is concerned. Im-

agination they have of something that is great and glorious, but what it is they know not. No wonder if such persons have no delight in, no use for, thoughts of heaven. When their imaginations have fluctuated up and down in all uncertainties for a while, they are swallowed up in nothing. Glorious, and therefore desirable, they take it for granted that it must be: but nothing can be so to them, but what is suitable to their present dispositions, inclinations, and principles: and hereof there is nothing in the true spiritual glory of heaven, or in the eternal enjoyment of God. These things are not suited to the wills of their minds and of the flesh, and therefore they cannot rise up to any constant desire of them. Hence to please themselves, they begin to imagine what is not. But whereas what is truly heaven, pleaseth them not, and what doth please them is not heaven, nor there to be found, they seldom or never endeavor, in good earnest, to exercise their thoughts about it.

It were well if darkness and ignorance of the true nature of the future state and eternal glory, did not exceedingly prejudice believers themselves, as to their delight in them and meditations about them. They have nothing fixed or stated in their minds, which they can betake themselves to in their thoughts, when they would contemplate about them. And by the way, whatever diverts the minds of men from the power and life of spiritual worship, as do all pompous solemnities in the performance of it, doth greatly hinder them as to right conceptions of our future state. There was a promise of eternal life given to the saints under the Old Testament: but whereas they were obliged to a worship that was carnal and outwardly pompous, they never had clear and distinct apprehensions of the future state of glory: for life and immortality were brought to light by the gospel. Wherefore, although no man living can see or find out the infinite riches of eternal glory; yet it is the duty of all to be acquainted with the nature of it in general, so as that they may have fixed thoughts of it, love to it, earnest desires after it, all under its own true and proper notion.

2. So great a part of mankind as the Mahometans, to whom God hath given all the principal and most desirable parts of the world to inhabit and possess, conceive the state of future blessedness to consist in the full satisfaction of their sensual lusts and pleasures. An evidence this is, that the religion which they profess hath no power or efficacy on their minds to change them from the love of sin, or placing their happiness in fulfilling the desires of the flesh. It doth not at all enlighten their minds to discern a beauty in spiritual things, nor excite their affections to the love of them, nor free the soul to look after blessedness in such things as alone are suited to its rational constitution; for if it did, they would place their happiness and blessedness in them. Wherefore, it is nothing but an artifice of the god of this world, to blind the eyes of men to their eternal destruction.

3. Some of the philosophers of old attained an apprehension, that the blessedness of men in another world doth consist in the soul's full satisfaction in the goodness and beauty of the Divine Nature: and there is a truth in this notion, which contemplative men have adorned with excellent and rational discourses: and sundry who have been and are learned among Christians, have greatly improved this truth by the light of the scripture. From reason they take up

with thoughts of the goodness, the amiableness, the self-sufficiency, the all-sufficient satisfactoriness of the infinite perfections of the Divine Nature. These things shine in themselves with such a glorious light, as that there is no more required to a perception of them, but that men do not wilfully shut their eyes against it, through bestial sensuality and love of sin. From reason also, they frame their conceptions concerning the capacity of the souls of men for the immediate enjoyment of God, and what is suited therein to their utmost blessedness. No more is required to these things, but a due consideration of the nature of God and man, with our relation to him and dependence on him. By the light of the Scripture they frame these things into that which they call the beatifical vision, whereby they intend all the ways in which God, in the highest and immediate instances, can and doth communicate of himself to the souls of men, and the utmost elevation of their intellectual capacities to receive those communications. It is such an intellectual apprehension of the Divine Nature and perfections, with ineffable love, as gives the soul the utmost rest and blessedness which its capacities can extend to.

These things are so; and they have been by many both piously and elegantly illustrated; howbeit, they are above the capacities of ordinary Christians; they know not how they manage them in their minds, nor exercise their thoughts about them; they cannot reduce them to present usefulness, nor make them subservient to the exercise and increase of grace: and the truth is, the Scripture gives us another notion of heaven and glory, not contrary to this, not inconsistent with it, but more suited to the faith and experience of believers, and which alone can convey a true and useful sense of these things to our minds. This, therefore, is diligently to be inquired into, and firmly stated in our thoughts and affections.

4. The principal notion which the Scripture gives us of the state of heavenly blessedness, and which the meanest believers are capable of improving in daily practice, is, that faith shall be turned into sight, and grace into glory. We walk now by faith and not by sight, saith the apostle. 2 Cor. iii. 7. Wherefore this is the difference between our present and our future state, that sight hereafter shall supply the room of faith. 1 John. iii. 2. And if sight come into the place of faith, then the object of that sight must be the same with the present object of our faith. So the apostle informs us, 1 Cor. xiii. 9—12. 'For we know in part, and we prophecy in part; but when that which is perfect is come, then that which is in part shall be done away. For now we see through a glass darkly, but then face to face.' Those things which we see now darkly, as in a glass, we shall then have an immediate sight, and full comprehension of; for that which is perfect, must come and do away that which is in part. What then is the principal present object of faith as it is evangelical, into whose room light must succeed? Is it not 'the manifestation of the glory of the infinite wisdom, grace, love, kindness and power of God in Christ, the revelation of the eternal counsels of his will, and the ways of their accomplishment to the eternal salvation of the church in and by him, with the glorious exaltation of Christ himself?' Wherefore, in the full, satisfactory representation of these things to our souls, received by sight, or a direct, immediate intuition, of them, doth

the glory of heaven principally consist. We behold them now darkly as in a glass; that is, the utmost which by faith we can attain to; in heaven they shall be openly and fully displayed. The infinite, incomprehensible excellencies of the divine nature, are not proposed in Scripture as the immediate object of our faith, nor shall they be so unto sight in heaven. The manifestation of them in Christ is the immediate object of our faith here, and shall be of our sight hereafter. Only through this manifestation of them we are led even by faith, ultimately to acquiesce in them; as we shall in heaven be led by love, perfectly to adhere to them with delight ineffable. This is our immediate objective glory in heaven; we hope for no other; and this, if God will I shall shortly more fully explain.

Whoever lives in the exercise of faith, and hath any experience of the life, power, and sweetness of these heavenly things, to whom they are a spring of grace and consolation, they are able to meditate on the glory of them in their full enjoyment. Think much of heaven, as that which will give you a perfect view and comprehension of the wisdom and love and grace of God in Christ, with those other things which shall be immediately declared.

Some, perhaps, will be ready to say, that if this be heaven, they can see no great glory in it, no such beauty as for which it should be desired. It may be so; for some have no instrument to take a view of invisible things but carnal imaginations; some have no light, no principle, no disposition of mind or soul whereto these things are either acceptable or suitable. Some will go no further in the consideration of the divine excellencies of God, and the faculties and actings of our souls, than reason will guide them, which may be of use: but we look for no other heaven, we desire none, but what we are led to, and prepared for, by the light of the gospel; that which shall perfect all the beginnings of God's grace in us; not what shall be quite of another nature, and destructive of them. We value not that heaven which is equally suited to the desires and inclinations of the worst of men, as well as the best; for we know that they who like not grace here, neither do nor can like that which is glory hereafter. No man who is not acquainted experimentally in some measure with the life, power, and evidence of faith here, hath any other heaven in his aim but what is erected in his own imagination. The glory of heaven which the gospel prepares us for, which faith leads and conducts us to, which the souls of believers long after, as that which shall give us full rest, satisfaction, and complacency, is the full, open, perfect manifestation of the glory, of the wisdom, goodness, and love of God in Christ, in his person and mediation, with the revelation of all his counsels concerning them and the communication of their effects to us. He that likes it not, to whom it is not desirable, may betake himself to Mahomet's paradise, or the philosophers speculations; in the gospel heaven he hath no interest. These are the things which we see now darkly as in a glass, by faith: in the view of them are our souls gradually changed into the likeness of God; and the comprehension of them is that which shall give us our utmost conformity and likeness to him, whereof our natures are capable. In a sense and experience of their reality and goodness given us by the Holy Ghost, do all our spiritual consolations and joys consist. The effects produced by them in our souls are the first fruits of glory. Our light, sense, experience, and enjoyment of these things, however were and frequently interrupted, our apprehensions of them, however dark and obscure, are the only means whereby we are made meet for the inheritance of the saints in light.

To have the eternal glory of God in Christ, with all the fruits of his wisdom and love, whilst we are ourselves under the full participation of the effects of them, immediately, directly, revealed, proposed, made known to us in a divine and glorious light, our souls being furnished with a capacity to behold and perfectly comprehend them; this is the heaven which, according to God's promise, we look for: but, as was said, these things shall be elsewhere more fully treated of.

It is true, that there are sundry other things in particular that belong to this state of glory; but what we have mentioned is the fountain and spring of them all. We can never have an immediate enjoyment of God in the immensity of his nature, nor can any created understanding conceive such things. God's communications of himself unto us, and our enjoyment of him, shall be in and by the manifestation of his glory in Christ. He who can see no glory, who is sensible of no blessedness in these things, is a stranger to that heaven which the scripture reveals, and which faith leads to.

It may be inquired, what is the subjective glory, or what change is to be wrought in ourselves, that we may enjoy this glory? Now that depends principally as to our souls in the 'perfection of all grace, which is initially wrought, and subjectively resides in us, in this world.' The grace which we have here shall not be done away as to its essence and nature, though somewhat of it shall cease as to the manner of its operation. What soul could think with joy of going to heaven, if thereby he must lose all his present light, faith, and love of God, though that he were told he should receive that in lieu of them which is more excellent, whereof he hath no experience, nor can understand of what nature it is? When the saints enter into rest, their good works do follow them; and how can they do so, if their grace do not accompany them, from whence they proceed? The perfection of our present graces, which are here weak, and interrupted in their operations, is a principal eminency of the state of glory; faith shall be heightened into vision, as was proved before; which doth not destroy its nature, but cause it to cease as to its manner of operation towards things invisible. If a man have a weak, small faith in this life, with little evidence, and no assurance, so that he doubts of all things, questions all things, and hath no comfort from what he doth believe; if afterwards, through supplies of grace, he hath a mighty prevailing evidence of the things believed, is filled with comfort and assurance; this is not by a faith or grace of another kind from what he had before, but by the same faith, raised to an higher degree of perfection. When our Saviour cured the blind man, and gave him his sight, (Mark viii.) at first he saw all things obscurely and imperfectly; he saw men, as trees walking, ver. 24; but on another application of virtue to him, he saw all things clearly—ver. 25. It was not a sight of another kind which he then received from what he had at first, only its imperfection, whereby he saw men like trees, walking, was taken away. Nor will our perfect vision of things above, be a grace absolutely of another kind from the light of faith which we here enjoy, only what is imperfect in it will be done away, and it will be made meet for the present enjoyment of things, here at a distance and invisible. Love shall have its perfection also, and the least alteration in its manner of operation of any grace whatever. And there is nothing that should more excite us to labor after a growth in love to God in Christ, than this, that it shall to all eternity be the same in its nature and in all its operations, only both the one and the other will be made absolutely perfect. The soul will be by it enabled to cleave unto God unchangeably, with eternal delight, satisfaction, and complacency. Hope will be perfect in enjoyment, which is all the perfection it is capable of. So shall it be as to other graces.

This subjective perfection of our natures, especially in all the faculties, powers, and affections of our souls, and all their operations, belongs to our blessedness, nor can we be blessed without it. All the objective glory in heaven would not, in our beholding and enjoying of it, (if it were possible,) make us blessed and happy, if our own natures were not made perfect, freed from all disorder, irregular motions, and weak, imperfect operations. What is it then that must give our nature this subjective perfection? It is that grace alone, whose beginnings we are here made partakers of; for therein consists the renovation of the image of God in us. And the immediate communication of that image to us, is the absolute perfection of our natures, the utmost which their capacity is suited to. And this gives us the last thing to be inquired into, namely, by what means in ourselves we shall eternally abide in that state! And this is by the unalterable adherence of our whole souls to God, in perfect love and delight. This is that whereby alone the soul reacheth to the essence of God, and the infinite, incomprehensible perfections of his nature: for the perfect nature hereof, divine revelation hath left under a veil, and so must we do also. Nor do I designedly handle these things in this place, but only in the way of a direction how to exercise our thoughts about them.

This is that notion of heaven, which those who are spiritually minded, ought to be conversant with; and the true acting of it by faith, is a discriminating character of believers. This is no heaven to any others. Those who have not an experience of the excellency of these things in their initial state in this world, and their incomparable transcendency to all other things, cannot conceive how heavenly glory and blessedness should consist in them. Unskilful men may cast away rough, unwrought diamonds, as useless stones; they know not what polishing will bring them to. Nor do men unskilful in the mystery of godliness, judge there can be any glory in rough unwrought grace; they know not what lustre and beauty the polishing of the heavenly hand will give to it.

It is generally supposed, that however men differ in and about religion here, yet they agree well enough about heaven; they would all go to the same heaven. But it is a great mistake, they differ in nothing more; they would not all go to the same heaven. How few are they, who value that heavenly state which we have treated of; or understand how any blessedness can consist in the enjoyment of it? But this and no other heaven would we go to. Other notions there may be, there are of it, which being but fruits and effects of mens's own imaginations, the more they dwell in the contemplation of them, the more carnal they may grow, at best the more superstitious. But spiritual thoughts of this heaven, consisting principally in freedom from all sin, in the perfection of all grace, in the vision of the glory of God in Christ, and all the excellencies of the divine nature as manifested in him, are an effectual means for the improvement of spiritual life, and the increase of all graces in us; for they cannot but effect an assimilation in the mind and heart to the things contemplated on, where the principles and seeds of them are already inlaid and begun. This is our first direction.

Secondly. Having fixed right notions and apprehensions of heavenly things in our minds, it is our duty to think and contemplate greatly on them, and our own concernment in them. Without this, all our speculations concerning the nature of eternal things, will be of no use to us; and for your encouragement and direction, take these few short rules relating to this duty. (1.) Here lies the great trial, whether we are spiritually minded or not, by virtue of this rule; if we are risen with Christ we will mind the things that are above. Col. iii. 3. (2.) This is the great means whereby we may attain further degrees in that blessed frame of mind, if it be already formed in us, by virtue of that rule; beholding the glory of God as in a glass, we are changed into the same image from glory to glory. 2 Cor. iii. 18. (3.) Here lies the great evidence whether we have a real interest in the things above or not; whether we place our portion and blessedness in them, according to that rule; where our treasure is, there will our hearts be also. Are they our treasure, our portion, our reward, in comparison whereof all other things are but loss and dung? then we shall assuredly be conversant in our minds about them. 4. It cannot be imagined, that a man should have in him a principle suited to things above, of the be under the conduct of those habits of grace, which strive after, and naturally tend to, perfection, laboring greatly here under the weight of their own weaknesses, (as it is with all who are truly spiritually minded,) and yet not have his thoughts greatly exercised about these things. 1 John iii. 3.

It were well if we would try ourselves by things such of uncontrolable evidence. What can any object to the truth of these things, or the necessity of this duty? If it be otherwise with us, it is from one of these two causes; either we are not convinced of the truth and reality of them, or we have no delight in them, because we are not spiritually minded. Do we think that men may turmoil themselves in earthly thoughts all the day long, and when they are freed of their affairs, betake themselves to those that are vain and useless, without any stated converse with things above, and yet enjoy life and peace? We must take other measures of things, if we intend to live to God, to be like him, and to come to the enjoyment of him.

What is the matter with men that they are so stupid? They all generally desire to go to heaven, at least when they can live here no longer. Some, indeed, have no other regard to it, but only that they would not go to hell. But most would die the death of the righteous, and have their latter end like his; yet few there are who endeavor to attain a right notion of it, to try how it is suited to their principles and desires; but content themselves with such general notions of it as please their imaginations. It is no wonder if such persons seldom exercise their minds or thoughts about it, nor do they so much as pretend to be spiritually minded. But as for those who are instructed in these things, who profess their chiefest same kind and nature with them ; that his soul should interest to lie in them, not to abound in meditation concerning them, it argues indeed, that whatever they profess, they are earthly and carnal.

Again; meditate and think of the glory of heaven, so as to compare it with the opposite state of death and eternal misery. Few men care to think much of hell, and the everlasting torments of the wicked therein. Those do so least, who are in most danger of falling therein : they put far from them the evil day, and suppose their covenant with death and hell to be sure. Some begin to advance an opinion that there is no such place, because it is their interest and desire that there should be none. Some out of profaneness, make a scoff at it, as though a future judgment were but a fable. Most seem to think there is a severity in thoughts about it, which it is not fit we should be too much terrified with. Some transient thoughts they will have of it, but not suffer them to abide in their minds, lest they should be too much discomposed. Or they think it not consistent with the goodness of Christ to leave any men in that condition; whereas there is more spoken directly of hell, its torments and their eternity, by himself, than in all the scripture besides. These thoughts, in most, proceed from an unwillingness to be troubled in their sins, and are useful to none. It is the height of folly for men to endeavor the hiding of themselves, for a few moments, from that which is unavoidably coming upon them unto eternity, and the due consideration whereof is a means for an escape from it. But I speak only of true believers: and the more they are conversant, in their thoughts, about the future state of eternal misery, the greater evidence they have of the life and confidence of faith· It is a necessary duty to consider it, as what we were by nature obnoxious to, as being children of wrath; what we have deserved by our personal sins, as the wages of sin is death; what we are delivered from through Jesus the deliverer, who saves us from the wrath to come; what an expression it is of the indignation of God against sin, who hath prepared this Tophet of old; that we may be delivered from sin, kept up to an abhorrency of it, walking in humility, self-abasement, and the admiration of divine grace. This, therefore, is required of us, that in our thoughts and meditations, we compare the state of blessedness and eternal glory, as a free and absolute effect of the grace of God in and through Christ Jesus, with that state of eternal misery which we had deserved. And if there be any spark of grace or of holy thankfulness in our hearts, it will be stirred up to its due exercise.

Some, it may be, will say, that they complained before that they cannot get their minds fixed on these things. Weakness, weariness, darkness, diversions, occasions, do prevalently obstruct their abiding in such thoughts. I shall speak further to this afterwards; at present I shall only suggest two things. (1.) If you cannot attain, yet continue to follow after; get your minds in a perpetual endeavor after an abode in spiritual thoughts. Let your minds be rising towards them every hour, yea. an hundred times a day, on all occasions, in a continual sense of duty; and sigh within yourselves for deliverance, when you find disappointments, or not a continuance, in them. It is the sense of that place, Rom. viii. 23—27. (2.) Take care you go not backwards, and lose what you have wrought. If you neglect these things for a season, you will quickly find yourselves neglected by them. So I observe it every day in the hearing of the word. Whilst persons keep up themselves to a diligent attendance on it, where they find it preached to their edification, they find great delight in it, and will undergo great difficulties for the enjoyment of it: let them be diverted from it for a season; after a while it grows indifferent to them; any thing will satisfy them that pretends to the same duty.

CHAPTER VII.

Especial objects of spiritual thoughts on the glorious state of heaven, and what belongs thereto. First, of Christ himself. Thoughts of heavenly glory, in opposition to thoughts of eternal misery. The use of such thoughts. Advantage in sufferings.

It will be to our advantage, having stated right notions of the glory of the blessed state above, in our minds, to fix on some particulars belonging to it, as the especial object of our thoughts and meditations. As, 1. Think much of him, who to us is the life and centre of all the glory of heaven, that is, Christ himself. I shall be very brief in treating hereof, because I have designed a particular treatise on this subject, of beholding the glory of Christ, both here and to eternity. At present, therefore, a few things only shall be mentioned, because on this occasion they are not to be omitted. The whole of the glory of the state above, is expressed by being ever with the Lord; where he is, to behold his glory. For in and through him, is the beatifical manifestation of God and his glory made for evermore: and through him are all communications of inward glory unto us. The present resplendency of heavenly glory consists in his mediatory ministry, as I have at large elsewhere declared:

and he will be the means of all glorious communications between God and the church to eternity.—Wherefore, if we are spiritually minded, we should fix our thoughts on Christ above, as the centre of all heavenly glory. To help us herein we may consider the things that follow.

(1.) Faith hath continual recourse to him on the account of what he did and suffered for us in this world: for thereon, pardon of sin, justification and peace with God, do depend. This ariseth, in the first place, from a sense of our own wants. But love of him is no less necessary to us than faith in him. And although we have powerful motives to love, from what he did and was in this world, yet the formal reason of our adherence to him thereby, is what he is in himself, as he is now exalted in heaven. If we rejoice not at the remembrance of his present glory, if the thoughts of it be not frequent with us, and refreshing to us, how dwelleth his love in us?

(2.) Our hope is that, ere long, we shall be ever with him; and if so, it is certainly our wisdom and duty to be here with him as much as we can. It is a vain thing for any to suppose, that they place their chiefest happiness in being forever in the presence of Christ, who care not at all to be with him here, as they may. And the only way of our being present with him here, is by faith and love, acting themselves in spiritual thoughts and affections; and it is an absurd thing for men to esteem themselves Christians, who scarce think of Christ all the day long. Yet some, as one complained of old, scarce ever think or speak of him, but when they swear by his name. I have read of them, who have lived and died in continual contemplation on him, so far as the imperfection of our present state will admit. I have known them, I do know them, who call themselves to a reproof, if at any time he hath been many minutes out of their thoughts. And it is strange that it should be otherwise with them who love him in sincerity; yet I wish I did not know more, who give evidences that it is a rare thing for them to be exercised in serious thoughts and meditations about him. Yea, there are some, who are not averse, upon occasions, to speak of God, of mercy, of pardon, of his power and goodness; who, if you mention Christ to them, with any thing of faith, love, trust in him, they seem to them as a strange thing. Few there are who are sensible of any religion beyond what is natural. The things of the wisdom and power of God in Christ, are foolishness to them. Take some directions for the discharge of this duty. (1.) In your thoughts of Christ, be very careful that they are conceived and directed according to the rule of the word, lest you deceive your own souls, and give up the conduct of your affections to vain imaginations. Spiritual notions, befalling carnal minds, did once, by the means of superstition, ruin the power of religion. A conviction men had that they must think much of Jesus Christ, and that this would make them conformable to him; but having no real evangelical faith, nor the wisdom of faith to exercise it in their thoughts and affections in a due manner; nor understanding what it was to be truly like unto him, they gave up themselves to many foolish inventions and imaginations; by which they thought to express their love and conformity to him. They would have images of him, which they would embrace, adore, and bedew with their tears. They would have crucifixes, as they called them, which they would carry about them, and wear next to their hearts, as if they resolved to lodge Christ always in their bosoms. They would go in pilgrimage to the place where he died and rose again, through a thousand dangers; and purchase a feigned chip of a tree whereon he suffered, at the price of all they had in the world. They would endeavor, by long thoughtfulness, fastings, and watchings, to cast their souls into raptures and ecstasies, wherein they fancied themselves in his presence. They came at last to make themselves like him, in getting impressions of wounds on their sides, their hands and feet. Unto all these things, and sundry others of a like nature and tendency, did superstition abuse and corrupt the minds of men, from a pretence of a principle of truth; for there is no more certain gospel truth than this, that believers ought continually to contemplate on Christ, by the actings of faith in their thoughts and affections; and that thereby they are changed and transformed into his image. 2 Cor. iii. 18. And we are not to forego our duty, because other men have been mistaken in theirs; nor part with practical fundamental principles of religion, because they have been abused by superstition. But we may see herein, how dangerous it is to depart in any thing from the conduct of scripture light and rule, when for want thereof, the best and most noble endeavors of the minds of men, even to love Christ, and to be like unto him, do issue in provocations of the highest nature.

Pray, therefore, that you may be kept unto the truth in all things, by a diligent attention to the only rule thereof, and conscientious subjection of soul to the authority of God in it. For we ought not to suffer our affections to be entangled with the paint or artificial beauty of any way or means of giving our love to Christ, which are not warranted by the word of truth. Yet I must say, that I had rather be among them, who, in the actings of their love and affections to Christ, fall into some irregularities and excesses in their manner of expressing it (provided their worship of him be neither superstitious nor idolatrous,) than among those who, professing themselves to be Christians, do almost disavow their having any thoughts of, or affection to, the person of Christ: but there is no need that we should foolishly run into either of these extremes. God hath, in the scripture, sufficiently provided against them both. He hath both showed us the necessity of our diligent acting of faith and love on the person of Christ; and hath limited out ways and means whereby we may so do. And let our designs be what they will, where in any thing we depart from his prescriptions, we are not under the conduct of his spirit, and so are sure to lose all that we do.

Wherefore, two things are required that we may thus think of Christ and meditate on him, according to the mind and will of God. (1.) That the means of bringing him to mind, be what God hath promised and appointed. (2.) That the continued proposal of him, as the object of our thoughts and meditations, be of the same kind. For both these ends, the superstitious minds of men invented the ways of images and crucifixes, with their appurtenances before mentioned. And this rendered all their devotion an abomination. That which tends to these ends among believers, is the promise of the spirit, and the institutions of the word. Would you then think of Christ as you ought, take these two directions. (1.) Pray that the holy spirit may abide with you continually, to mind you of him, which he will do in all in whom he doth abide; for it belongs to his office. (2.) For more fixed thoughts and meditations, take some express place of scripture, wherein he is set forth and proposed either in his person, office, or grace, to you. Gal. iii. 1.

4. This duty lies at the foundation of all that blessed communion and intercourse, that is between Jesus Christ and the souls of believers. This, I confess, is despised by some, and the very notion of it esteemed ridiculous. But they do therein no less than renounce Christianity, and turn the Lord Christ into an idol, that neither knoweth, seeth, nor heareth. But I speak to them who are not utter strangers to the life of faith, who know not what religion is, unless they have real, spiritual intercourse and communion with the Lord Christ thereby. Consider this, therefore, as it is in particular exemplified in the book of Canticles. There is not one instance of it to be found, which doth not suppose a continual thoughtfulness of him. And in answer to them, as they are actings of faith and love wherein he is delighted, doth he, by his spirit, insinuate into our minds and hearts, a gracious sense of his own love, kindness, and relation to us. The great variety wherein these things are mutually carried on between him and the church, the singular endearments which ensue thereon, and blessed estate in rest and complacency, make up the substance of that holy discourse. No thoughts, then, of Christ, proceeding from faith, accompanied with love and delight, shall be lost: they that sow this seed shall return with their sheaves; Christ will meet them with gracious intimations of his acceptance of them, delight in them,

and return a sense of his own love to them. He never will be, he never was, behind with any poor soul in returns of love. Those gracious and blessed promises which he hath made, of coming to them that believe in him, of making his abode with them, and of supping with them, all expressions of a gracious presence and intimate communion, all depend on this duty. Wherefore, we may consider three things concerning these thoughts of Christ. (1.) That they are exceeding acceptable to him, as the best pledge of our cordial affection. Cant. ii. 14. "O my dove, that art in the clefts of the rock, in the secret places of the stairs, let me see thy countenance, let me hear thy voice; for sweet is thy voice, and thy countenance is comely." When a soul, through manifold discouragements and despondencies, withdraws, and as it were hides itself from him, he calleth to see a poor, weeping, blubbered face, and to hear a broken voice, that scarce goes beyond sighs and groans. (2.) These thoughts are the only means, whereby we comply with the gracious intimations of his love mentioned before. By them do we hear his knocking, know his voice, and open the door of our hearts to give him entrance, that he may abide and sup with us. Sometimes, indeed, the soul is surprised into acts of gracious communion with Christ. Cant. vi. 11. But they are not to be expected, unless we abide in those ways and means which prepare and make our souls meet for the reception and entertainment of him. Wherefore, (3.) our want of experience in the power of this holy intercourse and communion with Christ, ariseth principally from our defect in this duty. I have known one, who, after a long profession of faith and holiness, fell into great darkness and distress, merely on this account, that he did not experience in himself the sweetness, life, and power of the testimonies given concerning the real communications of the love of Christ unto, and the intimation of his presence with, believers. He knew well enough the doctrine of it, but did not feel the power of it; at least he understood there was more in it, than he had experience of. God carried him by faith through that darkness; but taught him withal, that no sense of these things was to be let into the soul, but by constant thoughtfulness and contemplation on Christ. How many blessed visits do we lose, by not being exercised to this duty? See Cant. v. 1, 2, 3. Sometimes we are busy, sometimes careless and negligent, sometimes slothful, sometimes under the power of temptations, so that we neither inquire after, nor are ready to receive, them. This is not the way to have our joys abound.

Again: I speak now with especial respect to him in heaven. The glory of his presence, as God and man eternally united; the discharge of his mediatory office, as he is at the right hand of God; the glory of his present acting for the church, as he is the minister of the sanctuary, and the true tabernacle which God hath fixed, and not man; the love, power, and efficacy of his intercession, whereby he takes care for the accomplishment of the salvation of the church; the approach of his glorious coming to judgment; are to be the objects of our daily thoughts and meditations.

Let us not mistake ourselves. To be spiritually minded, is not to have the notions and knowledge of spiritual things in our minds; it is not to be constant, no, not to abound, in the performance of duties, both which may be where there is no grace in the heart at all. It is to have our minds really exercised with delight about heavenly things, the things that are above, especially Christ himself, as at the right hand of God.

Again: So think of eternal things, as continually to lay them in the balance against all the sufferings of this life. This use of it I have spoken to somewhat before; and it is necessary it should be pressed upon all occasions. It is very probable that we shall yet suffer more than we have done. Those who have gone before us, have done so; it is foretold in the scripture, that if we will live godly in Christ Jesus, we must do so; we stand in need of it, and the world is prepared to bring it on us. And as we must suffer, so it is necessary to the glory of God and our own salvation, that we suffer in due manner. Mere sufferings, will neither commend us to God, nor any way advantage our own souls. When we suffer according to the will of God, it is an eminent grace, gift, and privilege. Phil. i. 29. But many things are required hereto. It is not enough that men suppose themselves to suffer for conscience' sake, though if we do not so, all our sufferings are in vain. Nor is it enough that we suffer for this or that way of profession in religion, which we esteem to be true, and according to the mind of God in opposition to what is not so. The glory of sufferings on these accounts solely, hath been much sullied in the days wherein we live. It is evident that persons, out of a natural courage, accompanied with deep radical persuasions, and having their minds influenced with some sinister ends, may undergo things hard and difficult, in giving testimony to what is not according to the mind of God. Examples we have had hereof in all ages, and in that wherein we live in an especial manner. See 1 Pet. iv. 14—16. We have had enough to take off all paint and appearance of honor from them, who, in their sufferings, are deceived in what they profess. But men may, for the same principles, suffer for what is indeed according to the mind of God; yea, may give their bodies to be burned therein, and yet not to his glory, nor their own eternal advantage. Wherefore, we are duly to consider all things that are requisite to make our sufferings acceptable to God, and honorable to the gospel.

I have observed, in many, a frame of spirit with respect to sufferings, that I never saw good event of when it was tried to the uttermost. Boldness, confidence, a pretended contempt of hardships, and scorning other men, whom they suppose defective in these things, are the garment or livery they wear on this occasion. Such principles may carry men out in a bad cause, but they will never do so in a good one. Evangelical truth will not be honorably witnessed to, but by evangelical graces. Distrust of ourselves, a due apprehension of the nature of the evils to be undergone, and of our own frailty, with continual prayers to be delivered from them, or supported under them, and prudent care to avoid them without an inroad on conscience, or neglect of duty, are much better preparations for an entrance into a state of suffering. Many things belong to our learning aright this first and last lesson of the gospel, namely, of bearing the cross, or undergoing all sorts of sufferings for the profession of it. But they belong not to our present occasion. This only is that which we now press, as an evidence of our sincerity in our sufferings, and an effectual means to enable us cheerfully to undergo them, which is, to have such a continual prospect of the future state of glory, as to lay it in the balance against all that we may undergo. For,

(1.) To have our minds filled and possessed with thoughts thereof, will give us an alacrity in our entrance into sufferings in a way of duty. Other considerations will offer themselves to our relief, which will quickly fade and disappear. They are like a cordial water, which gives a little relief for a season, and then leaves the spirits to sink beneath what they were before it was taken. Some relieve themselves from the consideration of the nature of their sufferings; they are not so great but that they may conflict with them, and come off with safety. But there is nothing of that kind so small, but it will prove too hard and strong for us, unless we have especial assistance. Some do the same from their duration; they are but for ten days or six months, and then they shall be free. Some from the compassion and esteem of men. These and the like considerations are apt to occur to the minds of all sorts of persons, whether they are spiritually minded or not. But when our minds are accustomed to thoughts of the glory that shall be revealed, we shall cheerfully entertain every way and path that leads thereunto, as suffering for the truth doth in a peculiar manner. Through this medium we may look cheerfully and comfortably on the loss of name, reputation, goods, liberty, life itself, as "knowing in ourselves that we have better and more abiding comforts" to betake ourselves to. And we can no other way glorify God by our alacrity in the entrance on sufferings, than when it ariseth from a prospect into, and valuation of those invisible things which he hath promised, as an abundant recompense for all we can lose in this world.

(2.) The great aggravation of sufferings is their long continuance, without any rational appearance or hopes of relief. Many who have entered into sufferings with much courage and resolution, have been wearied and worn out with their continuance. Elijah himself was hereby reduced to pray that God would take away his life, to put an end to his ministry and calamities. And not a few in all ages have been hereby so broken in their natural spirits, and so shaken in the exercise of faith, as that they have lost the glory of their confession, in seeking deliverance by sinful compliances in the denial of the truth. And although this may be done out of mere weariness (as it is the design of Satan to wear out the saints of the Most High,) with reluctance of mind, and a love yet remaining to the truth in their hearts, yet hath it constantly one of these two effects. Some by the overwhelming sorrow that befals them on the account of their failure in profession, and out of a deep sense of their unkindness to the Lord Jesus, are stirred up immediately to higher acts of confession than ever they were before engaged in, and to an higher provocation of their adversaries, until their former troubles are doubled upon them, which they frequently undergo with great satisfaction. Instances of this nature occur in all histories of great persecutions. Others being cowed and discouraged in their profession, and perhaps neglected by them whose duty it was rather to restore them, have, by the craft of Satan, given place to their declensions, and become vile apostates. To prevent these evils arising from the duration of sufferings, without a prospect of deliverance, nothing is more prevalent than a constant contemplation on the future reward and glory. So the apostle declares it, Heb. xi. 35. When the mind is filled with the thoughts of the unseen glories of eternity, it hath in readiness what to lay in the balance against the longest continuance and duration of sufferings, which in comparison thereunto at their utmost extent are but for a moment.

I have insisted the longer on these things, because they are the peculiar object of the thoughts of them that are indeed spiritually minded.

CHAPTER VIII.

Spiritual thoughts of God himself. The opposition to them, and neglect of them; with their causes, and the way of their prevalency. Predominant corruptions expelling due thoughts of God, how to be discovered, &c. Thoughts of God, of what nature, and what they are to be accompanied with, &c.

I HAVE spoken very briefly to the first particular instance of the heavenly things that we are to fix our thoughts upon, namely, the person of Christ: and I have done it for the reason before mentioned, namely, that I intend a particular treatise on that subject, or an inquiry how we may behold the glory of Christ in this life, and how we shall do so to eternity. That which I have reserved to the last place, as to the exercise of their thoughts about who are spiritually minded, is that which is the absolute foundation and spring of all spiritual things, namely, God himself. He is the fountain whence all these things proceed, and the ocean wherein they issue: he is the centre and circumference wherein they all begin, meet, and end. So the apostle issues his profound discourse of the counsels of the divine will and mysteries of the gospel, Rom. xi. 36. "Of him, and through him, and to him are all things, to whom be glory for ever." All things arise from his power, and are disposed by his wisdom into a tendency to his glory; "of him, and through him, and to him are all things." Under that consideration alone are they to be the objects of our spiritual meditations, namely, as they come from him, and tend to him. All other things are finite and limited; but they begin and end in that which is immense and infinite. So God is all in all; he, therefore, is, or ought to be, the only supreme absolute object of our thoughts and desires; other things are from and for him only. Where our thoughts do not either immediately and directly, or mediately and by just consequence, tend to, and end in him, they are not spiritual. 1 Pet. i. 21.

To make way for directions how to exercise our thoughts on God himself, some things must be premised concerning a sinful defect herein, with the causes of it.

1. It is the great character of a man presumptuously and flagitiously wicked, that God is not in all his thoughts. Psal. x. 4. That is, he is in none of them. And of this want of thoughts of God there are many degrees; for all wicked men are not equally forgetful of him.

1. Some are under the power of atheistical thoughts: they deny or question, or do not avowedly acknowledge, the very being of God. This is the height of what the enmity of the carnal mind can rise to. To acknowledge God, and yet to refuse to be subject to his law or will, a man would think were as bad, if not worse, than to deny the being of God: but it is not so. That is a rebellion against his authority—this, an hatred to the only Fountain of all goodness, truth, and being; and that because they cannot own it, but, withal they must acknowledge it to be infinitely righteous, holy, and powerful, which would destroy all their desires and security. Such may be the person in the

Psalm, (for the words may be so read,) All his thoughts are, that there is no God. Howbeit the context describes him as one who rather despiseth his providence, than denieth his being. But such there are, whom the same Psalmist elsewhere brands for fools, though themselves seem to suppose that wisdom was born and will die with them. Psal. xiv. 1, & liii. 1.

It may be, never any age since the flood did more abound with open atheism, among such as pretended to the use and improvement of reason, than that wherein we live. Among the ancient civilized heathen, we hear ever and anon of a person branded for an atheist, yet are not certain whether it was done jùstly or not: but in all nations of Europe at this day, cities, courts, towns, fields, armies, abound with persons who, if any credit may be given to what they say or do, believe not that there is a God. And the reason hereof may be a little inquired into.

Now this is no other, in general, but that men have decocted and wasted the light and power of the Christian religion. It is the fullest revelation of God that ever he made; it is the last that ever he will make in this world. If this be despised, if men rebel against the light of it, if they break the cords of it, and are senseless of its power, nothing can preserve them from the highest atheism that the nature of man is capable of. It is in vain to expect relief or preservation from inferior means, where the highest and most noble is rejected. Reason, or the light of nature, gives evidences to the being of God, and arguments are still well pleaded from them to the confusion of atheists; and they were sufficient to retain men in an acknowledgment of the divine power and Godhead, who had no other, no higher evidences of them; but where men have had the benefit of divine revelation, where they have been educated in the principles of the Christian religion, have had some knowledge, and some profession of them; and have, through love of sin, and hatred of every thing that is truly good, rejected all convictions from them concerning the being, power, and rule of God, they will not be kept to a confession of them, by any considerations that the light of nature can suggest.

There are, therefore, among others, three reasons why there are more atheists among them who live where the Christian religion is professed, and the power of it rejected, than among any other sort of men, even than there were among the heathens themselves

1. God hath designed to magnify his word above all his name, or all other ways of the revelation of himself to the children of men. Ps. cxxxviii. 2. Where, therefore, this is rejected and despised, he will not give the honor to reason, or the light of nature, that they shall preserve the minds of men from any evil whatever. Reason shall not have the same power and efficacy on the minds of men who reject the light and power of divine revelation by the word, as it hath, or may have, on them whose best guide it is, who never enjoyed the light of the gospel; and, therefore, there is oft-times more common honesty among civilized heathens and Mahometans, than amongst degenerate Christians; and from the same reason, the children of professors are sometimes irrecoverably profligate. It will be said, many are recovered to God by afflictions, who have despised the word; but it is otherwise; never any were converted to God by afflictions who had rejected the word. Men may by afflictions be recalled to the

light of the word; but none are immediately turned to God by them. As a good shepherd, when a sheep wanders from a flock, and will not hear his call, sends out his dog, which stops him, and bites him; hereon he looks about him, and hearing the call of the shepherd, returns again to the flock. Job. xxxiii. 19—25. But with this sort of persons it is the way of God, that where the principal means of the revelation of himself, and wherein he doth most glorify his wisdom and his goodness, is despised, he will not only take off the efficacy of inferior means, but judicially harden the hearts, and blind the eyes of men, that such means shall be of no use to them. See Isa. vi. 8—12. Acts xiii. 40, 41. Rom. i. 21, 28. 2 Thess. ii. 11, 12.

2. The contempt of gospel light and the Christian religion, as it is supernatural, (which is the beginning of transgression to all atheists among us,) begets in, and leaves on the mind such a depraved corrupt habit, such a congress of all evils, that the hatred of the goodness, wisdom, and grace of God, can produce; that it cannot but be wholly inclined to the worst of evils, as all our original vicious inclinations succeed immediately on our rejection and loss of the image of God. The best things corrupted, yield the worst savor, as manna stank and bred worms; the knowledge of the gospel being rejected, stinking worms take the place of it in the mind, which grow into vipers and scorpions. Every degree of apostacy from gospel truth brings in a proportionate degree of inclination to wickedness into the hearts and minds of men. 2 Pet. ii. 21: and that which is total to all the evils that they are capable of in this world. Whereas, therefore, multitudes, from their darkness, unbelief, temptation, love of sin, pride, and contempt of God, fall off from all subjection of soul and

conscience to the gospel, either notionally or practically, deriding or despising all supernatural revelations; they are a thousand times more disposed to downright atheism, than persons who never had the light or benefit of such revelations. Take heed of decays; whatever ground the gospel loseth in our minds, sin possesseth itself of for its own ends.

Let none say it is otherwise with them. Men grow cold and negligent in the duties of gospel worship, public and private, which is to reject gospel light. Let them say and pretend what they please, that in other things in their minds and conversations, it is well with them; indeed it is not so. Sin will, sin doth, one way or other, make an increase in them, proportionate to these decays, and will sooner or later discover itself so to do. And themselves, if they are not utterly hardened, may greatly discover it, inwardly in their peace, or outwardly in their lives.

3. Where men are resolved not to see, the greater the light is that shines about them, the faster they must close their eyes. All atheism springs from a resolution not to see things invisible and eternal. Love of sin, a resolved continuance in the practice of it, the effectual power of vicious inclinations, in opposition to all that is good, make it the interest of such men that there should be no God to call them to an account. For a supreme unavoidable Judge, an eternal Rewarder of good and evil, is inseparable from the first notion of a Divine Being. Whereas, therefore, the most glorious light, and uncontrollable evidence of these things shines forth in the scripture, men that will abide by their interest to love and live in sin, must close their eyes with all the arts and powers that they have, or else they will pierce into their minds to their torment.

This they do by downright atheism, which alone pretends to give them security against the light of divine revelation. Against all other convictions, they might take shelter from their fears, under less degrees of it.

It is not, therefore, to the disparagement, but honor of the gospel, that so many avow themselves to be atheists, in those places wherein the truth of it is known and professed: for none can have the least inclination or temptation thereto, until they have beforehand rejected the gospel, which immediately exposeth them to the worst of evils.

Nor is there any means for the recovery of such persons. The opposition that hath been made to atheism, with arguments for the divine being and existence of God, taken from reason and natural light, in this and other ages, hath been of good use to cast contempt on the pretences of evil men, to justify themselves in their folly. But that they have so much as changed the minds of any, I much doubt. No man is under the power of atheistical thoughts, or can be so long, but he that is ensnared into them by his desire to live securely and uncontrollable in sin. Such persons know it to be their interest, that there should be no God, and are willing to take shelter under the bold expressions and reasonings of them, who by the same means have hardened and blinded their minds into such foolish thoughts. But the most rational arguments for the being of the Deity will never prove an effectual cure to a predominant love of, and habitual course in sin, in them who have resisted and rejected the means and motives to that end, declared in divine revelation. And unless the love of sin be cured in the heart, thoughts of the acknowledgement of God will not be fixed in the mind.

2. There are those of whom also it may be said, that God is not in all their thoughts, though they acknowledge his essence and being. For they are not practically influenced in any thing by the notions they have of him. Such is the person of whom this is affirmed, Psal. x. 4. He is one who, through pride and profligacy, with hardness in sin, regards not God in the rule of the world, ver. 4, 5, 11, 13. Such is the world filled with at this day, as they are described, Tit. i. 16. "They profess that they know God, but in their works deny him, being abominable and disobedient, and to every good work reprobate." They think, they live, they act in all things as if there were no God, at least as if they never thought of him with fear and reverence. And for the most part we need not seek far for evidences of their disregard of God; the pride of their countenances testifies against them. Psal. x. 4. And if they are followed further, cursed oaths, licentiousness of life, and hatred of all that is good, will confirm and evidence the same. Such as these may own God in words, may be afraid of him in dangers, may attend outwardly on his worship; but they think not of God at all in a due manner; he is not in all their thoughts.

3. There are yet less degrees of this disregard of God and forgetfulness of him. Some are so filled with thoughts of the world, and the occasions of life, that it is impossible they should think of God as they ought. For as the love of God and the love of the world in prevalent degrees are inconsistent, (for if a man loveth this world, how dwelleth the love of God in him?) so thoughts of God and of the world in the like degree, are inconsistent. This is the state of many, who yet would be esteemed spiritually minded. They are con-

tinually conversant in their minds about earthly things. Some things impose themselves on them under the notion of duty: they belong to their callings, they must be attended to. Some are suggested to their minds from daily occasions and occurrences. Common converse in the world engageth men into no other but worldly thoughts, love and desire of earthly things, their enjoyment and increase, exhaust the vigor of their spirits all the day long. In the midst of a multitude of thoughts arising from these and the like occasions, whilst their hearts and heads are reeking with the steam of them, many fall immediately in their seasons to the performance of holy duties. Those times may suffice for thoughts of God, but notwithstanding such duties, what through the want of a due preparation for them, what through the fulness of their minds and affections with other things, and what through a neglect of exercising grace in them, it may be said comparatively, that God is not in all their thoughts.

I pray God, that this, at least as to some degrees of it, be not the condition of many among us. I speak not now of men who visibly and openly live in sin, profane in their principles, and profligate in their lives. The prayers of such persons are an abomination to the Lord; neither have they ever any thoughts of him, which he doth accept: but I speak of them who are sober in their lives, industrious in their callings, and not openly negligent about the outward duties of religion. Such men are apt to approve of themselves, and others also to speak well of them; for these things are in themselves commendable and praise-worthy. But if they are traced home, it will be found, as to many of them, that God is not in all their thoughts as he ought to be. Their earthly conversation, their vain communication, with their foolish designs, do all manifest, that the vigor of their spirits, and the most intense contrivances of their minds, are engaged in things below. Some refuse, transient, unmanaged thoughts, are sometimes cast away on God, which he despiseth.

4. Where persons do cherish secret predominant lusts in their hearts and lives, God is not in their thoughts as he ought to be. He may be, he often is, much in the words of such persons, but in their thoughts he is not, he cannot be, in a due manner. And such persons, no doubt, there are. Ever and anon, we hear of one and another whose secret lusts break forth into a discovery. They flatter themselves for a season, but God oft-times so orders things in his holy providence, that their iniquity shall be found out to be hateful. Some hateful lust discovers itself to be predominant in them. One is drunken, another unclean, a third an oppressor. Such there were found among professors of the gospel, and that in the best of times; among the apostles, one was a traitor, a devil. Of the first professors of Christianity, there were those, whose God was their belly, whose end was destruction, who minded earthly things. Phil. iii. 18, 19. Some may take advantage at this acknowledgment, that there are such evils among such as are called professors. And it must be confessed, that great scandal is given hereby unto the world, casting both them that gave it, and them to whom it is given, under a most dreadful wo. But we must bear the reproach of it, as they did of old, and commit the issue of all things to the watchful care of God. However, it is good in such a season to be "jealous over ourselves and others, to exhort one another daily whilst it is called to-day, lest any be hardened through the deceitfulness of sin." See Heb. xii.

13—17. And because those with whom it is thus, cannot be spiritually minded, yet as there are some difficulties in the case, as to the predominancy of a secret lust or sin, I shall consider it somewhat more distinctly.

1. We must distinguish between a time of temptation in some, and the ordinary state of mind and affections in others. There may be a season, wherein God, in his holy wise orderings of all things towards us, and for his own glory, in his holy, blessed ends, may suffer a lust or corruption to break loose in the heart, to strive, tempt, suggest, and tumultuate, to the great trouble and disquietude of the mind and conscience. Neither can it be denied, but that falling in conjunction with some vigorous temptation, it may proceed so far as to surprise the person in whom it is, into actual sin, to his defilement and amazement. In this case no man can say " he is tempted of God, for God tempteth no man," but every man is " tempted of his own lust, and enticed." But yet temptations, of what sort soever they be, so far as they are afflictive, corrective, or penal, are ordered and disposed by God himself. For there is no evil of that nature, and he hath not done it. And where he will have the power of any corruption to be afflictive in any instance, two things may safely be ascribed to him.

1. He withholds the supplies of that grace, whereby it might be effectually mortified and subdued. He can give in a sufficiency of efficacious grace, to repel any temptation, to subdue any or all our lusts and sins. For he can and doth work in us to will and to do, according to his pleasure. Ordinarily he doth so in them that believe; so that although their lusts may rebel and war, they cannot defile or prevail. But to the

continual supplies of this actual prevailing grace, he is not obliged. When it may have a tendency to his holy ends, he may, and doth, withhold it. When it may be, a proud soul is to be humbled, a careless soul to be awakened, an unthankful soul to be convinced and rebuked, a backsliding soul to be recovered, a froward, selfish, passionate soul to be broken and meekened, he can leave them for a season to the sore exercise of a prevalent corruption, which, under his holy guidance, shall contribute greatly to his blessed ends. It was so in the temptation of Paul, 2 Cor. xi. 7—9. If a man, through disorder and excesses, is contracting any habitual distempers of body, which gradually and insensibly tend to his death; it may be an advantage to be cast into a violent fever, which threatens immediately to take away his life. For he will hereby be thoroughly awakened to the consideration of his danger, and not only labor to be freed from his fever, but also for the future to watch against those disorders and excesses which cast him into that condition. And sometimes a loose, careless soul, that walks in a secure formal profession, contracts many spiritual diseases, which tend to death and ruin. No arguments or considerations can prevail with him, to awaken himself, to shake himself out of the dust, and to betake himself to a more diligent and humble walking before God. In this state, it may be, through the permission of God, he is surprised into some open, actual sin. Hereon, through the vigorous actings of an enlightened conscience, and the stirrings of any sparks of grace which yet remain, he is amazed, terrified, and stirs up himself to seek after deliverance.

2. God may, and doth, in his providence, "administer objects and occasions of men's lusts," for their

trial. He will place them in such relations, in such circumstances, as shall be apt to provoke their affections, passions, desires, and inclinations, to those objects that are suited to them.

In this state, any lust will quickly get such power in the mind and affections, as to manage continual solicitations to sin. It will not only dispose the affections towards it, but multiply thoughts about it, and darken the mind as to those considerations which ought to prevail to its mortification. In this condition it is hard to conceive how God should be in the thoughts of men in a due manner. However, this state is very different from the habitual prevalency of any secret sin or corruption, in the ordinary course of men's walking in the world, and therefore I do not directly intend it.

If any one shall inquire how we know this difference, namely, that which is between the "occasional prevalency of any lust or corruption in conjunction with a temptation," and "the power of sin in any instance habitually and constantly complied with, or indulged in the mind:" I answer:

1. It is no great matter whether we are able to distinguish between them or not. For the end why God suffers any corruption to be such a snare and temptation, such a thorn and brier, is to awaken the souls of men out of their security, and to humble them for their pride and negligence. The more severe are their apprehensions concerning it, the more effectual it will be to this end and purpose. It is good, it may be, that the soul should apprehend more of what is sinful in it, as it is a corruption, than of what is afflictive in it, as it is a temptation. For if it be conceived as a predominant lust, if there be any spark of grace remaining in the soul, it will not rest until in some measure it be

subdued. It will also immediately put it upon a diligent search into itself, which will issue in deep self-abasement, the principal end designed. But,

2. For the relief of them that may be perplexed in their minds, about their state and condition, I say, there is an apparent difference between these things. A lust or corruption arising up or breaking forth into a violent temptation, is the continual burthen, grief, and affliction of the soul wherein it is. And as the temptation for the most part which befals such a person, will give him no rest from its reiterated solicitations; so he will give the temptation no rest, but will be continually conflicting with it, and contending against it. It fills the soul with an amazement at itself, and continual self-abhorrency, that any such seeds of filth and folly should be yet remaining in it. With them in whom any sin is ordinarily prevalent, it is otherwise. According to their light and renewed occasional convictions, they have trouble about it; they cannot but have so, unless their consciences are utterly seared. But this trouble respects principally, if not solely, its guilt and effects. They know not what may ensue on their compliance with it, in this world and another. Beyond this they like it well enough, and are not willing to part with it. It is of this latter sort of persons of whom we speak at present.

3. We must distinguish between the perplexing solicitation of any lust, and the conquering predominancy of it. The evil that is present with us, will be soliciting and pressing to sin of its own accord, even where there is no such especial temptation, as that spoken of before. So is the case stated, so are the nature and operations of it described, Rom. i. Gal. v. And sometimes an especial, particular lust, may be so warmed

and fomented by men's constitutions within, or be so exposed to provoking, exciting occasions without, as to bring perpetual trouble on the mind. Yet this may be where no sin hath the predominancy inquired after. And the difference between the perplexing solicitation of any corruption to sin, and the conquering prevalency of it, lies in this; that under the former, the thoughts, contrivances, and actings of the mind, are generally disposed and inclined to an opposition to it, and a conflict with it, how it may be obviated, defeated, destroyed; how an absolute victory may be obtained against it. Yea, death itself is sweet to such persons under this notion, as it is that which will deliver them from the perplexing power of their corruptions; so is the state of such a soul at large represented, Rom. vii. In the other case, namely, of its predominancy, it disposeth the thoughts actually for the most part, to make provision for the flesh, and to fulfil it in the lusts thereof. It fills the mind with pleasing contemplations of its object, and puts it on contrivances for satisfaction. Yea, part of the bitterness of death to such persons, is, that it will make an everlasting separation between them and the satisfaction they have received in their lusts. It is bitter in the thoughts of it to a worldly minded man, because it will take him from all his enjoyments, his wealth, profits, and advantages. It is so to the sensual person, as that which finally determines all his pleasures

3. There is a difference in the degrees of such a predominant corruption. In some, it taints the affections, vitiates the thoughts, and works over the will to acts of a secret complacency in sin, but proceeds no further. The whole mind may be vitiated by it, and rendered, in the multitude of its thoughts, vain, sen-

sual, or worldly, according as is the nature of the prevailing corruption. Yet here God puts bounds to the raging of some men's corruptions, and says to their proud waves, "thus far shall ye proceed, and no further." He either lays a restraint on their minds, that when lust hath fully conceived, it shall not bring forth sin, or he sets an hedge before them in his providence, that they shall not be able, in their circumstances, to find their way unto what perhaps they do most earnestly desire. A woful life it is that such persons lead. They are continually tortured between their corruptions and convictions, or the love of sin, and fear of the event. With others it pursues its course into outward actual sins, which in some are discovered in this world, in others they are not: for "some men's sins go before them unto judgment, and some follow after." Some fall into sin upon surprisal, from a concurrence of temptation with corruption and opportunities; some habituate themselves to a course in sin; though in many it be not discovered, in some it is. But among those who have received any spiritual light, and made profession of religion thereon, this seldom falls out, but from the great displeasure of God. For when men have long given way unto the prevalency of sin in their affections, inclinations, and thoughts, and God hath set many a hedge before them, to put bounds to their inclinations, and to shut up the womb of sin; sometimes by afflictions, sometimes by fears and dangers, sometimes by the word; and yet the bent of their spirits is toward their sin; God takes off his hand of restraint, removes his hinderances, and "gives them up to their own hearts' lusts, to do the things that are not convenient." All things hereon suit their desires, and they rush into actual sins and follies, setting their feet in the paths that go down to the chambers of death. The uncontrollable power of sin in such persons, and the greatness of God's displeasure against them, make their condition most deplorable.

Those that are in this state, of either sort, the former or the latter, are remote from being spiritually minded, nor is God in all their thoughts, as he ought to be. For,

1. They will not so think and meditate on God. Their delight is turned another way. Their affections, which are the spring of their thoughts, which feed them continually, cleave unto the things which are most adverse to him. Love of sin is gotten to be the spring in them, and the whole stream of the thoughts which they choose and delight in, is towards the pleasures of it. If any thoughts of God come in, as a faint tide for a few minutes, and drive back the other stream, they are quickly repelled and carried away with the strong current of those which proceed from their powerful inclinations. Yet may such persons abide in the "performance of outward holy duties," or attendance to them. Pride of, or satisfaction in, their gifts, may give them delight in their own performances, and something in those of others, they may be exceedingly pleased with; as it is expressly affirmed, Ezek. xxxiii. 31, 32. But in these things they have no immediate real thoughts of God, none that they delight in, none that they seek to stir up in themselves, and those which impose themselves on them they reject.

2. As they will not, so they dare not, think of God. They will not, because of the power of their lusts; they dare not, because of their guilt. No sooner should they begin to think of him in good earnest, but their sin would lose all its desirable forms and appearances,

and represent itself in the horror of guilt alone. And in that condition all the properties of the divine nature are suited to increase the dread and terror of the sinner. Adam had heard God's voice before with delight and satisfaction, but on the hearing of the same voice after he had sinned, he hid himself, and cried that he was afraid. There is a way for men to think of God with the guilt of sin upon them, which they intend to forsake; but none for any to do it with the guilt of sin which they resolve to continue in. Wherefore, of all these sorts of persons it may be said, that God is not in all their thoughts, and therefore are they far enough from being spiritually minded. For unless we have many thoughts of God, we cannot be so. Yea, moreover, there are two things required to those thoughts which we have of God, that they may be an evidence of our being so.

1. That we take delight in them. Psalm xxx. 4. "Sing unto the Lord, O ye saints of his, and give thanks at the remembrance of his holiness." The remembrance of God delighteth and refresheth the hearts of his saints, and stirs them up to thankfulness.

1. They rejoice in what God is in himself. Whatever is good, amiable, or desirable; whatever is holy, just, and powerful; whatever is gracious, wise, and merciful; and all that is so, they see and apprehend in God. That God is what he is, is the matter of their chiefest joy. Whatever befalls them in this world, whatever troubles and disquietment they are exercised with, the remembrance of God is a satisfactory refreshment to them. For therein they behold all that is good and excellent, the infinite centre of all perfections. Wicked men would have God to be any thing but what he is. Nothing that God is, really and truly, pleaseth

them. Whefore they either frame false notions of him in their minds, as Ps. l. 21; or they think not of him at all, at least as they ought, unless sometimes they tremble at his anger and power. Some benefit they suppose may be had, by what he can do, but how there can be any delight in what he is, they know not. Yea, all their trouble ariseth from hence, that he is what he is. It would be a relief to them, if they could make any abatement of his power, his holiness, his righteousness, his omnipresence; but his saints, as the Psalmist speaks, "give thanks at the remembrance of his holiness."

And when we can delight in the thoughts of what God is in himself, of his infinite excellencies and perfections, it gives us a threefold evidence of our being spiritually minded. (1.) In that it is such an evidence that we have a gracious interest in those excellencies and perfections, whereon we can say with rejoicing in ourselves, this God, thus holy, thus powerful, thus just, good, and gracious, "is our God, and he will be our guide unto death." So the Psalmist, under the consideration of his own frailty, and apprehensions of death in the midst of his years, comforts and refreshes himself with the thoughts of "God's eternity and immutability," with his interest in them, Ps. cii. 23—28. And God himself proposeth to us his infinite immutability, as the ground whereon we may expect safety and deliverance, Mal. iii. 6. When we can thus think of God, and what he is, with delight, it is, I say, an evidence, that we have a gracious covenant-interest, even in what God is in himself: which none have but those who are spiritually minded.

2. It is an evidence that the image of God is begun to be wrought in our own souls; and we approve of, and rejoice in it, more than in all other things what-

ever. Whatever notions men may have of the divine goodness, holiness, righteousness, and purity, they are all but barren, jejune, and fruitless, unless there be a similitude and conformity to them wrought in their minds and souls. Without this they cannot rejoice in the thoughts and remembrance of the divine excellencies. Wherefore, when we can do so, when such meditations of God are sweet to us, it is an evidence that we have some experience in ourselves of the excellency of the image of those perfections, and that we rejoice in them above all things in this world.

3. They are so also, in that they are manifest, that we discern and judge that our "eternal blessedness doth consist in the full manifestation, and our enjoyment of God in what he is, and of all his divine excellencies." This men for the most part take for granted; but how it should be so, they know not. They understand it in some measure, whose hearts are here deeply affected with delight in them; they are able to believe that the manifestation and enjoyment of the divine excellencies will give eternal rest, satisfaction, and complacency to their souls. No wicked man can look upon it otherwise than a torment, to abide for ever with eternal holiness, Isa. xxxiii. 14. And we ourselves can have no present prospect into the fulness of future glory, when God shall be all in all, but through the delight and satisfaction which we have here in contemplation of what he is in himself, as the centre of all divine perfections.

I would, therefore, press this unknown, this neglected duty, on the minds of those of us in an especial manner, who are visibly drawing nigh to eternity. The days are coming, wherein what God is in himself, that is, as manifest and exerted in Christ, shall alone be (as we hope) the eternal blessedness and reward of our souls. Is it possible that any thing should be more necessary for us, more useful to us, than to be exercised in such thoughts and contemplations? The benefits we may have hereby are not to be reckoned, some of them only may be named. As (1.) We shall have the best trial of ourselves, how our hearts really stand affected towards God. For if, upon examination, we find ourselves not really to delight and rejoice in God, for what he is in himself, and that all perfections are eternally resident in him, how dwelleth the love of God in us? But if we can truly rejoice at the remembrance of his holiness, in the thoughts of what he is, our hearts are upright with him. (2.) This is that which will effectually take off our thoughts and affections from things here below. One spiritual view of the divine goodness, beauty, and holiness, will have more efficacy to raise the heart to a contempt of all earthly things, than any other evidences whatever. (3.) It will increase the grace of being heavenly minded in us, on the grounds before declared. (4.) It is the best, I had almost said, it is the only preparation, for the future full enjoyment of God. This will gradually lead us into his presence, take away all fears of death, increase our longing after eternal rest, and even make us groan to be unclothed. Let us not then cease laboring with our hearts, until, through grace, we have a spiritually sensible delight and joy in the remembrances and thoughts of what God is in himself.

2. In thoughts of God, his saints rejoice at the "remembrance of what he is, and what he will be to them." Herein have they regard to all the holy relations that he hath taken on himself towards them, with all the effects of his covenant in Christ Jesus. To that purpose

were some of the last words of David, 2 Sam. xxiii. 5. "Although my house be not so with God, yet he hath made with me an everlasting covenant, ordered in all things, and sure this is all my salvation and all my desire." In the prospect he had of all the distresses that were to befall his family, he triumphantly rejoiceth in the everlasting covenant that God hath made with him. In these thoughts his saints take delight, they are sweet to them and full of refreshment. "Their meditations of him are sweet, they are glad in the Lord." Psal. civ. 34. Thus it is with them that are truly spiritually minded. They not only think much of God but they take delight in these thoughts; they are sweet to them; and not only so, but they have no solid joy nor delight, but in their thoughts of God, which therefore they retreat to continually. They do so especially on great occasions, which of themselves are apt to divert them from them. As, suppose a man hath received a signal mercy, with the matter whereof he is exceedingly affected and delighted. The minds of some men are apt on such occasions, to be "filled with thoughts of what they have received," and their affections to be wholly taken up with it. But he who is spiritually minded, will immediately retreat to thoughts of God, placing his delight and taking up his satisfaction in him. And so, on the other side, great distresses, prevalent sorrows, strong pains, violent distempers, are apt of themselves to take up and exercise all the thoughts of men about them. But those who are spiritually minded, will in and under them all, continually betake themselves to thoughts of God, wherein they find relief and refreshment against all that they feel or fear. In every state, their principal joy is in the remembrance of his holiness.

2. "That they may be accompained with godly fear and reverence." These are required of us, in all wherein we have to do with God, Heb. xii. 28, 29. And as the scripture doth not more abound with precepts to any duty, so the nature of God and our own, with the infinite distance between them, make it indispensably necessary, even in the light of the natural conscience. Infinite greatness, infinite holiness, infinite power, all which God is, command the uttermost reverential fear that our natures are capable of. The want hereof is the spring of innumerable evils, yea, indeed, of all that is so. Hence are blasphemous abuses of the holy name of God, in cursed oaths and execrations; hence it is taken in vain, in ordinary exclamations; hence is all formality in religion.

It is the spiritual mind alone that can reconcile those things which are prescribed us as our duty towards God. To delight and rejoice in him always, to triumph in the remembrance of him, to draw nigh to him with boldness and confidence, are on the one hand prescribed to us; and on the other it is so, that we fear and tremble before him, that we "fear that great and dreadful name, the Lord our God;" that we have grace to serve him with reverence and godly fear, because he is a consuming fire. These things carnal reason can comprehend no consistency in; what it is afraid of, it cannot delight in; and what it delights in, it will not long fear. But the consideration of faith (concerning what God is in himself, and what he will be to us) gives these different graces their distinct operations, and a blessed reconciliation in our souls. Wherefore all our thoughts of God ought to be accompanied with an holy awe and reverence, from a due sense of his greatness, holiness, and power. Two things will utterly vitiate all thoughts of God, and render them useless to us.

(1.) Vain curiosity. (2.) Carnal boldness. It is unimaginable how the subtle disquisitions and disputes of men, about the nature, properties, and counsels of God, have corrupted, rendered sapless and useless by vain curiosity, and striving for an artificial accuracy, in expression of men's apprehensions. When the wits and minds of men are engaged in such thoughts, 'God is not in all their thoughts,' even when all their thoughts are concerning him. When once men are got into their 'metaphysical curiosities, and logical niceties,' in their contemplations about God and his divine properties, they bid farewell, for the most part, to all godly fear and reverence. Others are under the power of carnal boldness, that they think of God with no other respect, than if they thought of worms of the earth like themselves. There is no holy awfulness upon their minds and souls in the mention of his name. By these things may our thoughts of God be so vitiated, that the heart in them shall not be affected with a reverence of him nor any evidence be given that we are spiritually minded.

It is this holy reverence that is the means of bringing sanctifying virtue into our souls, from God, upon our thoughts of him. None that think of God with a due reverence, but he shall be sensible of advantage by it. Hereby do we sanctify God in our access to him, and when we do so, he will sanctify and purify our hearts by those very thoughts in which we draw nigh to him.

We may have many sudden, occasional, transient thoughts of God, that are not introduced in our minds by a preceding reverential fear. But if they leave not that fear on our hearts, in proportion to their continuance with us, they are of no value, but will insensibly habituate us to a common bold frame of spirit, which he despises.

So it is in the case of thoughts of a contrary nature. Thoughts of sin, of sinful objects, may arise in our minds from the remainders of corruption; or be occasioned by the temptations and suggestions of Satan; if these are immediately rejected and cast out of us, the soul is not more prejudiced by their entrance, than it is advantaged by their rejection, through the power of grace. But if they make frequent returns into the minds of men, or make any abode or continuance in their soliciting of the affections, they greatly defile the mind and conscience, disposing the person to the further entertainment of them. So, if our occasional thoughts of God do immediately leave us, and pass away without much affecting our minds; we shall have little or no benefit by them. But if by their frequent visits, and some continuance with us, they dispose our souls to an holy reverence of God, they are blessed means of promoting our sanctification. Without this, I say, there may be thoughts of God to no advantage of the soul.

There is implanted in our nature such a sense of a divine power and presence, as that, on all sudden occasions and surprisals, it will act itself according to that sense and apprehension, *vox naturæ clamantis ad Dominum naturæ:* a voice in nature itself, upon any thing that is suddenly too hard for it, which cries out immediately to the God of nature. So men, on such occasions, without any consideration, are surprised into a calling on the name of God, and crying to him. And from the same natural apprehension it is, that wicked and profane persons will break forth on all occasions into cursed swearing by his name. So men in such ways have thoughts of God, without either reverence or godly fear, without giving any glory to him, and for the most part for their own disadvantage. Such are all thoughts of God that are not accompanied with holy fear and reverence.

There is scarce any duty that ought at present to be more pressed on the consciences of men, than this of keeping up a constant holy reverence of God in all wherein they have to do with him, both in private and public, in their inward thoughts and outward communication. Formality hath so prevailed in religion, and that under the most effectual means of its suppression, that very many manifest, that they have little or no reverence of God, in the most solemn duties of his worship; and less it may be in their secret thoughts. Some ways that have been found out to keep up a pretence and appearance of it, have been, and are, destructive to it.

But herein consists the very life of religion. The fear of God is, in the Old Testament, the usual expression of all the due respect of our souls to him; and that because where that is not in exercise, nothing is accepted with him. And thence the whole of our wisdom is said to consist therein, and if it be not in a prevalent exercise in all wherein we have to do with him immediately, all our duties are utterly lost as to the ends of his glory, and the spiritual advantage of our own souls.

CHAPTER IX.

What of God or in God we are to think and meditate upon. His being; reasons of it; oppositions to it; the way of their conquest. Thoughts of the omnipresence and omniscience of God, peculiarly necessary. The reasons hereof. As also of his omnipotency.— The use and benefit of such thoughts.

These things mentioned have been premised in general, as to the nature, manner, and way of exercise of our thoughts on God. That which remains, is to give some particular instances of what we are to think upon in an especial manner; and what we are conversant with in our thoughts, if so be we are spiritually minded. And I shall not insist at present on the things which concern his grace and love in Christ Jesus, which belong to another head, but on those which have an immediate respect to the divine nature itself, and its holy essential properties.

1. The abounding of atheism, both notional and practical. The reasons of it have been given before, and the matter of fact is evident to any ordinary observation. And on two accounts with respect hereto we ought to abound with thoughts of faith concerning the being of God. (1.) An especial testimony is required in us, in opposition to this effect of hell. He, therefore, who is spiritually minded, cannot but have many thoughts of the being of God, thereby giving glory to him. Isa. xlii. 9—12. 'Let all the nations be gathered together, and let the people be assembled: who among them can declare this, and show us former things? let them bring forth their witnesses, and be justified; or let them hear and say, it is truth. Ye

are my witnesses, saith the Lord, and my servant, whom I have chosen, that ye may know and believe me, and understand that I am he: before me there was no God formed, neither shall there be after me. I, even I, am the Lord, and beside me there is no Saviour. I have declared, and have saved, and I have showed when there was no strange God among you: therefore ye are my witnesses, saith the Lord, that I am God.' Chap. xliv. 8. 'Fear ye not, neither be afraid: have I not told thee from that time, and have declared it, ye are even my witnesses. Is there a God beside me? Yea, there is no God: I know not any.' (2.) Those atheistical impieties, principles, and practices, which abound amongst us, are grievous provocations to all pious souls. Without frequent retreat to thoughts of the being of God, there is no relief nor refreshment to be had under them. Such was the case of Noah in the old world, and of Lot in Sodom, which rendered their graces illustrious.

2. Because of the unaccountable confusion that all things are filled with at this day of the world. Whatever in former times hath been a temptation in human affairs to any of the people of God, abounds at this day. Never had men, profane and profligate, greater outward appearances to strengthen them in their atheism, nor those that are godly, greater trials for their faith, with respect to the visible state of things in the world. The Psalmist of old, on such an occasion, was almost surprised into unbelieving complaints, Ps. lxxiii. 2—4, &c., and such surprisals may now also befall us, that we may be ready to say with him, 'verily I have cleansed my heart in vain, and washed my hands in innocency; for all the day long have I been plagued, and chastened every morning.' Hence, when

the prophet Habakkuk was exercised with thoughts about such a state of things as is at this day in the world, which he declares, chap. i. 6—12, he lays the foundation of his consideration in the fresh exercise of faith on the being and properties of God, v. 12, 13. And David makes that his retreat on the like occasion. Ps. xi. 3—5.

In such a season as this is, upon both the accounts mentioned, those who are spiritually minded will much exercise their thoughts about the being and existence of God. They will say within themselves, 'verily there is a reward for the righteous; verily he is a God who judgeth in the earth.' Hence will follow such apprehensions of the immensity of his nature, of his eternal power, and infinite wisdom, of his absolute sovereignty, as will hold their souls firm and steadfast in the highest storms of temptation that may befall them.

Yet there are two things that the weaker sort of believers may be exercised with, in their thoughts of the divine being and existence, which may occasion them some trouble.

1. Satan, knowing the weakness of our minds in the immediate contemplation of things infinite and incomprehensible, will sometimes take advantage to insinuate blasphemous imaginations, in opposition to what we would fix upon and relieve ourselves with. He will take that very time, trusting to our weakness, and his own methods of subtilty, to suggest his temptations of atheism, by ensnaring inquiries, when we go about to refresh our souls with thoughts of divine being and excellencies. 'But is there a God indeed? How do you know that there is a God? and may it not be otherwise?' will be his language to our minds; for,

from his first temptation, by way of an ensnaring question, 'yea, and hath God said it, ye shall not eat of every tree of the garden?' he still proceeds much in the same methods. So he did with our Saviour himself, if thou be the Son of God. Is there a God? How if there should be none? In such a case the rule is given us by the apostle: 'above all, take the shield of faith, whereby ye shall be able to quench all the fiery darts of the wicked.' Eph. vi. 16, '*tou ponerou*,' of the wicked one, that is, the devil. And two ways will faith act itself on this occasion.

(1.) By a speedy rejection of such diabolical suggestions with detestation. So did our Saviour in a case not unlike it, Get thee behind me, Satan. Wherefore if any such thoughts are suggested, or seem to arise in our minds, know assuredly that they are no less immediately from the devil, than if he personally stood before you, and visibly appeared to you; if he did so, there is none of you but would arm yourselves with an utter defiance of what he should offer to you. It is no less necessary on this occasion, when you may feel him, though you see him not. Suffer not his fiery darts to abide one moment with you; reject them with indignation; and strengthen your rejection with some pertinent text of scripture, as our Saviour did. If a man have a grenado or a fire-ball cast into his clothes by his enemy, he doth not consider whether it will burn or not, but immediately shakes it off from him. Deal no otherwise with these fiery darts, lest by their abode with you they inflame your imagination to greater disturbance.

(2.) In case they utterly depart not upon this endeavor for their exclusion and casting out, return immediately, without further dispute, to your own experience. When the devil hath asked you the question, if you answer him, you will be ensnared; but if thereon you ask yourselves the question, and apply yourselves to your own experience for an answer to it, you will frustrate all his designs.

There are arguments to be taken, as was said, from the light of nature, and reason in its proper exercise, sufficient to defeat all objections of that kind. But these are not our proper weapons in case of our own temptation, which alone is now under consideration. It requires longer and more sedate reasonings, than such a state will admit of; nor is it a sanctified medium for our relief.

It is what is suited to suggestions on the occasion of our meditations that we inquire after. In them we are not to argue on such principles, but to take the shield of faith to quench these fiery darts. And if on such occasions Satan can divert us into long disputes about the being of God, he hath his end, by carrying us off from the meditation on him which we designed, and after a while he will prevail to make it a common road and trade, that no sooner shall we begin to think of God, but immediately we must dispute about his being.

Therefore the way in this case for him who is really a believer, is to retreat immediately to his own experience, which will pour shame and contempt on the suggestions of Satan. There is no believer who hath knowledge and time to exercise the wisdom of faith in the consideration of himself and of God's dealings with him, but hath a witness in himself of his eternal power and Godhead, as also of those other perfections of his nature, which he is pleased to manifest and glorify by Jesus Christ. Wherefore, on this suggestion of Satan, that there is no God, he will be able to say, that he might better tell me that I do not live nor breathe; that I am not fed by my meat, nor warmed by my clothes; that I know not myself nor any thing else: for I have spiritual sense and experience to the contrary; like him of old, who, when a cunning sophister would prove to him by syllogisms, that there was no such thing as motion, gave no answer to his arguments, but rose up and walked. How often, will he say, have I had experience of the power and presence of God in prayer; as though I had not only heard of him by the hearing of the ear, but also seen him by the seeing of the eye? How often hath he put forth his power and grace in me by his spirit and his word, with an uncontrollable evidence of being, goodness, love and grace? How often hath he refreshed my conscience with the sense of the pardon of sin, speaking that peace to my soul, which all the world could not communicate to me? In how many afflictions, dangers, troubles, hath he been a present help and relief? What sensible emanations of life and power from him have I obtained in meditation on his grace and glory? He who had been blind, answered the Pharisees to their ensnaring captious questions; be it what it will, one thing I know, that whereas I was blind, now I see. Whatever, saith such a soul, be in this temptation of Satan, one thing I know full well, that whereas I was dead, I am alive, whereas I was blind, now I see, and that by an effect of divine power.

This shield of faith, managed in the hand of experience, will quench the fiery darts of Satan; and he will fall under a double defeat. (1.) His temptation will be repelled by the proper way of resistance, whereon he will not only desist in his attempt, but even fly from you. Resist the devil, saith the apostle, and he will fly from you. He will not only depart and cease to trouble you, but will depart as one defeated and confounded. And it is for want of this resistance, lively made use of, that many hang so long in the briers of this temptation. (2.) Recalling the experiences we have had of God, will lead us to the exercise of all kinds of graces, which is the greatest disappointment of our adversary.

(2.) In thoughts of the divine being and existence, we are apt to be at a loss, to be as it were overwhelmed in our minds, because the object is too great and glorious for us to contemplate on. Eternity and immensity, every thing under the notion of infinite, take off the mind from its distinct actings, and reduces it as it were to nothing. Hereon in some, not able to abide in the strict reasons of things, vain and foolish imaginations are apt to arise, and inquiries how can these things be, which we cannot comprehend. Others are utterly at a loss, and turn away their thoughts from them, as they would do their eyes from the bright beams of the sun. Two things are advisable in this case.

1. That we betake ourselves to an holy admiration of what we cannot comprehend. In these things we cannot see God and live; nay, in life eternal itself, they are not absolutely to be comprehended, only what is infinite can fully comprehend what is so. Here they are the objects of faith and worship: in them we may find rest and satisfaction, when inquiries and reasonings will disquiet us, and it may be, overwhelm us. Infinite glory forbids us any near approach, but only by faith. The soul thereby bowing itself to God's adora-

ble greatness, and incomprehensible perfections; finding ourselves to be nothing, and God to be all, will give us rest and peace in these things, Rom. xi. 33—36. We have but unsteady thoughts of the greatness of the world, and all the nations and inhabitants of it, yet are it and these but as 'the dust of the balance and the drop of the bucket, as vanity, as nothing,' compared with God: what then can our thoughts concerning him issue in, but holy admiration?

2. In case we are brought to a loss and disorder in our minds, on the contemplation of any one infinite property of God, it is good to divert our thoughts to the effects of it, such as whereof we have, or may have experience; for what is too great or high for us in itself, is made suitable to our understandings in its effects. So the 'invisible things of God are known in, and by, the things that are seen.' And there is indeed no property of the divine nature, but we may have an experience of it, as to some of its effects in and upon ourselves. These we may consider, and in the streams taste of the fountain which we cannot approach. By them we are led to an holy admiration of what is in itself infinite, immense, incomprehensible. I cannot comprehend the immensity of God's nature; it may be, I cannot understand the nature of immensity; yet if I find by experience, and do strongly believe, that he is always present wherever I am, I have the faith of it, and satisfaction in it.

(2.) With thoughts of the divine being, those of his omnipresence and omniscience ought continually to accompany us. We cannot take one step in a walk before him, unless we remember, that always and in all places he is present with us; that the frame of our hearts, and our inward thoughts, are continually in his view, no less than our outward actions. And as we ought to be perpetually under an awe of, and in the fear of God, in these apprehensions, so there are some seasons wherein our minds ought to be in the actual conception and thoughts of them, without which we shall not be preserved in our duty.

1. The first season of this nature is, when times, places, with other occasions of temptation, and consequently of sinning, do come and meet. With some, company constitutes such a season; and with some, secresy with opportunity does the same. There are those who are ready, with a careless boldness, to put themselves on such societies as they know have been temptations to them, and occasions of sin; every such entrance into any society or company, to them who know how it hath formerly succeeded, is their actual sin, and it is just with God to leave them to all the evil consequences that ensue. Others also do either choose, or are frequently cast on such society; and no sooner are they engaged in it, but they forget all regard to God, and give themselves up, not only to vanity, but to various sorts of excess. David knew the evil and danger of such occasions; and gives us an account of his behavior in them. Psal. xxxix. 1—3. 'I said, I will take heed to my ways, that I sin not with my tongue: I will keep my mouth with a bridle, while the wicked is before me. I was dumb with silence; I held my peace, even from good, and my sorrow was stirred; my heart was hot within me; while I was musing, the fire burned: then spake I with my tongue.' As for their evil words and ways, he would have no communication with them. And as to good discourse, he judged it unseasonable to cast pearls before swine. He was therefore silent as to that also,

though it was a grief and trouble to him. But this occasioned in him afterwards those excellent meditations which he expresseth in the following verses. In the entrances of these occasions, if men would remember the presence of God with them, in these places, with the holy severity of the eye that is upon them, it would put an awe upon their spirits, and embitter those jollities, whose relish is given them by temptation and sin. He doth neither walk humbly nor circumspectly, who being unnecessarily cast on the society of men, wicked or profane, (on such occasions wherein the ordinary sort of men give more than usual liberty to corrupt communications or excess in any kind,) doth not in his entrance of them call to mind the presence and all-seeing eye of God, and at his departure from them, consider whether his deportment hath been such as became that presence, and his being under that eye. But, alas! pretences of business and necessary occasions, engagements of trade, carnal relations, and the common course of communication in the world, with a supposition that all sorts of society are allowed for diversion, have cast out the remembrance of God from the minds of most, even then when men cannot be preserved from sin without it.

This hath sullied the beauty of gospel conversation amongst the most, and left in very few any prevalent evidence of being spiritually minded.

Wherefore, as to them who, either by their voluntary choice, or necessity of their occasions, do enter and engage promiscuously into all societies and companies, let them know assuredly, that if they awe not their hearts and spirits continually with the thoughts and apprehensions of the omnipresence and omniscience of God, that he is always with them, and his eyes always upon them, they will not be preserved from snares and sinful miscarriages.

Yea, such thoughts are needful to the best of us all, and in the best of our societies, that we behave not ourselves indecently in them at any time.

Again, to some privacy, secrecy, and opportunity, are occasions of temptation and sin. They are so to persons under convictions not wholly turned to God. Many a good beginning hath been utterly ruined by this occasion and temptation. Privacy and opportunity have overthrown many such persons in the best of their resolutions. And they are so unto all persons not yet flagitiously wicked. Cursed fruits proceed every day from these occasions. We need no other demonstration of their power and efficacy in tempting unto sin, but the visible effects of them. And what they are to any, they may be to all, if not diligently watched against. So the apostle reflects on the shameful things that are done in the dark, in a concurrence of secrecy and opportunity. This, therefore, gives a just season to thoughts of the omnipresence and omniscience of God, and they will not be wanting in some measure in them that are spiritually minded.

'God is in this place; the darkness is no darkness unto him, light and darkness are with him both alike,' are sufficient considerations to lay in the balance against any temptations springing out of secrecy and opportunity. One thought of the actual presence of the holy God, and the open view of his all-seeing eye; will do more to cool those affections, which lust may put into a tumult on such occasions, than any other consideration whatever. A speedy retreat hereunto, upon the first perplexing thoughts wherewith temptation assaults the soul, will be its strong tower, where it shall be safe.

2. A second season calling for the exercise of our minds in thoughts of the omnipresence and omniscience of God, is made up of our solitudes and retirements. These give us the most genuine trials, whether we are spiritually minded or not. What we are in them, that we are, and no more. But yet in some of them, as in walkings and in journeyings, or the like, vain thoughts and foolish imaginations are exceedingly apt to solicit our minds. Whatever is stored up in the affections or memory, will at such a time offer itself for our present entertainment: and where men have accustomed themselves to any sort of things, they will press on them for the possession of their thoughts, as it were, whether they will or not. The Psalmist gives us the way to prevent this evil: Psal. xvi. 7, 8. 'I will bless the Lord, who hath given me counsel; my reins also instruct me in the night season. I have set the Lord always before me, because he is at my right hand.' His reins, that is, his affections, and secret thoughts, gave him counsel, and instructed him in all such seasons; but whence had they that wisdom and faithfulness? In themselves they are the seat of all lusts and corruptions; nor could they do any thing but seduce him into an evil frame. It was from hence alone, that he has set the Lord always before him. Continual apprehensions of the presence of God with him, kept his mind, his heart and affections, in that awe and reverence of him, as that they always instructed him to his duty. But as I remember, I spake somewhat as to the due management of our thoughts in this season before.

3. Times of great difficulties, dangers, and perplex-

ities of mind thereon, are a season calling for the same duty. Suppose a man is left alone in his trials for the profession of the gospel, as it was with Paul when all men forsook him, and no man stood by him. Suppose him to be brought before princes, rulers, or judges, that are filled with rage, and armed with power against him, all things being disposed to affect him with dread and terror. It is the duty of such a one to call off his thoughts from all things visibly present, and to fix them on the omnipresence and omniscience of God. He sits amongst those judges, though they acknowledge him not; he rules over them at his pleasure; he knows the cause of the oppressed, and justifies them whenever the world condemns; and can deliver them when he pleaseth. With the thoughts hereof did those holy souls support themselves, when they stood before the fiery countenance of the bloody tyrant on the one hand, and the burning fiery furnace on the other, Dan. iii. 14. 'Our God whom we serve is able to deliver us from the burning fiery furnace, and he will deliver us out of thine hand, O king; but if not, be it known unto thee, O king, that we will not serve thy gods, nor worship the golden image which thou hast set up.' Thoughts of the presence and power of God, gave them not only comfort and supportment under their distress, when they were alone and helpless, but courage and resolution to defy the tyrant to his face. And when the apostle was brought before Nero, that monster of cruelty and villany, and all men forsook him, he affirms that the Lord stood by him, and strengthened him. 2 Tim. iv. 17. He refreshed himself with thoughts of his presence, and had the blessed fruit of it.

Wherefore, on such occasions, when the hearts of

men are ready to quake, when they see all things about them filled with dread and terror, and all help far away, it is, I say, their duty and wisdom to abstract and take off their thoughts from all outward and present appearances, and to fix them on the presence of God. This will greatly change the scene of things in their minds; and they will find that strength, and power, and wisdom, are on their side alone; all that appears against them, being but vanity, folly and weakness.

So when the servant of Elisha saw the place where they were, compassed with an host, both horses and chariots, that came to take them, he cried out for fear, Alas, my master, how shall we do? But upon the praying of the prophet, the Lord opening the eyes of the young man, to see the heavenly guard that he had sent to him, the mountain being full of horses and chariots of fire round about Elisha, his fear and trouble departed, 2 Kings vi. 15—17. And when, in the like extremity, God opens the eye of faith to behold his glorious presence, we shall no more be afraid of the dread of men. Herein did the holy martyrs triumph of old, and even despised their bloody persecutors. Our Saviour himself made it the ground of his supportment on the like occasion, John, xvi. 32. Behold, saith he to his disciples, his only friends, 'the hour cometh, yea, is now come, that ye shall be scattered every one to his own, and leave me alone, and yet I am not alone, because the Father is with me.' Can we but possess our soul with the apprehension, that when we are left alone in our trials and dangers, from any countenance of friends, or help of men, yet that indeed we are not alone, because the Father is with us, it will support us under our despondencies, and enable us to our duties.

4. Especial providential warnings, call for thoughts of God's omnipresence and omniscience. So Jacob, in his nightly vision, instantly made this conclusion; God is in this place, and I knew it not. We have frequently such warnings given to us. Sometimes we have so in the things which are esteemed accidental, whence it may be we are strangely delivered. Sometimes we have so in the things which we see to befall others, by thunder, lightning, storms at sea or land. For all the works of God, especially those that are rare and strange, have a voice whereby he speaks to us. The first thing suggested to a spiritual mind, in such seasons, will be, God is in this place, he is present that liveth and seeth, as Hagar confessed on the like occasion, Gen. xvi. 13, 14.

(3.) Have frequent thoughts of God's omnipotency, or his almighty power. This most men, it may be, suppose they need not much exhortation to; for none ever doubted of it; who doth not grant it on all occasions? Men grant it indeed in general; for eternal power is inseparable from the first notion of the Divine Being. So are they conjoined by the apostle, his eternal power and godhead, Rom. i. 20. Yet few believe it for themselves, and as they ought. Indeed, to believe the almighty power of God, with reference to ourselves and all our concernments, temporal and eternal, is one of the highest and most noble acts of faith, which includes all others in it. For this is that which God at first proposed alone as the proper object of our faith, in our entrance into covenant with him, Gen. xvii. 1. I am God Almighty; that which Job arrived to, after his long exercise and trial; I know, saith he, thou canst do every thing, and no thought of thine can be hindered. Chap. xlii. 2. God hath spoken once, (saith the Psalmist,) twice have I heard this, that power belongs unto God. Psal. lxii. 11. It was that which God saw it necessary frequently to instruct him in. For we are ready to be affected with the appearances of present power in creatures, and to suppose that all things will go according to their wills, because of their power. But it is quite otherwise; all creatures are poor, feeble ciphers, that can do nothing; power belongs to God; it is a flower of his crown imperial, which he will suffer none to usurp; if the proudest of them go beyond the bounds and limits of his present permission, he will send worms to eat them up, as he did to Herod.

It is utterly impossible we should walk before God, to his glory, or with any real peace, comfort, or satisfaction in our own souls, unless our minds are continually exercised with thoughts of his almighty power. Every thing that befalls us, every thing that we hear of, which hath the least danger in it, will discompose our minds, and either make us tremble like the leaves of the forest, that are shaken with the wind, or betake ourselves to foolish or sinful relief, unless we are firmly established in the faith hereof. Consider the promises of God to the church, which are upon record, and yet unaccomplished; consider the present state of the church in the world, with all that belongs to it; in all the fears and dangers they are exposed to, in all the evils they are exercised with, and we shall quickly find, that unless this sheet-anchor be well fixed, we shall be tossed up and down at all uncertainties, and exposed to most violent temptations, Rev. xix. 6. Unto this end are we called hereunto by God himself, in his answer to the despondent complaints of the church in its greatest dangers and calamities. Isa. xl. 28—31. 'Hast thou not known, hast thou not heard, that the everlasting God, the Lord, the Creator of the ends of the earth, fainteth not, neither is weary? There is no searching of his understanding. He giveth power to the faint, and to them that have no might, he increaseth strength. Even the youths shall faint and be weary, and the young men shall utterly fall: but they that wait upon the Lord shall renew their strength: they shall mount up with wings as eagles, they shall run and not be weary, they shall walk and not faint.'

Take one instance, which is the continual concernment of us all. We are obnoxious to death every moment. It is never the further from any of us, because we think not of it as we ought. This will lay our bodies in the dust, from whence they will have no more disposition nor power in themselves to rise again, than any other part of the mould of the earth. Their recovery must be an act of external almighty power, when God shall have a desire to the work of his hands: when he shall call, and we shall answer him out of the dust. And it will transmit the soul into an invisible world, putting a final end to all relations, enjoyments, and circumstances here below. I speak not of them who are stout-hearted and far from righteousness, who live and die like beasts, or under the power of horrible presumption, without any due thoughts of their future and eternal state. But as to others, what comfort or satisfaction can any man have in his life, whereon his all depends, and which is passing from him every moment; unless he hath continual thoughts of the mighty power of God, whereby he is able to receive his departing soul, and to raise his body out of the dust.

Not to insist on more particulars; thus it is with them who are spiritually minded; thus must it be with all, if we pretend a title to that privilege. They are filled with thoughts of God, in opposition to that character of wicked men, that God is not in all their thoughts. And it is greatly to be feared, that many of us, when we come to be weighed in the balance, will be found too light. Men may be in the performance of outward duties; they may hear the word with some delight, and do many things gladly; they may escape the pollutions that are in the world through lust, and not run out into the same compass of excess and riot with other men; yet may they be strangers to inward thoughts of God with delight and complacency. I cannot understand how it can be otherwise with them, whose minds are over and over filled with earthly things, however they may satisfy themselves with pretences of their callings and lawful enjoyments, or not any way inordinately set on the pleasures or profits of the world.

To walk with God, to live to him, is not merely to be found in an abstinence from outward sins, and in the performance of outward duties, though with diligence in the multiplication of them. All this may be done upon such principles, for such ends, with such a frame of heart, as to find no acceptance with God. It is our hearts that he requireth, and we can no way give them to him, but by our affections and holy thoughts of him with delight. This is to be spiritually minded; this is to walk with God. Let no man deceive himself; unless he thus abound in holy thoughts of God, unless our meditation of him be sweet to us, all that we else pretend to will fail us in the day of our trial.

This is the first thing wherein we may evidence ourselves to ourselves, to be under the conduct of the minding of the Spirit, or to be spiritually minded. And I have insisted the longer on it, because it contains the first sensible egress of the spring of living waters in us, the first acting of spiritual life unto our own experience. I should now proceed to the consideration of our affections, of whose frame and state these thoughts are the only genuine exposition: but whereas there are, or may be, some who are sensible of their own weakness and deficiency in the discharge of that part of this duty in being spiritually minded, which we have passed through, and may fall into discouragements thereon, we must follow him, as we are able, who will not quench the smoking flax, nor break the bruised reed, by offering something to the relief of them that are sincere, under the sense of their own weakness.

CHAPTER X.

Sundry things tendered to such as complain that they know not how, that they are not able to abide in holy thoughts of God, and spiritual or heavenly things; for their relief, instruction, and direction. Rules concerning stated Spiritual Meditation.

SOME will say, yea, many on all occasions do say, that there is not any thing in all their duty towards God, wherein they are more at a loss, than they are in this one, of fixing or exercising their thoughts or meditations on things heavenly or spiritual. They acknowledge it a duty; they see an excellency in it, with inexpressible usefulness. But although they often try and attempt it, they cannot attain to any thing, but what makes them ashamed both of it and themselves. Their minds they find are unsteady, apt to rove and wander, or give entertainment to other things, and not to abide on the object which they design their meditation towards. Their abilities are small, their invention barren, their memories frail, and their judgments, to dispose of things into right order, weak and unable. They know not what to think on for the most part; and when they fix on any thing, they are immediately at a loss as to any progress, and so give over. Hence other things, or thoughts of other things, take advantage to impose themselves on them, and what began in spiritual meditation ends in carnal vanity. On these considerations, ofttimes they are discouraged to enter on the duty, ofttimes give it over so soon as it is begun, and are glad if they come off without being losers by their endeavors, which often befalls them. With respect to other duties, it is so with them. To such as are really concerned in these things: to whom their want and defect is a burden; who mourn under it, and desire to be freed from it, or refreshed in their conflict with it, I shall offer the things that ensue.

1. That sense of the vanity of our minds, which this consideration, duly attended to, will give us, ought greatly to humble and abase our souls. Whence is it thus with us, that we cannot abide in thoughts and meditations of things spiritual and heavenly? Is it because they are such things as we have no great concernment in? It may be they are things worthless and unprofitable, so that it is to no purpose to spend our thoughts about them: the truth is, they alone are

worthy, useful, and desirable; all other things, in comparison of them, are but loss and dung. Or is it because the faculties and powers of our souls were not originally suited to the contemplation of them, and delight in them? This also is otherwise: they were all given to us, all created of God for this end, all fitted with inclinations and power to abide with God in all things, without aversation or weariness. Nothing was so natural, easy, and pleasant to them, as steadiness in the contemplation of God and his works. The cause, therefore, of all this evil, lies at our own doors. All this, therefore, and all other evils, came upon us by the entrance of sin. And therefore Solomon, in his inquiry after all the causes and effects of vanity, brings it under this head; 'Lo, this only have I found, that God made man upright; but they have sought out many inventions.' Eccles. vii. 29. For hereby our minds, that were created in a state of blessed adherence to God, were wholly turned off from him, and not only so, but filled with enmity against him. In this state, that vanity which is prevalent in them, is both their sin and their punishment. Their sin, in a perpetual inclination to things vain, foolish, sensual and wicked. So the apostle describes it at large, Ephes. iv. 17—19. Tit. iii. 3. And their punishment, in that being turned off from the chiefest good, wherein alone rest is to be found, they are filled with darkness, confusion, and disquietment, being like a troubled sea that cannot rest, whose waters cast up mire and dirt.

By grace our minds are renewed; that is, changed and delivered from this frame; but they are so partially only. The principle of vanity is no longer predominant in us, to alienate us from the life of God, or to keep us in enmity against him. Those who are so renewed, do not walk in the vanity of their minds, as others do. Eph. iv. 17. They go up and down in all their ways and occasions, with a stream of vain thoughts in their minds. But the remainders of it are effectually operative in us, in all actings of our minds towards God, affecting them with uncertainty and instability. As he who hath received a great wound in any principal part of his body, though it may be so cured, as that death shall not immediately ensue thereon; yet it may make him go weak and lame all his days, and hinder him in the exercise of all the powers of life. The vanity of our minds is so cured, as to deliver us from spiritual death; but yet such a wound, such a weakness, doth remain, as both weakens and hinders us in all the operations of spiritual life. Hence those who have made any progress in grace, are sensible of their vanity, as the greatest burden of their souls, and do groan after such a complete renovation of their minds, as whereby they may be perfectly freed from it. This is that which they principally regard in that complaining desire, Rom. vii. 4. 'O wretched man that I am, who shall deliver me from this body of death?' Yea, they groan under a sense of it every day; nor is any thing such a trouble to them, observing how it defeats them in their designs to contemplate on heavenly things; how it frustrates their best resolutions to abide in the spiritual actings of faith and love; how they are imposed on by it, with the thoughts of things, which either in themselves, or in their consequences, they most abhor; nothing are they so afraid of, nothing is so grievous and burdensome to them, nothing do they more groan for deliverance from. When there is war in any place, it behooveth them that are concerned, to have an eye and regard to all their enemies, and their attempts against them. But if they are vigilant, and delight in their opposition to those that are without, that visibly contend with them, and in the mean time neglect such as traitorously act within among themselves, betraying their counsels, and weakening their strength, they will be undoubtedly ruined. Wise men do first take care of what is within, as knowing if they are there betrayed, all they do against their open enemies is to no purpose. In the warfare wherein we are engaged, we have enemies of all sorts, that openly and visibly, in various temptations, fight against our souls. These it is our duty to watch against, to conflict with, and to seek a conquest over. But it is this internal vanity of mind, that endeavors, in all things, to betray us, to weaken us in all our graces, or to hinder their due operations, and to open the doors of our hearts to our cursed enemies. If our principal endeavor be not to discover, suppress, and destroy this traitor, we shall not succeed in our spiritual warfare.

This, therefore, being the original cause of all that disability of mind as to steadiness in holy thoughts and meditations, whereof you do complain, when you are affected therewith, turn to the consideration of that from whence it doth proceed. Labor to be humbled greatly, and to walk humbly under a sense of the remainders of this vanity of mind. So some wholesome fruits may be taken from this bitter root, and meat may come out of this eater. If, when you cannot abide in holy thoughts of God, and your relation to him, you reflect on this cause of it to your further humiliation and self-abasement, your good designs and purposes are not lost. Let such a one say, 'I began to think of God, of his love and grace in Christ Jesus, of my duty towards him; and where now in a few minutes do I find myself? I am got into the ends of the earth, into things useless and earthly; or am at such a loss as that I have no mind to proceed in the work wherein I was engaged. O! wretched man that I am, what a cursed enemy have I within me! I am ashamed of myself, weary of myself, loathe myself, who shall deliver me from this body of death?' Such thoughts may be as useful to him, as those which he first designed.

True it is, we can never be freed absolutely from all the effects of this vanity and instability of mind in this world. Unchangeable cleaving to God, always, in all the powers and affections of our minds, is reserved for heaven. But yet great degrees may be attained in the conquest and expulsion of it, such as I fear few have experience of; yet ought all to labor after. If we apply ourselves as we ought, to the increase of spiritual light and grace; if we labor diligently to abide and abound in thoughts of spiritual things, and that in love to them, and delight in them; if we watch against the entertainment and approbation of such thoughts and things in our minds, as whereby this vain frame is pleased and confirmed; there is, though not an absolute perfection, yet a blessed degree of heavenly mindedness to be attained, and therein the nearest approach to glory, that in this world we are capable of. If a man cannot attain an athletic constitution of health, or a strength like that of Samson; yet, if he be wise, he will not omit the use of such means as may make him to be useful in the ordinary duties of life. And although we cannot attain perfection in this matter, which yet is our duty to be continually pressing after; yet, if we are wise, we will be endeavoring such a cure of this spiritual distemper, as that we may be able to discharge all the duties of the life of God. But if men, in all other things, feed the vanity of their own minds, if they permit them to rove continually after things foolish, sensual, and earthly; if they wilfully supply them with objects to that end, and labor not by all means for the mortification of this evil frame; in vain shall they desire or expect to bring them, at any time, on any occasion, to be steady in the thoughts of heavenly things. If it be thus with any, as it is to be feared it is with many, it is their duty to mind the words of our Lord Jesus Christ in the first place, make the tree good, and then the fruit will be good, and not before. When the power of sanctifying grace hath made the mind habitually spiritual and heavenly, thoughts of such things will be natural to it, and accompanied with delight. But they will not be so, until the God of peace have sanctified us in our whole spirits, souls and bodies, whereby we may be preserved blameless, to the coming of Jesus Christ.

2. Be always sensible of your own insufficiency to raise in your minds, or to manage spiritual thoughts, or thoughts of things spiritual and heavenly, in a due manner. But in this case, men are apt to suppose, that as they may, so they can, think of what they please. Thoughts are their own, and therefore, be they of what sort they will, they need no assistance for them. They cannot think as they ought, they can do nothing at all. And nothing will convince them of their folly, until they are burdened with experience of the contrary, as to spiritual things. But the advice given is expressly laid down by the apostle, in the instance of himself. 2 Cor. iii. 5. 'Not that we are

sufficient of ourselves to think any thing as of ourselves, but our sufficiency is of God.' He speaks principally of ministers of the gospel, and that of such as were most eminently furnished with spiritual gifts and graces, as he declares, v. 6. And if it be so with them, and that with respect to the work and duties of their calling, how much more is it so with others, who have not their graces nor their offices? Wherefore, if men, without regard to the present actual grace of God, and the supplies of his Spirit, do suppose that they can, of themselves, exercise their minds in spiritual thoughts, and so only fret at themselves when they fall into disappointment, not knowing what is the matter with them, they will live in a lifeless, barren frame, all their days.

By the strength of their natural abilities, men may frame thoughts of God and heavenly things in their minds, according to the knowledge they have of them. They may methodize them by rules of art, and express them elegantly to others; but even while they do so, they may be far enough from being spiritually minded; for there may be in their thoughts no actings of faith, love, or holy delight in God, nor any grace at all. But such alone are things which we inquire after; they are such only as wherein the graces of the spirit are in their proper exercise. With respect to them, we have no sufficiency in ourselves, all our sufficiency must be of God. There is no truth among persons of light and knowledge more generally granted in the notion of it than this, that of ourselves we can do nothing; and none more neglected in daily practice. Men profess they can do nothing of themselves, and yet go about their duties as if they could do all things

3. Remember, that I have not at present treated of solemn, stated meditation; concerning which, other rules and instructions ought to be given. By solemn or stated meditation, I intend the thoughts of some subject, spiritual and divine, with the fixing, forcing, and ordering our thoughts about it, with a design to affect our own hearts and souls with the matter of it, or the things contained in it. By this design it is distinguished from the study of the word, wherein our principal aim is to learn the truth, or to declare it to others. And so also from prayer, whereof God himself is the immediate object. But in meditation it is the affecting of our own hearts and minds, with love, delight, and humiliation. At present, I have only showed what it is to be spiritually minded, and that in this instance of our thoughts, as they proceed from the habitual frame of our hearts and affections; or of what sort the constant course of our thoughts ought to be, with respect to all the occasions of the life of God. This persons may be in a readiness for, who are yet unskilful in, and unable for, stated meditation. For there is required thereto such an exercise of our natural faculties and abilities, as some, through their weakness and ignorance, are incapable of. But as to what we have hitherto insisted on, it is not unattainable by any in whom is the spirit of faith and love. For it is but the frequent actings of them that I intend. Wherefore, do your hearts and affections lead you to many thoughts of God and spiritual things? Do they spring up in you, as water in a well of living waters? Are you ready, on all occasions, to entertain such thoughts, and to be conversant with them, as opportunity doth offer itself? Do you labor to have in readiness what is useful for you, with respect to temptations and du-

ties? Is God in Christ, and the things of the gospel, the ordinary retreat of your souls? Though you should not be able to carry on an ordinary, stated meditation in your minds, yet you may be spiritually minded.

A man may not have a capacity and ability to carry on a great trade of merchandise in the world. The knowledge of all sorts of commodities and seasons of the world, and nations of it, with those contrivances and accounts which belong to such trade, may be above his comprehension, and he may quickly ruin himself in undertaking such an employment. Yet may the abilities of this man serve him well enough to carry on a retail trade in a private shop, wherein perhaps he may thrive as well, and get as good an estate, as any of those whose greater capacities lead them forth to more large and hazardous employments. So it may be with some in this case. The natural faculties of their minds are not sufficient to enable them to stated meditation. They cannot cast things into that method and order which is required thereto; nor frame the conceptions of their minds into words significant and expressive; yet, as to frequency of thoughts of God, and a disposition of mind thereto, they may thrive and be skilful beyond most others of greater natural abilities. Howbeit, because even stated meditation is a necessary duty, yea, the principal way whereby our spiritual thoughts do profitably act themselves, I shall have regard thereto in the following direction; wherefore,

4. Whatever principle of grace we have in our minds, we cannot attain to a ready exercise of it, in a way of spiritual meditation or otherwise, without great diligence, nor without great difficulty,

It was showed at the entrance of this discourse, that there is a difference in this grace, between the essence, substance, or reality of it, which we would not exclude men from, under many failings or infirmities; and the useful degrees of it, wherein it hath its principal exercise. As there is a difference in life natural, and its actings, in a weak, diseased, sickly body, and in that which is of a good constitution, and in a vigorous health. Supposing the first, the reality of this grace, be wrought in us, or implanted in our minds by the Holy Ghost, as a principal part of that new nature which is the workmanship of God, created in Christ Jesus to good works; yet to the growth and improvement of it, as of all other graces, our own diligent care, watchfulness, and spiritual striving in all holy duties are required. Unless the most fruitful ground be manured, it will not bring forth a useful crop. Let not any think that this frame of a spiritual mind, wherein there is a disposition to and readiness for, all holy thoughts of God, of Christ, of spiritual and heavenly things, at all times and on all occasions, will befall him, and continue with him, he knows not how. As good it is for a poor man to expect to be rich in this world, without industry, or a weak man to be strong and healthy, without food and exercise; as to be spiritually minded without an earnest endeavor after it. It may be inquired, what is requisite thereto? And we may name some of those things, without which such an holy frame will not be attained. As,

1. A continual watch is to be kept in and on the soul against the incursions of vain thoughts and imaginations, especially in such seasons wherein they are apt to obtain advantage. If they are suffered to make an inroad into the mind, if we accustom ourselves

to give them entertainment, if they are wont to lodge within; in vain shall we hope or desire to be spiritually minded. Herein consists a principal part of that duty which our Saviour so frequently, so emphatically chargeth on us all; namely, to watch, Mark iii. 37. Unless we keep a strict watch herein, we shall be betrayed into the hands of our spiritual enemies; for all such thoughts are but making provision for the flesh, to fulfil its desires in the lust thereof, however they may be disappointed as to actual sin. This is the substance of the advice given us in charge, Prov. iv. 23. 'Keep thy heart with all diligence, for out of it are the issues of life.'

2. Careful avoidance of all societies and businesses of this life, which are apt, under various pretences, to draw and seduce the mind to an earthly or sensual frame. If men will venture on those things which they have found by experience, or may find by observation, seduce and draw off their minds from a heavenly frame to that which is contrary thereto, and will not watch to their avoidance, they will be filled with the fruit of their own ways. Indeed, the common converse of professors among themselves and others, walking, talking, and behaving themselves like other men, being as full of the world as the world is of itself, have lost the grace of being spiritually minded within, and stained the glory of profession without. The rule observed by David will manifest how careful we ought to be herein, Psal. xxxix. 1—3. 'I said, I will take heed to my ways, that I sin not with my tongue; I will keep my mouth with a bridle while the wicked is before me. I was dumb with silence; I held my peace even from good, and my sorrow was stirred. My heart was hot within me; while I was musing, the

fire burned; then spake I with my tongue:' which place was spoken to before.

3. An holy constraint put on the mind to abide in the duty of spiritual thoughts and meditations; pressing it continually with the consideration of their necessity and usefulness. The mind will be apt of itself to start aside from duties purely spiritual, through the mixture of the flesh abiding in it. The more inward and purely spiritual any duty is, which hath no outward advantages, the more prone will the mind be to decline from it. It will be so, more from private prayer than public, more from meditation than prayer. And other things will be apt to draw it aside from objects without, and various stirrings of the affections within. An holy constraint is to be put upon it, with a sudden rejection of what rises up to its diversion or disturbance. Wherefore, we are to call in all constraining motives, such as the consideration of the love of Christ, 2 Cor. v. 14, to keep the mind steady to its duty.

4. Diligent use of means to furnish the soul with that light and knowledge of heavenly things, which may administer continual matter of holy thoughts and meditations, from within ourselves. This hath been spoken to at large before. And the want hereof is that which keeps many from the least proficiency in these duties. As a man may have some skill or ability for a trade, yet if he have no materials to work upon, he must sit still, and let his trade alone. And so must men do to the work of holy meditation: whatever be the ability of the natural faculties, their inventions or memories, if they are not furnished with knowledge of things spiritual and heavenly, which are the subject matter of such meditations, they must let their work

alone. Hence the apostle prays for the Colossians, that the word of God might dwell in them richly in all wisdom, chap. iii. 16. That is, that they might abound in the knowledge of the mind of Christ, without which we shall be unfit for this duty.

5. Unweariedness in our conflict with Satan, who, by various artifices and the injection of fiery darts, labors continually to divert us from the duties. He is seldom or never wanting to this occasion. He who is furnished in any measure with spiritual wisdom and understanding, may find him more sensibly at work in his craft and opposition with respect to this duty, than any other way. When we stand thus before the Lord, he is always at our right hand to resist us; and ofttimes his strength is great. Hence, as was observed, ofttimes men design really to exercise themselves in holy thoughts, but end in vain imaginations, and rather take up with trifles than continue in this duty. Steadiness in the resistance of him, on these occasions, is one great part of our spiritual warfare. And we may know that he is at work, by his engines and methods. For they consist in his suggestion of vain, foolish, or corrupt imaginations. When they begin to rise in our minds, at such times as we would engage them in spiritual meditations, we may know assuredly from whence they are.

6. Continual watchful care, that no root of bitterness spring up and defile us, that no lust or corruption be predominant in us. When it is so, if persons, in compliance with their convictions, endeavor sometimes to be exercised in these duties, they shall labor in the very fire, where all their endeavors will be immediately consumed.

7. Mortifications to the world in our affections and

desires, with moderation in our endeavors after the needful things of it, are also necessary hereunto; yea, to that degree, that without them no man can in any sense be said to be spiritually minded. For otherwise our affections cannot be so preserved unto the power of grace, as that spiritual things may be always serviceable to us.

Some, it may be, will say, that 'if all these things are required thereunto; it will take up a man's whole life and time to be spiritually minded. They hope they may attain it at an easier rate, and not forget all other advantages and sweetnesses of life, which a strict observation of these things would cast them upon.'

I answer; that however it may prove a hard saying to some, yet I must say it, and my heart would reproach me if I should not say, that if the principal part of our time be not spent about these things, whatever we suppose, we have indeed neither life nor peace. The first fruits of all were to be offered to God; and in sacrifices he required the blood, and the fat of the inwards. If the best be not his, he will have nothing. It is so as to our time. Tell me, I pray you, how you can spend your time and your lives better, or to better purpose; and I shall say, Go on and prosper. I am sure some spend so much of their time so much worse, as it is a shame to see it. Do you think you came into this world to spend your whole time and strength in your employments, your trades, your pleasures, to the satisfaction of the will of the flesh and of the mind? Have you time enough to eat, to drink, to sleep, to talk unprofitably, it may be corruptly, in all sorts of unnecessary societies, but have not enough to live to God, in the very essentials of that life which consists in these things? Alas! you came into the world under the law, it is appointed unto men once to die, and after this the judgment; and the end why your life here is granted to you, is that you may be prepared for that judgment. If this be neglected, if the principal part of your time be not improved with respect to this end, you will fall under the sentence of it to eternity.

But men are apt to mistake in this matter. They may think that these things tend to take them off from their lawful employments and recreations, which they are generally afraid of, and unwilling to purchase any frame of mind at so dear a rate. They may suppose, that to have men spiritually minded, we would make them mopes, and to disregard all the lawful occasions of life. But let not any be mistaken; I am not upon a design that will be easily, or, it may be, honestly defeated. Men are able to defend themselves in their callings and enjoyments, and to satisfy their consciences against any persuasions to the contrary. Yet there is a season, wherein we are obliged to part with all we have, and give up ourselves wholly to follow Christ in all things. Mat. xix. 21. And if we neglect or refuse it in that season, it is an evidence that we are hypocrites. And there was a time when superstition had so much power on the minds of men, that multitudes were persuaded to forsake, to give up all their interest in relations, callings, goods, possessions, and betake themselves to tedious pilgrimages, yea, hard services in war, to comply with that superstition; and it is not the glory of our profession, that we have so few instances of men parting with all, and giving up themselves to heavenly retirement. But I am at present on no such design; I aim not to take men out of their lawful earthly occasions, but to bring spiritual affections and thoughts into the management of them all. The things mentioned will deprive you of no time you can lay a claim to, but will sanctify it all.

I confess, he must be a great proficient in spirituality, who dares venture on an absolute retirement, and he must be well satisfied that he is not called to a usefulness among men inconsistent therewith. To them it may prove a disadvantage. Yet this, also, is attainable, if other circumstances do concur. Men under the due exercise of grace, and the improvement of it, may attain to that fixedness in heavenly mindedness, that unconcernment in all things here below, as to give themselves up entirely and continually to heavenly meditation, and to a blessed advancement of all grace, and a near approach to glory. And I would hope it was so with many of them in ancient times who renounced the world, with all the circumstances of relations, state, inheritances, and betook themselves to retirement in wildernesses, to abide always in divine contemplation. But afterwards, when multitudes, whose minds were not so prepared, by a real growth in all grace, and mortification to the world, as they were, betook themselves under the same pretences to a monastical retirement, the devil, the world, sensual lusts, superstition, and all manner of evils, pursued them, found them out, possessed them, to the unspeakable damage and scandal of religion.

This, therefore, is not that which I invite the common sort of believers to. Let them that are able and free, receive it. The generality of Christians have lawful callings, employments, and businesses, which ordinarily they ought to abide in. That they also may live to God in their occasions, they may do well to consider two things.

1. Industry in men's callings, is a thing in itself very commendable. If in nothing else, it hath an advantage herein, that it is a means to preserve men from those excesses in lust and riot, which otherwise they are apt to run into. And if you consider the two sorts of men, whereunto the generality of men are distributed, namely, of them 'who are industrious in their affairs, and those who spend their time, as far as they are able, in idleness and pleasure,' the former sort are far more amiable and desirable. Howbeit, it is capable of being greatly abused. Earthly mindedness, covetousness, devouring things holy as to times and seasons of duty, uselessness, and the like pernicious vices, invade and possess the minds of men. There is no lawful calling that doth absolutely exclude this grace of being spiritually minded in them that are engaged in it, nor any that doth include it. Men may be in the meanest of lawful callings, and be so, and men may be in the best and highest, and not be so. Consider the calling of the ministry: the work and duty of it calls on those that are employed in it, to have their minds and thoughts conversant about spiritual and heavenly things. They are to study about them, to meditate on them, to commit them to memory, to speak them out to others. It will be said, surely such men must needs be spiritually minded. If they go no further than what is mentioned, I say they must needs be so, as printers must needs be learned, who are continually conversant about letters. A man may with great industry engage himself about these things, and yet his mind be most remote from being spiritual. The event doth declare that it may be so, and the reasons of it are manifest. It

requires as much, if not more watchfulness, m re care, more humility, for a minister to be spiritually minded in the discharge of his calling, than to any sort of men in theirs: and that, as for other reasons, so because the commonness of the exercise of such thoughts, with their design upon others in their expression, will take off their power and efficacy. And he will have little benefit by his own ministry, who endeavors not, in the first place, an experience in his own heart of the power of the truths which he doth teach to others. And there is evidently as great a failing herein among us, as among any other sort of Christians, as every occasion of trial doth demonstrate.

2. Although industry in any honest calling be allowable, yet unless men labor to be spiritually minded in the exercise of that industry, they have neither life nor peace. Hereunto all the things before mentioned are necessary; I know not how any of them can be abated, yea, more is required than is expressed in them. If you burn his roll, another must be written, and many like things must be added to it. And the objection from the expense of time in the observance of them, is of no force. For a man may do as much work whilst he is spiritually minded, as whilst he is carnal. Spiritual thoughts will no more hinder you in your callings, than those that are vain and earthly, which all sorts of men can find leisure for, in the midst of their employments. If you have filled a vessel with chaff, yet you may pour into it a great deal of water, which will be contained in the same space and vessel. And if it be necessary that you should take in much of the chaff of the world into your minds, yet are they capable of such measures of grace as shall preserve them sincere to God.

Fifthly. This frame will never be preserved, nor the duties mentioned be ever performed in a due manner, unless we dedicate some part of our time peculiarly to them. I speak to them only concerning whom I suppose that they do daily set apart some portion of time to holy duties, as prayer and reading of the word, and they find, by experience, that it succeeds well with them. For the most part, if they lose their seasons, they lose their duties. For some have complained, that the urgency of business, and multiplicity of occasions, driving them at first from the fixed time of their duties, hath brought them into a course of neglecting duty itself. Wherefore, it is our wisdom to set apart constantly some part of our time to the exercise of our thoughts about spiritual things in the way of meditation. And I shall close this discourse with some directions in this particular, to them who complain of their disability for the discharge of this duty.

(1.) Choose and separate a fit time or season, a time of freedom from other occasions and diversions. And because it is our duty to redeem time with respect to holy duties, such a season may be the more useful, the more the purchase of it stands us in. We are not at any time to serve God with what costs us nought, nor with any time that comes within the same rule. If we will allow only the refuse of our time to this duty, when we have nothing else to do, and it may be, through weariness of occasions, are fit for nothing else, we are not to expect any great success in it. This is one pregnant reason why men are so cold and formal, so lifeless in spiritual duties, namely, the times and seasons which they allot to them. When the body is wearied with the labors and occasions of the day, and it may be, the mind in its natural faculties indisposed, even by the means of necessary refreshment, men think themselves meet to treat with God about the great concernments of his glory, and their own souls. This is that which God condemneth by the prophet, Mal. i. 8. 'And if you offer the blind for sacrifice, is it not evil? And if you offer the lame and sick, is it not evil? Offer it now unto thy governor, will he be pleased with thee, or accept thy person?' Both the law of nature, and all the laws of holy institutions, require that we should serve God with the best that we have, as all the fat of the inwards was to be offered in sacrifice. And shall we think to offer that time to God, wherein we are unmeet to appear before an earthly ruler? Yet such, in my account, are the seasons, especially the evening seasons, that most men choose for the duties of their holy worship. And you may do well to consider, that beyond the day and time which he hath taken to himself by an everlasting law, how little of the choice of your time you have offered to God as a free will offering, that you may be excited to future diligence. If, therefore, you seriously intend this duty, choose the seasons for it wherein you are the most fit, when even the natural vigor of your spirits is most free and active. Possibly some will say, this may be such a time as when the occasions of the world call most earnestly for your attendance to them. I say, that is the season I would recommend. And if you can conquer your minds to redeem it for God at that rate, your endeavors in it will be prosperous. However, trust not to times that will offer themselves. Take them not up at hazard. Let the time itself be a free will offering to God, taken from the top of the heap, or the choicest part of your useful time.

(2.) Preparation of mind to a due reverence of God

and spiritual things, is required previously hereto. When we go about this duty, if we rush into thoughts of heavenly things without a due reverential preparation, we shall quickly find ourselves at a loss. See the rule, Eccles. v. 1, 2. Grace to serve God with reverence and godly fear, is required in all things wherein we have to do with him, as in this duty we have in an immediate and especial manner. Endeavor, therefore, in the first place, to get your hearts deeply affected with an awful reverence of God, and a holy regard to the heavenly nature of the things you would meditate upon. Hereby your minds will be composed, and the roots of other thoughts, be they vain or earthly, which are apt to arise and divert you from this duty, will be cast out. The principles of these contrary thoughts, are like Jacob and Esau, they struggle in the same womb, and oftentimes Esau will come first forth, and for a while seem to carry the birthright. If various thoughts do conflict in our minds, some for this world, and some for another, those for this world may carry it for a season. But where a due reverence of God hath cast out the bond woman and her children, the workings of the flesh in its vain thoughts and imaginations, the mind will be at liberty to exercise itself on spiritual things.

(3.) Earnest desires after a renewed sense and spirit of spiritual things, are required hereto. If we engage in this duty merely on a conviction of the necessity of it, or set ourselves about it because we think we ought to do so, and it will not be well utterly to neglect it, we may not expect to be successful in it: but when the soul hath at any time tasted that the Lord is gracious; when its meditations on him have been sweet; when spiritual things have had a savor and relish in the mind and affections; and hereon it comes to this duty with earnest desires to have the like tastes, the like experience, yea, to have them increased; then is it in the way of a hopeful progress. And this also will make us persevere in our endeavors to go through with what we undertake; namely, when we do know, by former experience, what is to be attained in it if we dig and search for it as treasure.

If you shall think that the right discharge of this duty may be otherwise attained; if you suppose that it deserves not all this cost and charge about it; judge by what is past, whether it be not advisable to give it over and let it alone. As good lie quietly on the ground, as continually attempt to rise, and never once effect it. Remember how many successive attempts you have made upon it, and all have come to nothing, or that which is as bad as nothing. I cannot say that in this way you shall always succeed; but I fear you will never have success in this duty without such things as are of the same nature and use with it.

When after this preparation you find yourselves yet perplexed and entangled, not able comfortably to persist in spiritual thoughts, to your refreshment, take these two directions for your relief.

1. Cry and sigh to God for help and relief. Bewail the darkness, weakness, and instability of your minds, so as to groan within yourselves for deliverance. And if your designed meditations do issue only in a renewed gracious sense of your own weakness and insufficiency, with application to God for supplies of strength, they are by no means lost as unto a spiritual account. The thoughts of Hezekiah, in his meditations, did not seem to have any great order or consistency, when he so expressed them; 'like a crane or a swallow, so did

I chatter: I did mourn as a dove: mine eyes failed with looking upwards; O Lord, I am oppressed, undertake for me.' Isa. xxxviii. 14. When the soul labors sincerely for communion with God, but sinks into broken confused thoughts under the weight of its own weakness, yet if he looks to God for relief, his chattering and mourning will be accepted with God, and profitable to himself.

2. Supply the brokenness of your thoughts with ejaculatory prayers, according as either the matter of them, or your defect in the management of them doth require. So was it with Hezekiah in the instance before mentioned; where his meditations were weak and broken, he cried out in the midst of them, O Lord, I am oppressed, undertake for me. And meditation is properly a mixture of spiritual apprehension of God and heavenly things, in the thoughts and conceptions of the mind, with desires and supplications thereon.

It is good and profitable to have some special designed subject of meditation in our thoughts. I have at large declared before what things are the proper objects of the thoughts of them that are spiritually minded. But they may be more peculiarly considered as the matter of designed meditation. And they may be taken out of some especial spiritual experience that we have lately had, or some warnings we have received of God, or something wherewith we have been peculiarly affected in the reading or preaching of the word, or what we find the present posture and frame of our minds and souls to require; or that which most frequently supplies all the person and grace of our Lord Jesus Christ. If any thing of this nature be peculiarly designed antecedently unto this duty, and a season be sought for it with respect thereto, the mind will be fixed and kept from wandering after variety of subjects, wherein it is apt to lose itself, and brings nothing to perfection.

Lastly, be not discouraged with an apprehension, that all that you can attain to in the discharge of this duty, is so little, so contemptible, as that it is to no purpose to persist in it. Nor be wearied with the difficulties you meet with in its performance. You have to do with him only in this matter, who will not break the bruised reed, nor quench the smoking flax; whose will it is that none should despise the day of small things. And if there be in this duty a ready mind, it is accepted, according to what a man hath, and not according to what he hath not. He that can bring into this treasury only the mites of broken desires and ejaculatory prayers, so they be his best, shall not come behind them who cast into it out of their great abundance in ability and skill. To faint and give out, because we cannot arise to such a height as we aim at, is a fruit of pride and unbelief. He who finds himself to gain nothing by continual endeavors after holy, fixed meditations, but only a living, active sense of his own vileness and unworthiness, is a sufficient gainer by all his pains, cost, and charge. But ordinarily it shall not be so; constancy in the duty, will give ability for it. Those who conscientiously abide in its performance, shall increase in light, wisdom, and experience, until they are able to manage it with great success. These few plain directions may possibly be of some use to the weaker sort of Christians, when they find a disability in themselves to the discharge of this duty, wherein those who are spiritually minded ought to be peculiarly exercised.

PART II.

CHAPTER XI.

The seat of Spiritual Mindedness in the Affections. The nature and use of them. The ways and means used by God himself, to call the affections of men from the World.

In the account given at the entrance of this discourse, of what it is to be spiritually minded, it was reduced to three heads.

The first was the habitual frame, disposition, and inclination of the mind in its affections.

The second was the usual exercise of the mind in its thoughts, meditations, and desires about heavenly things.

Whereunto, thirdly, was added, the complacency of mind in that relish and savor which it finds in spiritual things, so thought and meditated on.

The second of these hath hitherto alone been spoken to, as that which leads the way to the others, and gives the most sensible evidence of the state inquired after. Therein consists the stream, which, rising in the fountain of our affections, runs into a holy rest and complacency of mind.

The first and last I shall now handle together, and

therein comprehend the account of what it is to be spiritually minded.

'Spiritual affections, whereby the soul adheres to spiritual things, taking in such a savor and relish of them, as wherein it finds rest and satisfaction, is the peculiar spring and substance of our being spiritually minded.' This is that which I shall now further explain and confirm.

The greatest contest of heaven and earth is about the affections of the poor worm, which we call man. That the world should contend for them, is no wonder. It is the best that it can pretend to. All things here below are capable of no higher ambition than to be possessed of the affections of men. And as they lie under the curse, it can do us no greater mischief than by prevailing in this design. But that the holy God should, as it were, engage in the contest, and strive for the affections of man, is an effect of infinite condescension and grace. This he doth expressly; my son, saith he, give me thy heart, Prov. xxiii. 26. It is our affections he asketh for, and comparatively nothing else; to be sure he will accept of nothing from us without them. The most fat and costly sacrifice will not be accepted, if it be without a heart. All the ways and methods of the dispensation of his will, by his word; all the designs of his effectual grace, are suited to, and prepared for, this end, namely, to recover the affections of man to himself. So he expresseth himself concerning his word, Deut. x. 12. 'And now, Israel, what doth the Lord thy God require of thee, but to fear the Lord thy God, to walk in all his ways, and to love and to serve the Lord thy God with all thy heart, and with all thy soul?' And as to the word of his grace, he declares it to the same purpose,

Deut. xxx. 6. 'And the Lord thy God will circumcise thy heart, and the heart of thy seed; to love the Lord thy God with all thy heart, and with all thy soul.'

And on the other side, all the artifices of the world, all the paint it puts on its face, all the great promises it makes, all the false appearances and attires it clothes itself with, by the help of Satan, have no other end but to draw and keep the affections of men to itself. And if the world be preferred before God, in this address which is made to us for our affections, we shall justly perish with the world to eternity; and be rejected by him whom we have rejected. Prov. i. 24, 25, 31.

Our affections are, upon the matter, our all. They are all we have to give or bestow; the only power of our souls, whereby, if we may, we give away ourselves from ourselves, and become another's. Other faculties of our souls, even the most noble of them, are suited to receive in to our own advantage; by our affections we can give away what we are, and have. Hereby, we give our hearts to God, as he requireth. Wherefore to him we give our affections, to whom we give our all, ourselves, and all that we have; and to whom we give them not, whatever we give, upon the matter, we give nothing at all.

In what we do to or for others; whatsoever is good, valuable, or praiseworthy in it proceeds from the affections wherewith we do it. To do any thing for others without an animating affection, is but a contempt of them; for we judge them really unworthy that we should do any thing for them: to give to the poor upon their importunity, without pity or compassion; to supply the wants of saints without love and kindness, with other actings and duties of the like nature, are things of no value, things that can recommend us neither to God nor man. It is so in general with God and the world. Whatever we do in the service of God, whatever duty we perform on his command, whatever we undergo or suffer for his name's sake, if it proceed not from the cleaving of our souls to him by our affections, it is despised by him; he owns us not. 'As if a man would give all the substance of his house for love, it would utterly be contemned:' Cant. v.; so if a man would give to God all the substance of his house without love, it would in like manner be despised. And however, on the other hand, we may be diligent, industrious, and sedulous in and about the things of this world, yet, if it have not our affections, we are not of the world, we belong not to it. They are the seat of all sincerity, which is the jewel of divine and human conversation, the life and soul of every thing that is good and praiseworthy; whatever men pretend, as their affections are, so are they. Hypocrisy is a deceitful interposition of the mind, on various reasons and pretences, between men's affections and their profession, whereby a man appears to be what he is not. Sincerity is the open avowment of the reality of men's affections, which renders them good and useful.

Affections are in the soul as the helm in the ship; if it be laid hold on by a skilful hand, he turneth the whole vessel which way he pleaseth. If God hath the powerful hand of his grace upon our affections, he turns our soul to a compliance with his institutions, instructions, afflictions, trials, all sorts of providences, and in mercy holds them firm against all winds and storms of temptations, that they shall not hurry them on pernicious dangers. Such a soul alone is tractable and pliable to all intimations of God's will.

All others are stubborn and obstinate, stout hearted, and far from righteousness. And when the world hath the hand on our affections, it turns the mind, with the whole industry of the soul, to its interest and concerns. And it is in vain to contend with any thing that hath the power of our affections in its disposal, it will prevail at last.

On all these considerations, it is of the highest importance to consider aright how things are stated in our affections, and what is the prevailing bent of them. Iron sharpeneth iron, so a man sharpeneth the countenance of his friend, saith the wise man, Prov. xxvii. 17. Every man hath his edge, which may be sharpened by outward helps and advantages: the predominant inclination of a man's affections is his edge. According as that is set, so he cutteth and works; that way he is sharp and keen, but blunt to all other things.

Now because it must be, that our affections are either spiritual or earthly in a prevailing degree; that either God hath our hearts, or the world; that our edge is towards heaven, or towards things here below; before I come to give an account of the nature and operations of spiritual affections, I shall consider and propose some of these arguments and motives which God is pleased to make use of, to call off our affections from the desirable things of this world: for as they are weighty and cogent, such as cannot be neglected without the greatest contempt of divine wisdom and goodness, so they serve to press and enforce those arguments and motives that are proposed to us, to set our affections on things that are above, which is to be spiritually minded.

First. He hath, in all manner of instances, poured contempt on the things of this world, in comparison of things spiritual and heavenly. All things here below were at first made beautiful and in order, and were declared by God himself to be exceeding good, and that not only in their being and nature, but in the use whereunto they were designed. They were then desirable to men, and the enjoyment of them would have been a blessing, without danger of temptation; for they were the ordinance of God, to lead us to the knowledge of him, and love to him: but since the entrance of sin, whereby the world fell under the curse, and into the power of Satan, the things of it in his management, are become effectual means to draw off the heart and affections from God; for it is the world and the things of it, as summed up by the apostle, 1 John ii. 15, 16, that alone strive for our affections to be the object of them. Sin and Satan do but woo for the world to take them off from God: by them doth the god of this world blind the eyes of them that believe not: and the principal way whereby he worketh in them is by promises of satisfaction to all the lusts of the minds of men, with a proposal of whatever is dreadful and terrible in the want of them. Being now in this state and condition, and used to this end, through the craft of Satan, and the folly of the minds of men, God hath showed, by various instances, that they are all vain, empty, unsatisfactory, and every way to be despised, in comparison of things eternal.

First. He did it most eminently and signally in the life, death, and cross, of Christ. What can be seen or found in this world, after the Son of God hath spent his life in it, not having where to lay his head; and after he went out of it on the cross? Had there been aught of real worth here below, certainly he had enjoyed, if not crowns and empires, which were all in his power; yet such goods and possessions as men of sober reasonings and moderate affections esteem a competency. But things were quite otherwise disposed, to manifest that there is nothing of value or use in these things, but only to support nature to the performance of service to God, wherein they are serviceable to eternity. He never attained, he never enjoyed, more than daily supplies of bread out of the stores of Providence, and which alone he hath instructed us to pray for. Matt. viii. 20. In his cross the world proclaimed all its good qualities, and all its powers; and hath given to them that believe, its naked face to view and contemplate. Nor is it now one jot more comely than it was when it had gotten Christ on the cross. Hence is that inference and conclusion of the apostle, Gal. yi. 14. 'But God forbid that I should glory, save in the cross of our Lord Jesus Christ, whereby the world is crucified to me, and I to the world.' Since I have believed, since I have a sense of the power and virtue of the cross of Christ, I have done with all things in this world: it is a dead thing to me, nor have I any affection for it. This is that which made the difference between the promises of the old covenant and the new: for they were many of them about temporal things, the good things of this world and this life; those of the new are mostly of things spiritual and eternal. God would not call off the church wholly from a regard to these things, until he had given a demonstration of their emptiness, vanity, and insufficiency, in the cross of Christ. 2 Cor. iv. 16—18.

Whither so fast, my friend? 'What meaneth this rising so early, and going to bed late, eating the bread of carefulness?' Why this diligence? Why these contrivances? Why these savings and hoardings of riches and wealth? To what end is all this care and counsel? Alas! saith one, it is to get that which is enough in and of this world for me and my children, to prefer them, to raise an estate for them, which, if not so great as others, may yet be a competency, to give them some satisfaction in their lives, and some reputation in the world. Fair pretences! neither shall I ever discourage any from the exercise of industry in their lawful callings: but yet I know, that with many, this is but a pretence and covering for a shameful engagement of their affections to the world. Wherefore, in all these things, be persuaded sometimes to have an eye to Jesus, the author and finisher of our faith: behold how he is set before us in the gospel, poor, despised, reproached, persecuted, nailed to the cross, and all this by the world. Whatever be your designs and aims, let his cross continually interpose between your affections and this world. If you are believers, your hopes are, within a few days, to be with him for evermore. To him you must give an account of yourselves, and what you have done in this world: will it be accepted with him to declare what you have saved of this world; what you have gained; what you have preserved and embraced yourselves in; and what you have left behind you? Was this any part of his employment and business in this world? Hath he left us an example for any such course? Wherefore no man can set his affections on things here below, who hath any regard to the pattern of Christ, or is in any measure influenced with the power and efficacy of his cross. My love is crucified, said a holy martyr of old; he whom his soul loved was so, and in him his love to all things here below. Do you, therefore, find your affections ready to be engaged to, or too much entangled with the things of this world? Are your desires of increasing them, your hopes of keeping them, your fears of losing them, your love to them, and delight in them, operative in your minds, possessing your thoughts, and influencing your conversations? Turn aside a little, and by faith contemplate the life and death of the Son of God; a blessed glass will it be, where you may see what contemptible things they are which you perplex yourselves about. Oh! that any of us should love or esteem the things of this world, the power, riches, goods, or reputation of it, who have had a spiritual view of them in the cross of Christ!

Perhaps it will be said, that the circumstances mentioned were necessary to the Lord Christ, with respect to the especial work he had to do, as the Saviour and Redeemer of the church: and, therefore, it doth not thence follow that we ought to be poor, and want all things, as he did. I confess it doth not; and, therefore, do all along make an allowance for honest industry in our callings. But this follows unavoidably hereon, that what he did forego and trample on for our sake, that ought not to be the object of our affections; nor can such affections prevail in us, if he dwell in our hearts by faith.

Secondly. He hath done the same in his dealings with the apostles, and generally with all that have been most dear to him, and instrumental to the interest of his glory in the world, especially since life and immortality were brought to light by the gospel. He had great work to do by the apostles, and that of the greatest use to his interest and kingdom. The laying of the foundations of the glorious kingdom of Christ in the world, was committed to them. Who would not think that he should provide for them, if not principalities or popedoms, yet at least arch-bishoprics and bishoprics, with other good ecclesiastical dignities and preferments? Hereby might they have been made meet to converse with princes, and had been freed from the contempt of the vulgar; but Infinite Wisdom did otherwise dispose of them and their concerns in this world: for as God was pleased to exercise them with the common afflictions and calamities of this life, which he makes use of to take off the sweetness of present enjoyments, so they lived and died in a condition of poverty, distress, persecution, and reproach. God set them forth as examples as to other ends, namely, of light, grace, zeal, and holiness in their lives, so to manifest of how little concernment to our own blessedness, or an interest in his love, is the abundance of all things here below, as also, that the want of them all may consist with the highest participation of his love and favor. 1 Cor. iv. 9, 11—13. 'For I think that God hath set forth us the apostles last, as it were, appointed to death. For we are made a spectacle to the world, and to angels, and to men. Even to this present hour we both hunger and thirst, and are naked, and are buffeted, and have no certain dwelling place, and labor, working with our own hands: being reviled, we bless; being persecuted, we suffer it; being defamed, we entreat: we are made as the filth of the world, and are the offscouring of all things to this day.' And if the consideration hereof be not of weight with others, undoubtedly it ought to be so with them who are called to preach the gospel, and are the successors to the apostles. There can be nothing more uncouth, absurd, and shameful, nothing more opposite to the intimation of the wisdom and will of God, in his dealings with those first and most honorable dispensers of it, than for such persons to seek and follow greedily after secular advantages, in worldly powers, riches, wealth, and honor. Hence there hath been, in former ages, an endeavor to separate such persons as were by any means dedicated to the ministry of the gospel from all secular dignities and revenues. Yea, some maintained, that they were to enjoy nothing of their own, but were to live on alms, or the free contributions of the people. But this was quickly condemned as heresy, in Wickliff and others. Yet another sort set up, that would pretend thereto, as to themselves, though they would not oblige all others to the same rule. This produced some swarms of begging friars, whom they of the church, who were in possession of wealth and power, thought meet to laugh at and let alone; of late years this contest is at an end. The clergy have happily gotten the victory, and esteem all due to them, that they can by any ways obtain; nor is there any greater crime, than for a man to be otherwise minded. But these things are not our present concernment. From the beginning it was not so. And it is well if, in such a way, men are able to maintain the frame of mind inquired after, which is life and peace.

Thirdly. God continues to cast contempt on these things, by giving always incomparably the greatest portion of them to the vilest men, and his own avowed enemies. This was a temptation under the old covenant, but is highly instructive under the new. None will judge those things to be of real value, which 'a wise man casts out daily unto swine, making little or no use of them in his family.' Those monsters of men, Nero and Heliogabalus, had more interest in, and more power over, the things of this world, than ever had the best of men. Such villains in nature, so pernicious to human society, that their not being was the interest of mankind; but yet more of the world poured on them, than they knew either how to enjoy, possess, use, or abuse. Look on all the principal treasures and powers of this world, as in the hands of one of these monsters, and there disposed of by Divine Providence, and you may see at what rate God values them.

At this day, the greatest, most noble, wealthy, and fruitful parts of the earth, are given to the great Turk, with some other eastern potentates, either Mahometans or Pagans, who are prepared for eternal destruction. And if we look nearer home, we may see in whose hands is the power of the chiefest nations of Europe, and to what end it is used. The utmost of what some Christian professors among ourselves are intent and designing upon, as that which would render them wondrous happy in their own apprehensions, put hundreds of them together, and it would not answer the waste made by the forementioned beasts every day.

Doth not God proclaim herein, that the things of this world are not to be valued or esteemed? If they were so, and had a real worth in themselves, would the holy and righteous God make such a distribution of them? The most of those whom he loves, who enjoy his favor; not only comparatively, have the meanest share of them, but are exercised with all the evils that the destitution and want of them can be accompanied with. His open and avowed enemies, in the mean time, have more than they know what to do with. Who would set his heart and affections on those things which God poureth into the bosoms of the vilest men, to be a snare to them here, and an aggravation of their condemnation for ever? It seems, you may go and take the world, and take the curse, death and hell, along with it; and what will it profit a man to gain the whole world and lose his own soul? What can any man do on the consideration hereof, who will not forego all his hopes and expectations from God, but retreat to the faith of things spiritual and eternal, as containing an excellency in them incomparably above all that may be enjoyed here below?

Fourthly. He doth continue to give perpetual instances of their uncertainty and unsatisfactoriness, in the utter disappointment of men that have had expectations from them. The ways hereof are various, and the instances so multiplied, as that most men in the world, unless they are like the fool in the gospel, who bade his soul take its ease for many years, because his barns were full, live in perpetual fears and apprehensions, that they shall speedily lose whatever they enjoy; or are under the power of a stupid security. But as to this consideration of them, there is such an account given by the wise man, as to which nothing can be added, or which no reason or experience is able to contradict. Eccl. ii. By these and the like ways, doth God cast contempt on all things here below; discovering the folly and falseness of the promises which the world makes use of to allure our affections to itself. This, therefore, is to be laid as the foundation in all our considerations, to what or whom we shall cleave by our affections, that God hath not only declared the insufficiency of these things to give us that rest and happiness which we seek after, but also poured contempt upon them, in his holy, wise disposal of them in the world.

Secondly. God hath added to their vanity, by shortening the lives of men, reducing their continuance in this world to so short and uncertain a season, as it is impossible they should take any solid satisfaction in what they enjoy here below. So it is expressed by the Psalmist. 'Behold thou hast made my days as an hand breadth, and my age is nothing before thee.' Hence he draws two conclusions.

First. That every man, at his best estate, is but vanity.

Second. That every 'man walks in a vain show; surely they are disquieted in vain; he heapeth up riches, and knoweth not who shall gather them.' Psal. xxxix. 5, 6. The uncertainty and shortness of the lives of men render all their endeavors and contrivances about earthly things both vain and foolish. When men lived eight or nine hundred years, they had an opportunity to suck out all the sweetness that was in creature comforts, to make large provisions of them, and to have long projections about them. But when they had so, they all issued in that violence, oppression, and wickedness, which brought the flood on the world of ungodly men. And it still so abides; the more of, and the longer men enjoy these things, the more, without the sovereign preservative of grace, will they abound in sin and provocations of God. But God hath reduced the life of man to the small pittance of seventy years; casting what may fall out of a longer continuance into travail and sorrow. Besides, that space is shortened with the most, by various and innumerable incidences and occasions. Wherefore, in these seventy years, consider how long it is before men begin to have a taste or relish of the things of this life; how many things fall in cross, to make us weary of them before the end of our days; how few among us, not one of a thousand, attain that age; what is the uncertainty of all men living, as to the continuance of their lives to the next day; and we shall see that the holy, wise God, hath left no such season for their enjoyment, as might put a value upon them. And when, on the other hand, it is remembered, that this man, who is of such short continuance in this world, is yet made for eternity, eternal blessedness or misery, which state depends wholly on his interest in things above, and setting his affections on them, they must forfeit all their reason, as well as bid defiance to the grace of God, who gives them up for things below.

Moreover, God hath openly and fully declared the danger that is in these things, as to their enjoyment and use; and what multitudes of souls miscarry, by an inordinate adherence to them! For they are the matter of those temptations, whereby the souls of men are ruined forever; the fuel that supplies the fire of their lusts, until they are consumed by it.

Men, under the power of spiritual convictions, fall not into sin, fail not eternally, but by the means of temptation. That is the mire wherein this rush doth grow. For others who live and die in the madness and wildness of nature, without any restraint in their minds from the power of convictions, they need no external temptations, but only opportunities to exert their lusts. But for those who by any means are convinced of sin, righteousness, and judgment, so as to design the ordering of their lives, with respect to the sense they have of them, they fall not into actual sin, but upon temptations. That, whatever it be, which causeth, occasioneth, and prevaileth on a convinced person, to sin, that is temptation. Wherefore, this is the great means of the ruin of the souls of men.

Now, though there are many principles of temptation, many causes that actually concur in its efficacy, as sin, Satan, and other men, yet the matter of almost all ruinous temptations is taken out of this world, and the things of it. Thence doth Satan take all his darts; thence do evil men derive all the ways and means whereby they corrupt others, and from thence is all the fuel of sin and lust taken. And which adds to this evil, all that is in the world contributes its utmost thereto. 'All that is in the world, is the lust of the flesh, the lust of the eyes, and the pride of life.' 1 John ii. 16. It is not a direct formal enumeration of the things that are in the world, nor a distribution of them under several heads; but it is so of the principal lusts of the minds of men, whereto all things are subservient. Wherefore, not only the matter of all temptations is taken out of the world, but every thing that is in the world is apt and fit to be abused to that end. For it were easy to show, that there is nothing desirable or valuable in this whole world, but it is reducible to a subserviency to one or other of these lusts, and is applicable to the interest and service of temptations and sins.

When men hear of these things, they are apt to say, 'let the dream be to them that are openly wicked, and the interpretation of it to them that are profligate in sin.' To unclean persons, drunkards, oppressors, proud, ambitious persons, it may be, it is so; but as to them, they use the things of this world with a due moderation, so as they are no snare to them. But to own they are used to what end soever, if the affections of men are set upon them, one way or other, there is nothing in the world, but is thus a snare and temptation. However, we should be very careful how we adhere to or undervalue, that which is the cause and means of the ruin of multitudes of souls. By the warnings given us hereof, doth God design, as to the use of means, to teach us the vanity and danger of fixing our affections on things below.

Lastly. Things are so ordered in the holy, wise dispensation of God's providence, that it requires much spiritual wisdom to distinguish between the use and the abuse of these things, between a lawful care about them, and an inordinate cleaving to them. Few distinguish aright here; and therefore in these things will many find their great mistake at the last day. The disappointments that they will fall under, as to what concerns their earthly enjoyments and the use of them, wherewith they were intrusted. See Mat. xxv. 34, to the end of the chapter.

It is granted that there is a lawful use of these things, a lawful care and industry about them. So it is also acknowledged, it cannot be denied, that there is an abuse of them, springing from an inordinate love and cleaving to them. But here men deceive themselves, taking their measures by the most crooked, uncertain rules. Some make their own inclinations the rule and measure of what is lawful and allowable; some the example of others; some the course of the world; some their own real or pretended necessities. They confess that there is an inordinate love of those things, and an abuse of them, in excesses of various sorts, which the scripture plainly affirms, and which experience gives open testimony to. But as to their state and circumstances, their care, love, and industry, are all allowable. That which influenceth all these persons, is self love, which inveterate, corrupt affections, and false reasonings, make an application of to these occasions.

Hence we may have men approving of themselves as just stewards of their enjoyments, whilst others judge them hard, covetous, earthly minded; no way laying out what they are intrusted with, to the glory of God, in any due proportion. Others also think not amiss of themselves in this kind, who live in palpable excesses, either of pride of life or sensual pleasures, vain apparel, and the like. So, in particular, most men in their feastings and entertainments, walk in direct contempt of the rules which our Saviour gives in that case; Luke xiv. 12—14, and yet approve themselves therein

But what if any of us should be mistaken in our rule and application of it to our conditions? Men at sea may have a fair gale of wind, wherewith they may sail freely and smoothly for a season, and yet, instead of being brought into a port, be cast by it at last on destructive shoals or rocks.

And what if that which we esteem allowable, love, care, and industry, should prove to be the fruit of earthly affections, inordinate and predominant in us; what if we miss in our measures, and that which we approve of in ourselves should be disapproved of God; we are cast forever, we belong to the world, and with the world we shall perish.

It may be said, that if it be so difficult to distinguish between these things, namely, the lawful use of things here below, and their abuse; the allowable industry about them, and the inordinate love of them, on the knowledge whereof our eternal condition depends, it is impossible but men must spend their time in solicitous anxiety of mind, as not knowing when they have aright discharged their duty.

Ans. (1.) I press these things at present no further, but only to show how dangerous a thing it is for any to incline in his affections to the things of this world, wherein an excess is ruinous, and hardly discoverable. Surely, no wise man will venture freely and frequently to the edge of such a precipice. He will be jealous of his measures, lest they will not hold by the rule of the word. And a due sense hereof is the best preservative of the soul, from cleaving inordinately to these things below. And when God, in any instance, by afflictions, or otherwise, shows to believers their transgression herein, and how they have exceeded, Job xxxviii. 8, 9, it makes them careful for the future. They will now or never be diligent, that they fall not under that peremptory rule. 1 John ii. 14.

Secondly. Where the soul is upright and sincere, there is no need in this case of any more solicitousness or anxiety of mind, than there is to or about other duties. But when it is biased and actuated by self love, and its more strong inclinations are to things present, it is impossible men should enjoy solid peace, or be freed from severe reflections on them by their own consciences, in such seasons wherein they are awakened to their duty, and the consideration of their state; nor have I any thing to tender for their relief. With others it is not so; and therefore I shall so far digress in this place, as to give some directions to those who in sincerity would be satisfied in this lawful use and enjoyment of earthly things; so as not to adhere to them with inordinate affections.

First. Remember always that you are not proprietors, nor absolute possessors of these things, but only stewards of them. With respect to men, you are, or may be, just proprietors of what you enjoy; with respect to him who is the great possessor of heaven and earth, you are but stewards. This stewardship we are to give an account of, as we are taught in the parable, Luke xvi. 1, 2. This rule always attended to, will be a blessed guide in all instances and occasions of duty.

But if a man be left in trust with houses and large possessions, as a steward for the right lord, owner, and proprietor of them; if he fall into a pleasing dream, that they are all his own, and use them accordingly, it will be a woful surprisal to him, when he shall be called to account for all he hath received and laid out, whether he will or not; and when indeed he hath nothing to pay. It will scarce be otherwise with them at the great day, who forget the trust which is committed to them, and suppose they may do what they will, with what they call their own.

Secondly. There is nothing in the ways of getting, enjoying, or using of these things, but giveth its own evidence to spiritual wisdom, whether it be within the bounds of duty or not. Men are not lightly deceived herein, but when they are evidently under the power of corrupt affections, or will not at all attend to themselves, and the language of their own consciences. It is a man's own fault alone, if he know not wherein he doth exceed.

A due examination of ourselves in the sight of God, with respect to these things, the frame and actings of our minds in them, will greatly give check to our corrupt inclinations, and discover the folly of those reasonings, whereby we deceive ourselves into the love of earthly things, or justify ourselves therein, and bring to light the secret principle of self love, which is the root of all this evil.

Thirdly. If you would be able to make a right judgment in this case, be sure that you have another object for your affections, which hath a predominant interest in your minds, and which will evidence itself so to have on all occasions. Let a man be never so observant of himself, as to all outward duties required of him, with respect to these earthly things; let him be liberal in the disposal of them on all occasions; let him be watchful against all intemperance and excesses in the use of them; yet if he hath not another object for his affections, which hath a prevailing influence upon them; if they are not set upon the things that are above; one way or other, it is the world that hath the possession of his heart. For the affections of our minds will and must be placed, in chief, on things below or things above; there will be a predominant love in us, and therefore, although all our actions should testify another frame, yet if God, and the things of God, be not the principal object of our affections; by one way or other, unto the world we do belong; this is that which is taught us so expressly by our Saviour, Luke xvi. 9—13. 'And I say unto you, make to yourselves friends of the mammon of unrighteousness, that when you fail, they may receive you into everlasting habitations. He that is faithful in that which is the least, is faithful also in much; and he that is unjust in the least, is unjust also in much. If therefore you have not been faithful in the unrighteous mammon, who will commit to your trust the true riches? And if you have not been faithful in that which is another man's, who shall give you that which is your own? No servant can serve two masters; for either he will hate the one, and love the other; or else he will hold to the one, and despise the other; ye canot serve God and mammon.'

Fourthly. Labor continually for the mortification of your affections to the things of this world. They are in the state of corrupted nature, set and fixed on them; nor will any reasonings or considerations effectually divert them, or take them off in a due manner, unless they are mortified to them by the cross of Christ. Whatever change be otherwise wrought in them, it will be of no advantage to us. It is mortification alone, that will take them off from earthly things, to the glory of God. Hence the apostle, having given us that charge, set your affections on things above, and not on things below on the earth, Col. iii. 2, adds this, as the only way and means whereby we may do so: Mortify therefore your members that are on the earth, v. 5. Let no man think that his affections will fall off from earthly things of their own accord. The keenness and sharpness of them, in many things, may be abated by the decay of their natural powers in age, and the like. They may be abated by frequent disappointments, by sickness, pains, and afflictions, as we shall see immediately; or they may be willing to a distribution of earthly enjoyments, to have the reputation of it, wherein they still cleave to the world, but under another shape and appearance. They may be startled by convictions, so as to do many things gladly, that belong to another frame. But on one pretence or other, under one appearance or other, they will forever adhere and cleave to earthly things, unless they are mortified to them, through faith in the blood and cross of

Christ. Gal. vi. 14. Whatever thoughts you may have of yourselves in this matter, unless you have the experience of a work of mortification on your affections, you can have no refreshing ground of assurance, that you are in any thing spiritually minded.

Fifthly. In all instances of duty belonging to your stewardship of earthly things, attend diligently to the rule of the word; without this, the grace exhorted to may be abused. So of old, under a pretence of a relinquishment of the things of this world, because of the danger in adhering to them, their own superstition, and the craft of other men, prevailed with many, to part with all they had, to the service of others, not better, it may be, nor so good as themselves This evil wholly arose from want of attendance to the rule of truth, which gives no such direction in ordinary cases. But there is not much seen, in these days, of an excess in that kind. On the other hand, in all instances of duties of this nature, most men's minds are habitually influenced with pretences, reasonings, and considerations, that turn the scales as to what they ought to do in proportion, in this duty, on the side of the world. If you would be safe, you must in all instances of duty, as in works of charity, piety, and compassion, give authority in and over your souls, to the rule of the word. Let neither self, nor unbelief, nor the custom and example of others, be heard to speak; but let the rule alone be attended to, and to what that speaks, yield obedience.

Unless these things are found in us, none of us, no man living, if it be not so with him, can have any refreshing evidence or assurance, that he is not under the power of an inordidate, yea, and predominant love to this world.

And indeed, to add a little further on the occasion of this digression, it is a sad thing to have this exception made against the state of any man, on just grounds; yea, but he loves the world. He is sober and industrious, he is constant in duties of religion, it may be, an earnest preacher of them, a man of sound principles, and blameless as to the excesses of life: but he loves the world. The question is, how doth this appear? It may be, what you say, is but one of those evil surmises which all things are filled with. Wherefore, I speak it not at all to give countenance to the rash judging of others, which none are more prone to, than those who one way or other are eminently guilty themselves. But I would have every man judge himself, that we be none of us condemned of the Lord. If notwithstanding the things mentioned, any of us do centre in self, which is supplied and filled with the world; if we prefer self above all other things, aim at the satisfaction of self in what we do well or ill, are useless to the only good and blessed ends of these earthly things, in supplying the wants of others, according to the proportions wherewith we are intrusted; it is to be feared, that the world, and the things that are in it, have the principal interest in our affections.

And the danger is yet greater with them who divert on the other extreme. Such are they who, in pride of life, vanity in apparel, excess in drinking, pampering the flesh every day, tread close on the heels of the world, if they do not also fully keep company with it. Altogether in vain is it for such persons to countenance themselves with an appearance of other graces in them, or the sedulous performance of other duties. This one rule will eternally prevail against them; if any man love the world, the love of the Father is not in him. And by the way, let men take heed how they walk in any instance against the known judgment and practice of the wiser or more experienced sort of Christians, to their regret and sorrow, if not to their offence and scandal, or in any way whereto they win the consent of their own light and conscience, by such reasonings and considerations as will not hold weight in the balance of the sanctuary. Yet thus, and no otherwise, is it with all those who, under a profession of religion, indulge to any excesses wherein they are conformed to the world.

Fifthly. God makes a hedge against the excesses of the affections of men, rational and any way enlightened, to the things of this world, by suffering the generality of men to carry the use of them, and to be carried by the abuse of them, into actings so filthy, so abominable, so ridiculous, as reason itself cannot but abhor. Men by them transform themselves into beasts and monsters, as might be manifested by all sorts of instances: hence the wise man prayed against riches, lest he should not be able to manage the temptations wherewith they are accompanied. Prov. xxx. 8, 9.

Lastly. To close this matter, and to show us what we are to expect, in case we set our affections on things here below, and they have thereby a predominant interest in our hearts, God hath positively determined and declared, that if it be so, he will have nothing to do with us, nor will accept of those affections which, we pretend, we can and do spare for him, and spiritual things. If we abstain from open sins, if we abhor the lewdness and uncleanness of men in the world, if we are constant in religious duties, and give ourselves up to walk after the most strict sort in religion, like Paul in his Pharisaism, may we not, will some say or think, find acceptance with God, though our hearts cleave inordinately to the things of this world? I say, God hath peremptorily determined the contrary; and if other arguments will not prevail with us, he leaves us at last to this, go love the world and the things of it, but know assuredly you do it to the eternal loss of your souls. 1 John ii. 15. Jam. 4. These few instances have I given of the arguments and motives whereby God is pleased to deter us from fixing our affections on things here below. And they are most of them such only as he maketh use of in the administration of his providence. There are two other heads of things that offer themselves to our consideration.

First. The ways, means, arguings, and enticements, which the world makes use of to draw, keep, and secure the affections of men to itself.

Secondly. The secret, powerful efficacy of grace, in taking off the heart from these things, turning and drawing it to God, with the arguments and motives that the Holy Spirit maketh use of, in and by the word, to this end; and wherein we must show what is the act of conquering grace, wherein the heart is finally prevailed on to choose and adhere to God in love immutable. But these things cannot be handled in any measure according to their nature and importance, without such length of discourse, as I cannot here divert to. I shall therefore proceed to that which is the proper and peculiar subject before us.

CHAPTER XII.

What is required in and to our affections, that they may be spiritual. A threefold work on the affections described.

To declare the interest of our affections in this frame of being spiritually minded, and what they contribute thereto, I shall do these three things:

First. Declare what is required hereto, that our affections may be spiritual, wherein lies the foundation of the whole duty.

Secondly. What are their actings when they are so spiritual.

Thirdly. What are the means whereby they may be kept and preserved in that frame, with sundry other things of the like nature. How our affections are concerned in, or belong to, the frame of mind inquired after, hath been before declared. Without spiritual affections, we cannot be spiritually minded. And that they may be of this use, three things are required:

First. Their principle.

Secondly. Their object.

Thirdly. The way and manner of their application to their proper object, by virtue of that principle.

First. As to the principle, acting in them, that our affections may be spiritual, and the spring of our being spiritually minded, it is required that they be changed, renewed, and inlaid with grace, spiritual and supernatural. To clear the sense hereof, we must a little consider, what is their state by nature, and then, by what means they may be wrought upon, as to a change, or a renovation. For they are like to some things, which in themselves, and their own nature, are poisonous; but being corrected, and receiving a due temperament, from a mixture of other ingredients, become medicinal, and of excellent use.

First. By nature, our affections all of them, are depraved and corrupted. Nothing in the whole nature of man, no power or faculty of the soul, is fallen under greater disorder and depravation by the entrance of sin, than our affections are. In and by them is the heart wholly gone and turned off from God. Tit. iii. 3. It were a long work to set forth this depravation of our affections, nor doth it belong to our present design. Some few things I shall briefly observe concerning it, to make way for what is proposed concerning their change.

First. This is the only corruption and depravation of our nature by the fall, evident in and to reason, or the light of nature itself. Those who were wise among the heathen, both saw it and complained of it. They found a weakness in the mind, but saw nothing of its darkness and depravation as unto things spiritual. But they were sensible of this disorder and tumult of the affections in things moral, which renders the minds of men like a troubled sea, whose waters cast up mire and dirt. This greatly aggravates the neglect of them who are not sensible of it in themselves, seeing it is discernible in the light of nature.

Secondly. They are as depraved, the seat and subject of all lusts, both of the flesh and of the spirit Yea, lust or evil concupiscence, is nothing but the irregular motion and acting of our affections, as depraved, defiled, corrupted. Rom. vii. 9. Hence, no one sin can be mortified without a change wrought in the affections.

Thirdly. They are the spring, root, and cause of

all actual sin in the world. Mat. xv. 19. The evil heart in the scripture, is the corrupt affections of it, with the imaginations of the minds, whereby they are excited and acted. Gen. vi. 5. These are they which at this time fill the whole world with wickedness, darkness, confusion, and terror. And we may learn what is their force and efficacy from these effects. So the nature of the plague is most evident, when we see thousands dying of it every week.

Fourthly. They are the way and means whereby the soul applies itself to all sinful objects and actings. Hence are they called our members, our earthly members; because, as the body applies itself to its operations by its members, so doth the soul apply itself to what belongs to it, by its affections. Rom. vi. 13. Col. iii. 5.

Fifthly. They will not be under the conduct of the mind, its light, or convictions. Rebellion against the light of the mind, is the very form whereby their corruption acts itself. Job xxiv. 13. Let the apprehensions of the mind, and its notions of good and evil, be what they will, they reject them, and lead the soul in pursuit of their inclinations. Hence no natural man whatsoever doth in any measure answer the light of his mind, or the convictions of his understanding; but he sees and approves of better things, following those that are worse. And there is no greater spiritual judgment, than for men to be given up to themselves, and their own evil affections. Rom i. 26.

Many other instances might be given of the greatness of that depravation which our affections are fallen under by sin; these may suffice for our present purpose.

In general, this depravation of our affections by nature may be reduced to two heads.

First. An utter aversation from God and all spiritual things. In this lies the spring of all that dislike of God and his ways, that the hearts of men are filled with. Yea, they do not only produce an aversation from them, and dislike of them, but they fill the mind with an enmity against them. Therefore, 'men say in their hearts to God, depart from us, for we desire not the knowledge of thy ways; what is the Almighty, that we should serve him? Or what profit should we have, if we pray to him?' Job xxi. 14, 15. See Rom. i. 28. Chap. viii. 7, 8.

Secondly. An inordinate cleaving to things vain, earthly, and sensual; causing the soul to engage in the pursuit of them, as the horse rushes into the battle.

Whilst our affections are in this state and condition, we are far enough from being spiritually minded; nor is it possible to engage them in an adherence to, or delight in, spiritual things.

In this state, they may be two ways wrought upon, and yet not so renewed, as to be serviceable to this end.

First. There may be various temporary impressions made on them, sometimes they are so by the preaching of the word. Hereon men may hear it with joy, and do many things gladly. Sometimes it is so by judgments, dangers, sickness, apprehensions of the approach of death. Psal. xxxiv. 78; xxxv. 37. These things take men off for a season from their greedy delight in earthly things, and the pursuit of the interest of lust, in making provision for the flesh. On many other occasions, by great variety of causes, there may be temporary impressions made on the affections, that shall seem, for a season, to have turned the stream of them. And thereon we have many, who every day will be wholly, as it were, for God, resolved to forsake sin, and all the pleasures of it; but the next, return to all their former excesses. For this is the effect of those impressions, that whereas men ordinarily are predominantly actuated by love, desire, and delight, which lead them to act according to the true natural principles of the soul; now they are for a season actuated by fear and dread, which put a kind of force on all their inclinations. Hereon they have other thoughts of good and evil, of things eternal and temporal, of God, and their own duty, for a season. And hereon, some of them may, and do, persuade themselves, that there is a change in their hearts and affections, which there is not; like a man who persuades himself that he hath lost his ague, because his present fit is over. The next trial of temptation carries them away again to the world and sin.

There are sometimes sudden impressions made on spiritual affections, which are always of great advantage to the soul, renewing its engagements to God and duty. So was it with Jacob, Gen. xxviii. 16—20. So is it often with believers in hearing the word, and other occasions. On all of them they renew their cleavings to God with love and delight. But the effect of these impressions on unrenewed affections, is neither spiritual nor durable. Yea, for the most part, they are but checks given in the providence of God to the raging of their lusts. Psal. ix. 2.

Secondly. They are liable to an habitual change This the experience of all ages gives testimony to. There may be an habitual change wrought in the passions and affections of the mind, as to the inordinate and violent pursuit of their inclinations, without any gracious renovation of them. Education, philosophy, or reason, long afflictions, spiritual light and gifts, have wrought this change. So Saul, upon his call to be King, became another man. Hereby persons, naturally passionate and furious, have been made sedate and moderate; and those who have been sensual, have become temperate; yea, and haters of religion, to be professors of it. All these things, and many more of the like nature, have proceeded from a change wrought upon the affections only; whilst the mind, will, and conscience, have been totally unsanctified.

By this change, where it is alone, no man ever became spiritually minded. For whereas there are two parts of the depravation of our affections; that whereby they are turned off from God, and that whereby they inordinately cleave to other things, their change principally, if not only, respects the latter. They are brought into some order with respect to present things. The mind is not continually tossed up and down by them, as the waves of the sea, that are troubled, and cast up mire and dirt. They do not carry those in whom they are into vicious, sensual actions, but allow them to make virtue in moderation, sobriety, temperance, fidelity, and usefulness in several ways, to be their design. And it is admirable to think what degrees of eminency in all sorts of moral virtues, upon this one principle of moderating the affections, even many among the heathens attained to. But as to their aversation from God and spiritual things, in the true spiritual notion of them, they are not cured by this change. At least this change may be, and yet this latter not be wrought.

Again, this alteration doth not turn the course or stream of men's affections, it doth not change the nature of them. They are the same in their spring and fountain as ever they were, only they are habituated to another course than what of themselves they are inclined to. You may take a young whelp of the most fierce and savage creatures, as of a tiger, or a wolf, and by custom or usage, make it as tame and harmless as any domestic creature, a dog, or the like. But although it may be turned to quite another way or course of acting than what it was of itself inclined to, yet its nature is not changed. And, therefore, frequently on occasion, opportunity, or provocation, it will fall into its own savage inclination; and having tasted of the blood of creatures, it will never be reclaimed. So is it with the depraved affections of men with respect to their change; their streams are turned, they are habituated to a new course; their nature is not altered, at least not from rational to spiritual, from earthly to heavenly. Yet this is that which was most beautiful and desirable in nature, the glory of it, and the utmost of its attainments. He who has by any means proceeded to such a moderation of his affections, as to render him kind, benign, patient, useful, preferring public good before private; ordinate and temperate in all things, will rise up in judgment against those who, professing themselves to be under the conduct of the light of grace, do yet, by being morose, angry, selfish, worldly, manifest that their affections are not subdued by the power of that grace. Wherefore, that we may be spiritually minded, there is yet another work upon our affections required, which is their internal renovation, whereby not only the course of their actings is changed, but their nature is altered, and spiritually renewed. I intend that which i expressed in that great evangelical promise, Isa. xvii 6—9. 'The wolf shall dwell with the lamb, the leopard shall lie down with the kid, and the calf, and the young lion, and the fatlings together, and a little child shall lead them; and the cow and the bear shall feed, their young ones shall lie down together, and the lion shall eat straw like the ox; and the sucking child shall play on the hole of the asp, and the weaned child shall put his hand on the cockatrice's den. They shall not hurt nor destroy in all my holy mountain.' A change and alteration is promised in the natures, principles, and first inclinations of the worst and most savage sinners who pass under the power of gospel grace.

This is that which is required of us in a way of duty. Eph. iv. 13. 'And be ye renewed in the spirit of your minds.' There is a renovation of the mind itself, by the communication of spiritual saving light and understanding thereto, whereof I have treated elsewhere at large. See Rom. xii. 2. Eph. i. 17, 18. But the spirit of the mind, that whereby it is enlivened, led, and disposed to its actings, that is to be renewed also. The spirit of the mind is in this place opposed to the old man, which is corrupt, according to deceitful lust, or depraved affections. (v. 22.) These, therefore, are that spirit of the mind which incline, bend, and lead it to act suitably to its inclinations, which is to be renewed. And when our affections are inclined by the saving grace of the Holy Spirit, then are they renewed, and not else; no other change will give them a spiritual renovation. Hereby, those things which are only natural affections in themselves, in them that believe, become fruits of the spirit. Gal. v.

22. The fruit of the Spirit is love, joy, peace, &c. They continue the same as they were in their essence, substance, and natural powers, but are changed in their properties, qualities, inclinations, whenever a new nature is given to them. So the waters at Marah were the same waters still, before and after their cure; but of themselves, and in their own nature, they were bitter, so as that the people could not drink them; in the casting of a tree into them, they were made sweet and useful. Exod. xv. 25, 26. So was it with the waters of Jericho, which were cured by casting salt into them. 2 Kings x. 20, 21. Our affections continue the same as they were, in their nature and essence, but they are so cured by grace, as that their properties, qualities, and inclinations, are all cleansed or renewed. The tree or salt that is cast into these waters, whereby the cure is wrought, is the love of God above all, proceeding from faith in him by Christ Jesus.

CHAPTER XIII.

The work of the renovation of our affections. How differenced from any other impression on, or change wrought in them; and how it is evidenced so to be. The first instance in the universality accompanying of affections spiritually renewed. The order of the exercise of our affections with respect to their objects.

That which is our concernment herein, is to inquire of what nature that work is which hath been on our own affections, or in them, and how it differs from those which, whatever they do or effect, yet will not render us nor themselves spiritual.

And we ought to use the best of our diligence herein; because the great means whereby multitudes delude and deceive their own souls, persuading themselves that there has been an effectual work of the grace of the gospel in them, is the change that they find in their affections, which may be, on many occasions, without any spiritual renovation.

First. As to the temporary and occasional impressions in the affections before mentioned, whether from the word, or any other divine warning, by afflictions or mercies, they are common to all sorts of persons. Some there are, whose consciences are seared with a hot iron, (1 Tim. iv. 2,) who thereon being past feeling, (senseless of all calls, warnings, and rebukes,) do give themselves over to lasciviousness, to work all uncleanness with greediness. Eph. iv. 19. Such persons having hardened themselves in a long course of sin, and being given up to a reprobate mind or vile affections in a way of judgment, have, it may be, no such impressions on their affections on any occasion, as to move them with a sense of things spiritual and eternal. They may be terrified with danger, sudden judgments, and other revelations of the wrath of God from heaven against the ungodliness of men; but they are not drawn to take shelter in thoughts of spiritual things. Nothing but hell will awaken them to a due consideration of themselves and things eternal.

It is otherwise with the generality of men, who are not profligate and impudent in sinning: for, although they are in a natural condition, and a course of sin, in the neglect of known duties, yet by one means or other, most frequently by the preaching of the word, their affections are stirred towards heavenly things.

Sometimes they are afraid, sometimes they have hopes and desires about them. These put them on resolutions and some temporary endeavors to change their lives, to abstain from sin, and to perform holy duties. But, as the prophet complains, 'their goodness is as the morning cloud, and as the early dew, so passeth it away.' Yet by means hereof do many poor ignorant souls deceive themselves, and cry, Peace, Peace, when there is no peace. And they will sometimes so express how they are affected with complaints of themselves as to their long neglect of spiritual things, that others may entertain good hopes concerning them; but all comes to nothing in the trial.

There is no dificulty to spiritual light to distinguish between these occasional impressions on the affections, and that spiritual renovation of them which we inquire after. This alone is sufficient to do it, that they are all of them temporary and evanescent. They abide for a while only, as our Savior speaks, and every occasion defeats all their efficacy. They may be frequently renewed, but they never abide. Some of them immediately pass away, and are utterly lost between the place where they hear the word and their own habitations, and in vain shall they inquire after them again; they are gone forever. Some have a larger continuance, endure longer in the mind, and produce some outward effects; none of them will hold any trial, or shock of temptation.

Yet I have somewhat to say to those who have such impressions on their affections, and warning by them.

(1.) Despise them not, for God is in them. Although he may not be in them in a way of saving grace, yet he is in them in that which may be preparatory thereto. They are not common human accidents, but especial divine warnings.

(2.) Labor to retain them, or a sense of them, upon your hearts and consciences. You have got nothing by losing so many of them already; and if you proceed in their neglect, after a while you will hear of them no more.

(3.) Put no more in them than belongs to them. Do not presently conclude that your state is good, because you have been affected at the hearing of the word, or under a sickness, or in a danger. Hereon many think that now all is well with them, wherewith they please themselves, until they are wholly immersed in their former security.

Secondly. We may consider the difference that is between the habitual change of the affections before described, and that renovation by grace which renders them spiritual; and this is of great concernment to us all, to inquire into it with diligence. Multitudes are herein deceived, and that to their ruin; for they resolve their present peace in, and build their hopes of eternal life on, such a change in themselves as will not abide the trial. This difference, therefore, is to be examined by scripture light, and the experience of them that do believe. And,

1. There is a double universality with respect to the spiritual renovation of our actions.

(1.) That which is subjective, with respect to the affections themselves: and,

(2.) That which is objective, with respect to spiritual things.

First. Sanctification extends itself to the whole spirit, soul, and body. 1 Thes. v. 23. When we say that we are sanctified in part only, we do not say that any part, power, or faculty of the soul is unsanctified, but only that the work is not absolutely perfect in any of them. All sin may retain power in some one affection, as anger, fear, or love, as to actual irruptions and effects, more than in all the rest; as one affection may be more eminently sanctified in some than in others. For it may have advantages to this end from men's natural tempers, and various outward circumstances. Hence some find little difficulty in the mortification of all other lusts or corruptions, in comparison of what they meet with in some one inordinate affection or corruption. This, it may be, David had regard to, Psal. xviii. 23. I have known persons shining exemplarily in all other graces, who have been scarce free from giving great scandal by the excess of their passions, and easy provocations thereunto. And yet they have known that the setting themselves to the sincere vigorous mortification of that disorder, is the most eminent pledge of their sincerity in other things. For the trial of our self-denial lies in the things that our natural inclinations lie strongest towards. Howbeit, as was said, there is no affection where there is this work of renovation, but it is sanctified and renewed; none of them is left absolutely to the service of sin and Satan. And, therefore, whereas by reason of the advantages mentioned, sin doth greatly contend to use some of them to its interest and service in a peculiar manner, yet are they enabled to, and made meet for, gracious actings, and do in their proper seasons put forth themselves accordingly. There is no affection of the mind from whence the soul and conscience hath received the greatest damage, that was, as it were, the field wherein the contest is managed between sin and grace, but hath its spiritual use and exercise, when the mind is renewed.

There are some so inordinately subject to anger and

passion therein, if they were absolutely under the power and dominion of it: yet do they also know how to be angry, and sin not in being angry at sin in themselves and others. Yea, what indignation; yea, what revenge, 2 Cor. vii. 7. Yea, God is pleased sometimes to leave somewhat more than ordinary of the power of corruption in one affection, that it may be an occasion of the continual exercise of grace in the other affections. Yet are they all sanctified in their degree; that which is relieved, as well as that which doth relieve: and, therefore, as the remainder of sin in them that believe, is called the old man, which is to be crucified in all the members of it, because of its adherence to the whole person in all its powers and faculties, so the grace implanted in our natures is called the new man, there being nothing in us that is not seasoned and affected with it. As nothing in our natures escaped the the taint of sin, so nothing in our natures is excepted from the renovation that is by grace. He in whom any one affection is utterly unrenewed, hath no one graciously renewed in him. Let men take heed how they indulge any depraved affection, for it will be an unavoidable impeachment of their sincerity. Think not to say, with Naaman, God be merciful to me in this thing, in all others I will be for him.

He requires the whole heart, and will have it, or none. The chief work of a Christian is to make all his affections, in all their operations, subservient to the life of God. Rom. vi. 17. And he who is wise will keep a continual watch over those wherein he finds the greatest reluctancy thereunto. And every affection is originally sanctified, according to the use it is to be of, in the life of holiness and obedience.

To be entirely for God, to follow him wholly, to

cleave to him with purpose of heart, to have the heart circumcised to love him, is to have all our affections renewed and sanctified, without which we can do none of them. When it is otherwise, there is a double heart, an heart, and a heart which he abhors; Their heart is divided, now shall they be found faulty. Hosea x. 2.

So it is in the other change mentioned. Whatever is or may be wrought upon our affections when they are not spiritually renewed; that very change, as to the degree of it, is not universal; it doth not affect the whole mind in all its powers and affections: until a vital prevailing principle and habit of grace is implanted in the soul, sin will not only radically adhere to all the faculties, powers, and affections; but it will, under any change that may befall them, refer the rule and dominion in some of them to itself. So was it with the young man that came to our Lord Jesus Christ, to know what he should do to obtain eternal life. Mark x. 17—22.

Thus there are many who in other things are reduced to moderation, sobriety and temperance, yet there remaineth in them the love of money, in a predominant degree, which to them is the root of all evil, as the apostle speaks; some seem to be religious, but they bridle not their tongues; through anger, envy, hatred, and the like, their religion is vain.

The most of men, in their several ways of profession, pretend not only to religion, but to zeal in it; yet set no bounds to their affections to earthly enjoyments. Some of old, who had most eminently in all other things subdued their passions and affections, were the greatest enemies to, and persecutors of, the gospel.

Some who seem to have had a mighty change wrought in them by a superstitious devotion, do yet walk in the spirit of Cain towards all the disciples of Christ, as it is with the principal devotionalists in the church of Rome; and elsewhere we may see some go soberly about the persecution and destruction of other Christians. Some will cherish one secret lust or other, which they cannot but know to be pernicious to their souls.

Some love the praise of men, which will never permit them to be truly spiritually minded; so our Saviour testifieth of some, that they could not believe, because they loved the praise of men. This was the known vice of all the ancient philosophers; they had many of them, on the principles of reason, and by severe exercise, subdued their affections to great moderation about temporary things; but in the mean time, were all of them slaves to vain glory, and the praise of men, until by the public observation of it, and some contradictions in their lives to their pretences to virtue, they lost that, also, among wise and considerate men. And generally, if men, not spiritually renewed, were able to search themselves, they would find that some of their affections are so far from having any change wrought in them, as, that they are a quiet habitation for sin, where it exerciseth its rule and dominion.

Secondly. There is a universality that is objective in spiritual things, with respect to the renovation of our affections; that is, affections spiritually renewed fix themselves upon, and cleave to, all spiritual things in their proper places, and to their proper ends. For the ground and reason of our adherence to any one of them, are the same with respect to them all; that is, their relation to God in Christ. Wherefore, when our affections are renewed, we make no choice in spiritual things, cleaving to some, and refusing others, making use of Naaman's restraint; but our adherence is the same to them all, in their proper places and degrees. And if, by reason of darkness and ignorance, we know not any of them to be from God, as for instance, the observation of the Lord's day, it is of unspeakable disadvantage to us. An equal respect is required in us to all God's commands: yet there are various distinctions in spiritual things: and thereon a man may and ought to value one above another, as to the degrees of his love and esteem, although he is to be sincere, with respect to them all.

First. God himself, that is, as revealed in and by Christ, is in the first and chiefest place, the proper and adequate object of our affections, as they are renewed. He is so for himself, or his own sake alone. This is the spring, the centre, and chief object, of our love. He that loves not God for himself, that is, for what he is in himself, and, what from himself alone he is, and will be to us in Christ, which considerations are inseparable, hath no true affection for any spiritual thing whatever. And not a few here deceive themselves, or are deceived, which should make us the more strict and diligent in the examination of ourselves. They suppose that they love heaven and heavenly things, and the duties of divine worship, which persuasion may befall them on many grounds and occasions, which will not endure the trial. But as to God himself, they can give no evidence that they have any love to him, either on the account of the glorious excellencies of his nature, with their natural relation to him, and dependence on him, nor on the account of the manifestation of himself in Christ, and the exercise of his grace therein. But whatever be pretended, there is no love to God, whereof these things are not the formal reason, that proceed not from these springs. And because that all men pretend that they love God, and defy them that think them so vile as not so to do, though they live in open enmity against him, and hatred of him; it becomes us strictly to examine ourselves on what grounds we pretend so to do. It is because, indeed, we see an excellency, a beauty, a desirableness, in the glorious properties of his nature, such as our souls are refreshed and satisfied with the thoughts of by faith, and in whose enjoyment our blessedness will consist, so that we always rejoice at the remembrance of his holiness: It is our great joy and satisfaction that God is what he is; is it from the glorious manifestation that he hath made of himself and all his holy excellencies in Christ, with the communication of himself to us in him and by him? If it be so indeed, then is our Lord generous, and gracious, from the renovation of our affections. But if we say we love God, yet truly know not why, or upon principles of education, because it is esteemed the height of wickedness to do, otherwise we shall be at a loss when we are called to our trial. This is the first object of our affections.

Secondly. In other spiritual things, renewed affections cleave to them, according as God is in them. God alone is loved for himself, all other things for him, in the measure and degree of his presence in them. This alone gives them pre-eminence in renewed affections; for instance, God is in Christ, in the human nature of the man Christ Jesus, in a way and manner singular, in concern alike incomprehensible, so as he is in the same kind in nothing else. Therefore is the Lord Christ, even as to his human nature, the object of our love and affections, in such a way and degree as no other thing, spiritual or eternal, but God himself, is or ought to be; all other spiritual things become so from the presence of God in them; and from the degree of that presence have they their nature and use. Accordingly they are, or ought to be, the object of our affections, as to the degree of their exercise. Evidence of the presence of God in things and persons, is the only attractive of renewed affections.

Thirdly. In those things which seem to stand in an equality as to what is of God in them, yet on some especial occasions and reasons, our love may go forth eminently to one more than another. Some particular truth, with the grace communicated by it, may have been the means of our conversion to God, of our edification in an especial manner, of our consolation in distress; it cannot be, but that the mind will have a peculiar respect to, and valuation of, such truths, and the grace administered by them. And so it is as to duties. We may have found such a lively intercourse and communion with God in some of them, as may give us a peculiar delight in them.

But notwithstanding these differences, affections, spiritually renewed, do cleave to all spiritual things, as such. For the true formal reason of their so doing, is the same in them all, namely, God in them; only they have several ways of acting themselves towards them, whereof I shall give one instance.

Our Saviour distributes spiritual things into those that are heavenly, and those that are earthly, that is, comparatively so. John iii. 12. 'If I have told you earthly things, and you believe not, how shall ye believe if I tell you heavenly things?'

The heavenly things are the deep and mysterious counsels of the will of God. These renewed affections cleave to, with holy admiration, and satisfactory submission, captivating the understanding to what it cannot comprehend. So the apostle declares it, Rom. xi. 33—36. 'O the depth of the riches both of the wisdom and knowledge of God! How unsearchable are his judgments, and his ways past finding out! for who hath known the mind of the Lord, or who hath been his counselor? Or who hath first given to him, and it shall be recompensed to him again? For of him, and through him, and to him, are all things, to whom be glory for ever. Amen.' What the mind cannot comprehend, the heart doth admire and adore, delighting in God, and giving glory to him in all.

The earthly things intended by our Saviour in that place, are the work of God upon the souls of men in their regeneration, wrought here in the earth. Towards these the affections act themselves with delight, and with great thanksgiving. The experience of the grace of God in and upon believers is sweet to their souls. But one way or other they cleave to them all, they have not a prevailing aversation to any of them. They have a regard to all God's precepts, a delight in all his counsels, a love to himself and all his ways.

Whatever other change is wrought on the affections, if they be not spiritually renewed, it is not so with them. For as they do not cleave to any spiritual things, in their own true, proper nature, in a due manner, because of the evidences of the presence of God in them; so there are always some of them, whereto those whose affections are not renewed, maintain an aversation and an enmity. And although this frame doth not instantly discover itself, yet it will do so upon any especial trial. So was it with the hearers of our Saviour, John vi. There was a great impression made on their affections, by what he taught them concerning the bread of God, that came down from heaven, and gave life to the world. For they cried thereon, Lord, evermore give us of this bread, v. 34. But when the mystery of it was further explained to them, they liked it not, but cried, This is a hard saying, who can bear it? v. 60; and thereon fell off both from him and his doctrine, although they had followed him so long as to be esteemed his disciples, v. 66.

I say, therefore, whensoever men's affections are not renewed, whatever other change may have been wrought upon them, as they have no true delight in any spiritual things, or truths, for themselves, and in their own nature, so there are some instances, wherein they will maintain their natural enmity and aversation to them. This is the first difference between affections spiritually renewed, and those which, from any other causes, may have some kind of change wrought in them.

CHAPTER XIV.

The second difference between Affections spiritually renewed, and those which have been only changed by light and conviction. Grounds and reasons of men's delight in duties of divine worship, and of their diligence in their performance, whose minds are not spiritually minded.

The second difference lieth herein, That there may be a change in the affections, wherein men may have delight in the duties of religious worship, and diligence in their observance; but it is the spiritual renovation of the affections that gives delight in God, through Christ, in any duty of religious worship whatever.

Where the truth of the gospel is known and publicly professed; there is great variety in the minds, ways, and practices of men, about the duties of religious worship. Many are profane in their minds and lives, who, practically at least, despise, or wholly neglect, the observance of them. These are stout hearted, and far from righteousness, Tit. i. 16. Some attend to them formally and cursorily, from the principles of their education, and it may be, out of some convictions they have of their necessity. But many there are, who, in the way they choose and are pleased with, are diligent in their observance, and that with great delight, who yet give no evidence of the spiritual renovation of their minds. Yea, the way whereby some express their devotion in them, being superstitious and idolatrous, is inconsistent with that or any other saving grace. This therefore we must diligently inquire into, or search into the grounds and reasons of men's delight in divine worship, according to their convictions of the way of it, who yet continue in their minds altogether unrenewed. And,

(1.) Men may be greatly affected with the outward part of divine worship, and the manner of the performance thereof, who have no delight in what is internal, real, and spiritual, therein. John v. 35. 'He was a burning and a shining light; and ye were willing for a season to rejoice in this light.' So many were delighted in the preaching of Ezekiel, because of his eloquence and the elegance of his parables, chap.

xxxiii. 31, 32. This gave them both delight and diligence in hearing, whereon they called themselves the people of God, though they continued to live in sin; their hearts went after covetousness. The same may befall many at present, with reference to the spiritual gifts of those by whom the word is dispensed. I deny not but that men may be more delighted, more satisfied with the gifts, the preaching of one than another, and yet be sincere in their delight in the dispensation of the word; for they may find more spiritual advantage thereby, than by the gifts of others, and things so prepared as to be suited to their edification more than elsewhere. But that which at present we insist on, hath respect only to some outward circumstances pleasing the minds of men. 2 Tim. ii. 3, 4.

This was principally evident under the Old Testament, whilst they had carnal ordinances and a worldly sanctuary. Ofttimes under that dispensation, the people were given up to all sorts of idolatry and superstition. And when they were not so, yet were the body of them carnal and unholy, as is evident from the whole track of God's dealings with them by his prophets, and in his providences. Yet had they great delight in the outward solemnities of their worship, placing all their trust of acceptance with God therein. They who did truly and really believe, looked through them all to Christ, whom they did fore-signify; without which, the things were a yoke to them, and a burthen almost insupportable. Acts xv. But those who were carnal, delighted in the things themselves, and for their sakes rejected him who was the life and substance of them all. And this proved the great means of the apostasy of the Christian church also. For to maintain some appearance of spiritual affections, men introduced carnal incitations of them into evangelical worship, such as singing with music and pompous ceremonies. For they find such things needful to reconcile the worship of God to their minds and affections, and through them they appear to have great delight therein. Could some men but in their thoughts separate divine service from that outward order, those methods of variety, show, and melody, wherewith they are affected, they would have no delight in it, but look upon it as a thing that must be endured. How can it be otherwise conceived of among the Papists? They will, with much earnestness, many evidences of devotion, sometimes with difficulty and danger, repair to their solemn worship; and yet, when they are present, understand not one word, whereby their minds might be excited to the real actings of faith, love, and delight in God. Only order, ceremony, music, and other incentives of carnal affections, make great impressions on them. Affections spiritually renewed, are not concerned in these things. Yea, if those in whom they are, should be engaged in the use of them, they would find them means of diverting their minds from the proper work of divine worship, rather than an advantage therein. It will appear so to themselves, unless they are content to lose their spiritual affections, acting themselves in faith and love, embracing in their stead a carnal, imaginary devotion. Hence, two persons may at the same time attend to the same ordinances of divine worship, with equal delight, on very distinct principles, as if two men should come into the same garden, planted and adorned with every variety of herbs and flowers; one ignorant of the nature of them, the other a skilful herbalist. Both may be equally delighted, the one with the colors and smell of the flowers, the other with the consideration of their various natures, their uses in physical remedies, or the like. So it may be in the hearing of the word. For instance, one may be delighted with the outward administration, another with its spiritual efficacy, at the same time. Hence, Austin tells us, that singing in the church was laid aside by Athanasius at Alexandria; not the people's singing of psalms, but a kind of singing in the reading of the scripture, and some offices of worship, which began then to be introduced into the church. And the reason he gave why he did it, was, that the modulation of the voice and musical tune, might not divert the minds of men from that spiritual affection which is required of them in sacred duties. What there is of real order in the worship of God, as there is that order which is an effect of divine wisdom; it is suited and useful to spiritual affections, because proceeding from the same Spirit, whereby they are internally renewed. 'Beholding your order.' Col. ii. 5. Every thing of God's appointment is both helpful and delightful to them. None can say with higher raptures of admiration, How amiable are thy tabernacles, O Lord! Psal. lxxxiv. 1, 2, than they whose affections are renewed. Yet is not their delight terminated on them, as we shall see immediately.

Secondly. 'Men may be delighted in the performance of outward duties of divine worship, because in them they comply with, and give some kind of satisfaction to, their convictions.' When conscience is awakened to a sense of the necessities of such duties, namely, of those wherein divine worship doth consist, it will give the mind no rest or peace in the neglect of them. Let them be attended to in the seasons which light, conviction, and custom call for, it will be so far satisfied, as that the mind shall find present ease and refreshment in it. And when the soul is wonted to this relief, it will not only be diligent in the performance of such duties; it will not only not omit them, but it will delight in them, as those which bring them in great advantage. Hence many will not omit the duty of prayer every morning, who upon the matter are resolved to live in sin all the day long. And there are but few who sedulously endeavor to live and walk in the frame of their hearts and ways, answerable to their own prayers; yet all that is in our prayers beyond our endeavors to answer it in a conformity of heart and life, is but the exercise of gifts in answer to conviction. Others find them an allay of troubles in them, like that which sick persons may find by drinking cold water in a fever, whose flames are assuaged for a season by it. They make them as an antidote against the poison and sting of sin, which allayeth its rage, but cannot expel its venom.

Or these duties are to them, like the sacrifices for sin under the law: they gave a guilty person present ease; but as the apostle speaks, they made not men perfect. They took not away utterly a conscience condemning for sin. Presently, on the first omission of duty, a sense of sin again returned on them, and that not only as the fact, but as the person himself was condemned by the law. Then were the sacrifices to be repeated for renewed propitiation. This gave that carnal people such delight and satisfaction in those sacrifices, that they trusted to them for righteousness, life, and salvation. So it is with persons who are constant in spiritual duties merely from conviction. The performance of those duties gives them a present relief and ease; though it heal not their wounds, it assuageth their pain, and dispelleth their present fears. Hence are they frequent in them, and that ofttimes not without delight; because they find ease thereby. And their condition is somewhat dangerous, who, upon the sense of the guilt of any sin, do betake themselves for relief to their prayers; which having discharged, they are much at ease in their minds and consciences, although they have obtained no real sense of the pardon of sin, nor any strength against it.

It will be said, do not all men, the best of men, perform all spiritual duties out of a conviction of their necessity? Do they not know it would be their sin to omit them, and so find satisfaction in their minds upon their performance? I say they do; but it is one thing to perform a duty out of conviction of necessity, as it is God's ordinance, which conviction respects only the duty itself, another thing to perform it, to give satisfaction to convictions of other sins, or to quiet conscience under its trouble about them; which latter we speak to. This begins and ends in self; self-satisfaction is the sole design of it. By it men aim at some rest and quietness in their own minds, which otherwise they cannot attain. But in the performance of duties in faith, from a conviction of their necessity as God's ordinance, and their use in the way of his grace, the soul begins and ends in God. It seeks no satisfaction in them, nor finds it from them, but in and from God alone by them.

Thirdly. The principal reason why men whose affections are only changed, not spiritually renewed, delight in holy duties of divine worship, is, because they place their righteousness before God in them, whereon they hope to be accepted with him. They know not, they seek not after, any other righteousness but what is of their own working out. Whatever notions they may have of the righteousness of faith, of the righteousness of Christ, that which they practically trust to is their own; and it discovers itself so to be, in their own consciences, on every trial that befalls them. Yea, when they cry to the Lord, and pretend to faith in Christ, they quickly make it evident that their principal trust is resolved in themselves. Now in all that they can plead in a way of duties or obedience, nothing carrieth a fairer pretence to a righteousness, than what they do in the worship of God, and the exercise of the acts of religion towards him. This is that which he expects at their hands, what is due to him, in the light of their consciences, the best that they can do to please him; which therefore they must put their trust in, or nothing. They secretly suppose, not only that there is a righteousness in these things, which will answer for itself, but such also as will make compensation in some measure for their sins; and therefore, whereas they cannot but frequently fall into sin, they relieve themselves from the reflection of their consciences by a multiplication of duties, and renewed diligence in them.

It is inconceivable what delight and satisfaction men will take in any think that seems to contribute so much to a righteousness of their own: for it is suitable to, and pleaseth all the principles of nature, as corrupt, after it is brought under the power of a conviction concerning sin, righteousness, and judgment.

This made the Jews of old so pertinaciously adhere to the ceremonies and sacrifices of the law, and to prefer them above the gospel, the kingdom of God, and the righteousness thereof. Rom. x. 3, 4. They looked and sought for righteousness by them. Those who for many generations were kept up with great difficulty to any tolerable observance of them, when they had learned to place all their hopes of a righteousness in them, would, and did adhere to them, to their temporal and eternal ruin. Rom. ix. 31—33. And when men were persuaded that righteousness was to be attained by works of munificence and supposed charity, in the dedication of their substance to the use of the church; they who otherwise were covetous, and greedy, and oppressing, would lavish gold out of the bag, and give up their whole patrimony with all their ill gotten goods to obtain it, so powerful an influence hath the desire of self-righteousness upon the minds of men. It is the best fortification of the soul against Christ and the gospel, the last reserve whereby it maintains the interest of self against the grace of God.

Hence I say, those that place their righteousness, or that which is the principal part of it, in the duties of religious worship, will not only be diligent in them, but ofttimes abound in a multiplication of them. Especially will they do so, if they may be performed in such a way and manner as pleaseth their affections with a show of humility and devotion, requiring nothing of the exercise of faith, or sincere divine love therein. So is it with many in all kinds of religion, whether the way of their worship be true or false; whether it be appointed of God, or rejected by him. And the declaration hereof is the subject of the discourse of the prophet, Isaiah i. 11—19. Also, Mich. vi. 7, 8.

Fourthly. The reputation of devotion in religious duties, may insensibly affect the unrenewed minds of men with great diligence and delight in their performance. However men are divided in their apprehension and practice about religion; however different from and contrary to each other, their ways of divine worship are; yet it is amongst all sorts of men, yea, in the secret thoughts of them who outwardly contemn these things, a matter of reputation to be devout, to be diligent, to be strict in and about those duties of religion, which, according to their own light and persuasion, they judge incumbent on them. This greatly affects the minds of men, whilst pride is secretly predominant in them, and they love the praise of men more than the praise of God.

Especially will this consideration prevail on them, when they suppose that the credit and honor of the way which they profess, in competition with others, depends much on their reputation as to their strictness in duties of devotion. For then will they not only be diligent in themselves, but zealous in drawing others to the same observances. These two principles, their own reputation, and that of their sect, constituted the life and soul of Pharisaism of old. According as the minds of men are influenced with these apprehensions, so will a love to, and a delight in, those duties whereby their reputation is attained, thrive and grow in them.

I am far from apprehending that any men are, (at least I speak not of them who are,) such vile hypocrites, as to do all that they do in religion to be seen and praised of men, being influenced in all public duties thereby, which some among the Pharisees were given up to. But I speak of them, who, being under the convictions and motives before mentioned, do also yet give admittance to this corrupt end of desire of reputation, or the praise of men. For every such end being admitted and prevalent in the mind, will universally influence the affections to a delight in those duties, whereby that end may be attained, until the person with whom it is so be habituated to them with great satisfaction.

Fifthly. I should, in the last place, insist on superstition. As this is an undue fear of the divine nature, will, and operations, built on false notions and apprehensions of them, it may befall the minds of men in all religions, true and false. It is an internal vice of the mind. As it respects the outward way and means of religious service, and consists in the devout performance of such duties as God indeed accepts not, but forbids; so it belongs only to religion as it is false and corrupt. How in both respects it will engage the minds of men into the performance of religious duties, and for the most part with the most scrupulous diligence, and sometimes with prodigious attempts to exceed the measures of human nature in what they design, is too long a work here to be declared. It may suffice to have mentioned it among the causes and reasons why men, whose affections are not spiritually renewed, may yet greatly delight in the diligent performance of the outward duties of religion. Our design in these things is the discovery of the true nature of this grace and duty of being spiritually minded. Hereto we have declared that it is necessary that our affections be spiritually and supernaturally renewed. And because there may be a great change wrought on the affections of men, with respect to spiritual things, where there is nothing of this supernatural renovation; our present inquiry is, what are the differences that are between the actings of the affections of the one sort and of the other; whether spiritually renewed, or occasionally changed, and wherein the great exercise of them consists in the duties of religious worship. I have declared what are the grounds and reasons, whence men of unrenewed minds delight ofttimes in the duties of divine worship, and are diligent in the performance of them.

From these, and the like considerations, it may be made manifest that the greatest part of the devotion that is in the world, doth not spring from the spiritual renovation of the minds of men, without which it is not accepted with God. That which remains to give in instance, further evidence to the discovery we are in the pursuit of, is, what are the grounds and reasons whereon those, whose minds and affections are spiritually renewed, do delight in the institutions of divine worship; and attend to their observance with great heed and diligence? And because this is an inquiry of great importance, and is of great use to be stated in other cases, as well as that before us; I shall treat of it by itself in the ensuing chapter, that the reader may the more distinctly comprehend it, both in the nature of the doctrine concerning it, and in the place it holds in our present discourse.

CHAPTER XV.

Delight of believers in the holy institutions of divine worship. The grounds and reasons thereof. The evidence of being spiritually minded thereby, &c.

That all true believers, whose minds are spiritually renewed, have a singular delight in all the institutions and ordinances of divine worship, is fully evident, both in the examples of the saints in the scripture, and their own experience, which they will never forego.

For this hath been the greatest cause of their suffering persecution, and martyrdom itself, in all ages. If the primitive Christians under the power of the pagan emperors, or the witnesses for Christ under the antichristian apostasy, would, or could have omitted the observance of them (according to the advice and practice of the gnostics,) they might have escaped the rage of their adversaries. But they loved not their lives, in comparison to that delight which they had in the observance of the commands of Christ, as to the duties of evangelical worship. David gives us frequently an instance hereof in himself. Psal. xlii. 1—4. 'As the hart panteth after the water brooks, so panteth my soul after thee, O God. My soul thirsteth for God, for the living God: When shall I come and appear before God? My tears have been my meat day and night, while they continually say unto me, Where is thy God? When I remember these things, I pour out my soul in me: for I had gone with the multitude; I went with them to the house of God; with the voice of joy and praise, with a multitude that kept holy-day.' Psal. lxiii. 1—5. 'O God, thou art my God, early will I seek thee, my soul thirsteth for thee, my flesh longeth for thee in a dry and thirsty land, where no water is. To see thy power and thy glory, so as I have seen thee in thy sanctuary. Because thy loving kindness is better than life: my lips shall praise thee. Thus will I bless thee while I live. I will lift up my hands in thy name. My soul shall be satisfied as with marrow and fatness, and my mouth shall praise thee with joyful lips.' Psal. lxxxiv. 1—4. 'How amiable are thy tabernacles, O Lord of Hosts! My soul longeth, yea, even fainteth for the courts of the Lord: my heart crieth out for the living God. The sparrow hath found an house, and the swallow a nest for herself, where she may lay her young, even thy altars, O Lord of hosts, my King and my God. Blessed are they that dwell in thy house: they will be still praising thee. Selah.'

But a greater than David is here. Our Lord Jesus Christ himself did upon all occasions declare his delight in, and zeal for, all the ordinances of divine worship, which were then in force by virtue of divine institution and command. For although he severely reproved and rejected whatever men had added thereto, under the pretence of a supererogating strictness, or outward order, laying it all under that dreadful sentence, Every plant which my heavenly Father hath not planted shall be plucked up, and cast into the fire; yet as to what was of divine appointment, his delight therein was singular, and exemplary to all his disciples. With respect hereto was it said of him, that the zeal of God's house had eaten him up, by reason of the affliction which he had in his spirit, to see the worship of it neglected, polluted, and despised. This caused him to cleanse the temple, the seat of divine worship, from the pollutors and pollutions of it, not long before his sufferings, in the face and to the high provocation of all his adversaries. So with earnest desire he longed for the celebration of his last passover. Luke xxii. 15. 'With desire have I desired to eat this passover with you before I suffer.' And it is a sufficient evidence of the frame of spirit and practice of his disciples afterwards. In reference to the duties of evangelical worship by his appointment; that the apostle gives it as an assured token of an unsound condition, and that which tendeth to final cursed apostasy, when any 'fall into a neglect of them.' Heb. x. 25—27.

These things are manifest and unquestionable. But our present inquiry is only, what it is which believers do so delight in, in the ordinances and institutions of divine gospel worship, and what it is that engageth their hearts and minds to a diligent observance of them; as also how and wherein they exercise their love and delight? And I say, in general, that their delight in all ordinances of divine worship, as is evident in the testimonies before produced, is in Christ himself, or God in Christ. This alone is that which they seek after, cleave to, and are satisfied with. They make use of the streams but only as means of communication from the spring. When men are really renewed in the spirit of their minds, it is so. Their regard to ordinances and duties of divine worship, is, as they are appointed of God, a blessed means of communion and intercourse between himself in Christ, and their souls. By them doth Christ communicate of his love and grace to us; in and by them do we act faith and love on him. It is the treasure hid in the field, which, when a man hath found, he purchaseth the whole field; but it is that he may enjoy the treasure which is hid therein. Mat. xiii. 14. This field is the gospel, and all the ordinances of it. This men do purchase sometimes at a dear rate, even with the loss of all they enjoy. But yet if they obtain nothing but the field, they will have little cause to rejoice in their bargain. It is Christ the treasure alone, that pearl of price, that will certainly enrich the soul. The field is to be used only, as to find and dig up the treasure that is in it. It is, I say, Christ alone, that in the preaching of the gospel, renewed affections cleave to as the treasure, and to all other things according as their relation is to him, or they have a participation of him. Wherefore, in all duties of religion, in all ordinances of worship, their inquiry is after him whom their souls love. Cant. i. 7.

But yet we must treat more particularly and distinctly of these things. Those whose affections are spiritually renewed, do love, adhere to, and delight in, ordinances of divine service and duties of worship; on the grounds and reasons ensuing.

First. In general they do so, as they find faith and love, and delight in God through Christ, excited and acted in and by them. This is their first and immediate end in their institution. It is a pernicious mistake to suppose that any external duties of worship, as hearing the word, prayer, or the sacraments, are appointed for themselves, or accepted for themselves.

Such thoughts the Jews of old had concerning their sacrifices; namely, that they were appointed for their own sakes, and were acceptable service to God, merely on their own account. Wherefore God, to deliver them from their pernicious mistake, affirms ofttimes, that he never appointed them at all: that is, for any such end. Jer. vii. 22, 23. Isa. i. 12, 13, &c. And now under the gospel, sundry things destructive to the souls of men have proceeded from such a supposition. Some hereon have always satisfied and contented themselves with the external observance of them, without desiring or endeavoring any holy communion with God in them, or by them. This constitutes the state and condition mentioned, Rev. iii. 1. And by following this track, the generality of Christians wander out of the way; they cannot leave them, nor know how to use them to their advantage, until they come wholly to that woful state. Isa. xxix. 13. And some, to establish this deceit, have taught that there is much more in the outward work of these duties, than ever God put into them, and that they are sanctified merely by virtue of the work wrought.

But all the duties of the second commandment, as are all instituted ordinances of worship, are but means to express and exercise those of the first, as faith, love, fear, trust, and delight in God. The end of them all is, that through them, and by them, we may act those graces on God in Christ. Where this is not attended to, when the souls of men do not apply themselves to this exercise of grace in them, let them be never so solemn as to their outward performance, be attended to with diligence, be performed with earnestness and delight, they are neither acceptable to God, nor beneficial to themselves. Isa. i. 11. This therefore is the first general spring of the love of believers, of them whose affections are spiritually renewed, under the ordinances of divine worship, and their delight in them. They have experience, that in and by them, their faith and love are excited to a gracious exercise of themselves on God in Christ. And when they find it otherwise with them, they can have no rest in their souls. For this end are they ordained, sanctified, and blessed of God, and therefore, are effectual means of it, when their efficacy is not defeated by unbelief.

And those who have no experience hereof in their attendance to them, do, as hath been said, fall into pernicious extremes. Some continue their observance with little regard to God, in cursed formality. So they make them a means of their ruin by countenancing of them in their security.

Others utterly reject them, at least the most solemn of them, and therein the wisdom, and grace, and authority of God, by whom they are appointed. Because, through the power of their own unbelief, they find nothing in them.

This being the immediate end of all divine institutions, this being the only way whereby we may give glory to God in their observance, which is their ultimate end in this world; and this being the design in general of believers in that obedience, they yield to the Lord Christ in their diligent observation of them; we may consider how, in what way, and by what means, those whose affections are spiritually renewed, do and ought to apply their minds and souls to their observance. And we may consider herein, first, What they design, and then what they endeavor to be found in the exercise and practice of, in their use and enjoyment.

First. They come to them with this desire, design, and expectation, namely, to be enabled, directed, and excited by them to the exercise of divine faith and love. When it is not so with any, where there is not this design, they do in various degrees take the name of God in vain in their observance. These are *approximationes Dei*, the ways of drawing nigh to God, as they are every where called in scripture. To suppose that a drawing nigh to God may consist merely in the outward performance of duty, whatever be its solemnity, is to reject all due reverence of him. Forasmuch, saith the Lord, as this people draw near to me with their mouths, and with their lips do honor me, but have removed their hearts far from me, therefore I will proceed against them. Isaiah xxix. 13. The mouth and lips are put by a synecdoche, for all the means of outward worship and honor. These men may use, and diligently attend to, whilst their hearts are far from God, that is, when they do not draw nigh to him by faith and love. But all this worship is rejected of God with the highest tokens of his displeasure and indignation against it.

First. Our souls then have no way of approach to God in duties of worship, but by faith; no way of adherence or cleaving to him, but by love; no way of abiding in him, but by fear, reverence, and delight. Whenever these are not in exercise, outward duties of worship are so far from being a means of such an approach to him, as that they set us at a greater distance from him than we were before, at least are utterly useless and fruitless to us. So indeed they are to the most who come to them, they know not why, and behave themselves under them, they care not how: nor is there any evil in the hearts and ways of men, whereof God complaineth more in his word, as that which is accompanied with the highest contempt of him. And because these ordinances of divine worship are means which the wisdom and grace of God have appointed to this end, namely, the exercise and increase of divine faith and love, and therefore do sanctify and bless them thereto. I do not believe that they have any delight in the exercise of these graces, nor design growth in them, by whom these great means of them are despised or neglected.

And although I have seen those vallies of public worship forsaken, either on pretences of higher attainments in faith, light, and love, than to stand in need of them any more, or on a foolish opinion, that they cease upon the dispensation of the Spirit, which is given to us to make them useful and effectual, or on some provocations that have been given to some men, or which they have taken to themselves, which they have thought they could revenge by a neglect of public administrations, or through slavish peace and negligence in times of difficulty, as is the manner of some, who forsake the assemblies of the saints. Heb. vi. 25. Yet, I never saw, but it issued in a great decay, if not in an utter loss of all exercise of faith and love, and sometimes in open profaneness. For such persons contemn the ways and means, which God in his infinite wisdom and goodness hath appointed for their exercise and increase; and this shall not prosper. We may therefore do well to consider, that the principal way whereby we may sanctify the name of God, in all duties of his worship, and obtain the benefit of them to our own souls, is by a conscientious approach to them with a holy desire and design to be found in the exercise of faith and love on God in Christ, and to be helped and guided therein by them.

To be under an efficacious influence from this design, is the best preparation for any duty. So David expresseth his delight in the worship of God. 'How amiable are thy tabernacles, O Lord of hosts! My soul longeth, yea, even fainteth for the courts of the Lord: my heart and my flesh cry out for the living God.' Psal. lxxxiv. 1, 2. He longed for the tabernacle, and the courts of it, but it was the enjoyment of God himself, the living God, that he desired and sought after. This was that which made him so fervent in his desires after those ordinances of God. So he expresseth it, Psal. lxiii. 2. 'To see thy power and thy glory, so as I have seen thee in the sanctuary.' David had had great communion with and delight in God by faith and love in the solemn duties of his worship. And this was that which inflamed him with desires after renewed opportunities to the same end.

Secondly. This design is not general, inactive, useless, and slothful. But such persons diligently endeavor, in the use of these ordinances, and attendance to them, to be found in the exercise of these graces. They have not only an antecedent design to be so, but a diligent actual endeavor after it, not suffering their minds by any thing to be diverted from the pursuit of that design. Eccl. v. 1. Whatever is not quickened and enlivened hereby, they esteem utterly lost. Neither outward administrations nor order will give them satisfaction, when these things are wanting in themselves. Without the internal actings of the life of faith, external administrations of ordinances of worship are but dead things. Nor can any believer obtain real satisfaction in them, or refreshment by them, without an inward experience of faith and love in them, and by them. And it is that which, if we are wise, we shall continually attend to the consideration of. A watchful Christian will be careful lest he lose any one duty, by taking up the carcass of it. And the danger of so doing is not small. Our affections are renewed but in part. And as they are still liable to be diverted, and seduced from spirituality in duty, even by things earthly and carnal, through the corruption that remaineth in them; so there is a disposition abiding in them, to be pleased with those external things in religious duties, which others, as we have showed before, who are no way graciously renewed, satisfy themselves with. The grace and oratory of the speaker in preaching the word, especially in these days wherein the foppery of fine language, even in sacred things, is so much extolled, the order and circumstances of other duties, with inclination and love to a party, are apt to insinuate themselves with great complacency in our affections, so far as they are unrenewed. And these things discover the true grounds whence it is that the ordinances of divine worship are so useless as they are, to many who seem to attend to them with diligence. They may be referred to these two heads:

(1.) They do not come to them, as the means appointed of God, for the exercise of faith and love to Christ, so as to make it their design in their approaches to them, without which, all that is spoken of advantage in and by other duties is utterly lost.

(2.) They do not in and under them labor to stir up faith and love to their due exercise.

(3.) They suffer their minds to be diverted from the exercise of these graces, partly by occasional temptations, partly by attendance to what is outward only in the ordinances themselves.

Spiritual affections find no place of rest in any of these things; such proposals of God in Christ, of his will, and their own duty, as may draw out their faith, love, godly fear, and delight, into their due exercise, is that which they inquire after, and acquiesce in.

Two things alone doth faith regard in all duties of worship, as to the outward administration of it. The one absolutely, the other comparatively; both with respect to the end mentioned, or the exercise, growth, and increase of grace in us. The first is, that they be of divine appointment. Where their original and observance are resolved into divine authority, there, and there alone, will they have a divine efficacy. In all these things, faith hath regard to nothing but divine precepts and promises. Whatever hath regard to any thing else, is not faith, but fancy. And therefore these uncommanded duties in religion, which so abound in the papal church, as that, if not the whole, yet all the principal parts of their worship consist in them, are such as in whose discharge it is impossible faith should be in a due exercise. That which it hath comparative respect to, is the spiritual gifts of them to whom the administration of the ordinances of the gospel, in the public worship of the church, is committed. With respect to them, believers may have more delight and satisfaction in the ministry of one than of another, as was touched before. But this is not because one is more learned than another, or more elegant than another, hath more ability of speech than another, or fervency in utterance than another, is more fervent and earnest in his delivery; but because they find the gifts of one more suited, and more effectual to stir up faith and love to a holy exercise in their minds and hearts, than what they find in some others. Hence they have a peculiar value for, and delight in, the ministry of such persons, especially when they can enjoy it in due order, and without the offence of others. And ministers that are wise, will, in holy administrations, neglect all other things, and attend to this alone, how they may be helpful to the faith, and love, and joy of believers, so far as they are the object of their ministry. This is the first reason and ground whereon affections spiritually renewed cleave to ordinances of divine worship with delight and satisfaction; namely, because they are the means appointed and blessed of God for the exercise and increase of faith and love, with an experience of their efficacy to that end.

Secondly. The second is, Because they are the means of the communication of a sense of divine love, and supplies of divine grace, to the souls of them that believe. So far as our affections are renewed, this is the principal attractive to cleave to them with delight and complacency.

They are, as was observed before, the ways of our approaching to God. Now we do not draw nigh to God, as himself speaks, as a dry heath, or a barren wilderness, where no refreshment is to be obtained. To make a pretence of coming to God, and not with expectation of receiving good and great things from him, is to despise God himself, to overthrow the nature of the duty, and deprive our own souls of all benefit thereby; and the want hereof is that which renders the worship of the most, useless, and fruitless to themselves. We are always to come to God, as to an eternal spring of goodness, grace, and mercy, of all that our souls stand in need of, of all that we can desire in order to our everlasting blessedness; and all these things, as to believers, may be reduced to the two heads before mentioned.

First. They come for a communication of a sense of his love in Jesus Christ. Hence do all our peace, consolation, and joy, all our encouragement to do and suffer according to the will of God, all our supportments under our sufferings, solely depend; in these things do our souls live, and without them we are of all men the most miserable.

It is the Holy Spirit who is the immediate efficient cause of all these things in us. He sheds abroad the love of God in our hearts. Rom. v. 5. He witnesseth our adoption to us, (chap. viii. 15, 16,) and thereby an interest in the love of the Father, in God, as he is love. But the outward way and means whereby he communicates these things to us, and effects them in us, is by the dispensation of the gospel, or the preaching of it ordinarily. He doth the same work also in prayer, and ofttimes in other holy administrations. For this end, for a participation of this grace, of these mercies, do believers come to God by them. They use them as means to draw water from the well of salvation, and to receive in that spiritual sense of divine love, which God by them will communicate.

So Christ, by his word, knocks at the door of the heart; if it be opened by faith, he cometh in, and suppeth with men, giving them a gracious refreshment, by the testimony of his own love, and the love of the Father. Rev. iii. 23. John xiv. 3. This believers look for in, and this they do, in various measures, receive by the ordinances of divine worship. And although some, through their fears and temptations, are not sensible hereof, yet do they secretly receive those blessed gracious supplies, whereby their souls are held in life, without which they would pine away and perish. So he dealeth with them. Cant. iv. 5, 6. These are the gardens and galleries of Christ, wherein he gives us of his love. Cant. vii. 12. Those who are humble and sincere, know how often their souls have been refreshed in them, and how long sometimes the impressions they have received of divine grace and love have continued with them, to their unspeakable consolation. They remember what they have received in the opening and application of the exceeding great and precious promises that are given to them, whereby they are gradually more and more made partakers of the divine nature; how many a time they have received light in darkness, refreshment under despondencies, relief in their conflicts with dangers and temptations, in and by them. For this cause do affections that are spiritually renewed cleave to them. Who can but love and delight in that which he hath found, by experience, to be the way and means of communicating to him the most invaluable mercy, the most inestimable benefit, whereof in this life he can be made partaker? He who hath found a hidden treasure, although he should at once take away the whole of it, yet will he esteem the place where he found it; but if it be of that nature, that no more can be found or taken of it at once but what is sufficient for the present occasion, yet is so full and boundless, as that whenever he comes again to seek for it, he shall be sure to obtain present supply, he will always value it, and constantly apply himself to it. And such is the treasure of grace and divine love, that is in the ordinances of divine worship.

If we are strangers to these things, if we never received efficacious intimations of divine love to our souls, in and by the duties of divine worship, we cannot love them and delight in them as we ought. What do men come to hear the word of God for? What do they pray for? What do they expect to receive from him? Do they come to God as the eternal fountain of living waters? as the God of all grace, peace, and consolation? Or do they come to his worship without any design, as to a dry and empty show? Do they fight uncertainly with these things, as men beating the air? Or think they bring something to God, but receive nothing from him? That the best of their business is to please him in doing what he commands; but to receive any thing from him, they expect not, nor do ever examine themselves whether they have done so or not? It is not for persons who walk in such ways, ever to attain a due delight in the ordinances of divine worship.

Believers have other designs herein; and, among the rest, this in the first place, that they may be afresh made partakers of refreshing, comforting pledges of the love of God in Christ, and thereby of their adoption, of the pardon of their sins, and acceptance of their persons. According as they meet with these things in the duties of holy worship, public or private, so will they love, value, and adhere to them. Some men are full of other thoughts and affections, so as that these things are not their principal design or desire, or are contented with that measure of them which they suppose themselves to have attained; or, at least, are not sensible of the need they stand in to have fresh communications of them made to their souls; supposing that they can do well enough without a renewed sense of divine love every day: some are so ignorant of what they ought to design to look after, in the duties of gospel worship, as that it is impossible they should have any real design in them. Many of the better sort of professors are too negligent in this matter: they do not long and pant in the inward man after renewed pledges of the love of God; they do not consider how much they have need of them, that they may be encouraged and strengthened to all other duties of obedience; they do not prepare their minds for the reception of them, nor come with the expectation of their communication to them; they do not rightly fix their faith on this truth, namely, that these holy administrations and duties are appointed of God, in the first place, as the ways and means of conveying his love, and a sense of it, to our souls. From hence spring that lukewarmness, coldness and indifferency in and to the duties of holy worship, that are growing among us: for if men have lost the principal design of faith in them, and disesteem the chiefest benefit which is to be obtained by them, whence should zeal for them, delight in them, or diligence in attendance to them, arise? Let not any please themselves under the powers of such decays; they are indications of their inward frame, and those infallible. Such persons will grow cold, careless, and negligent, as to the duties of public worship; they will put themselves neither to charge nor trouble about them; every occasion of life diverts them, and finds ready entertainment in their minds; and when they do attend upon them, it is with great indifferency and unconcernedness. Yet would they have it thought that all is still well within as ever it was, they have as good a respect to religion as any. But these things openly discover an ulcerous disease in the very souls of men, as evidently as if it were written on their foreheads; whatever they pretend to the contrary, they are under the power of woful decays from all due regard to spiritual and eternal things. And I would avoid the society of such persons, as those who carry an infectious disease about them, unless it were to help on their cure.

Secondly. They come for supplies of internal, sanctifying, strengthening grace. This is the second great design of believers in their approaches to God in his worship. The want hereof, as to measures and degrees, they find in themselves, and are sensible of it. Yea, therein lies the great burden of the souls of believers in this world. All that we do in the life of God may be referred to two heads.

First. The observance of all duties of obedience. And,

Secondly. The conflict with, and conquest over, temptations. About these things are we continually exercised. Hence the great thing which we desire, labor for, and pant after, is spiritual strength and ability for the discharge of ourselves in a due manner with respect to these things. This is that which every true believer groaneth after in the inward man, and which he preferreth infinitely above all earthly things. So he may have grace sufficient in any competent measure for these ends; let what will befall him, he desireth no more in this world. God in Christ is the fountain of all his grace. There is not one drachm of it to be obtained but from him alone. And as he doth communicate it to us of his own sovereign goodness and pleasure; so the ordinary way and means whereby he will do it, are the duties of his worship. Isa. xl. 28—31. 'Hast thou not known, hast thou not heard, that the everlasting God, the Lord, the Creator of the ends of the earth, fainteth not, neither is weary? There is no searching of his understanding. He giveth power to the faint, and to them that have no might he increaseth strength. Even the youth shall faint and be weary, and the young men shall utterly fail. But they that wait upon the Lord shall renew their strength: they shall mount up with wings, as eagles; they shall run, and not be weary; they shall walk, and not faint.'

All grace and spiritual strength is originally seated in the nature of God; (v. 28,) but, what relief can that afford to us, who are weak, feeble, fainting? He will act suitably to his nature in the communication of this grace and power; (v. 29,) but, how shall we have an interest in this grace, in these operations? Wait on him in the ordinances of his worship, (v. 31.) The word, as preached, is the food of our souls, whereby God administereth growth and strength to them. (John

xvii. 17. 1 Pet. ii. 23.) 'Desire, saith he, the sincere milk of the word, that ye may grow thereby.' But what encouragement have we thereto? if so be, saith he, you have tasted that the Lord is gracious! If, in and by the dispensation of this word, you have had experience of the grace, the goodness, the kindness of God to your souls, you cannot but desire and delight in it; and otherwise you will not do so. When men have sat some good while under the dispensation of the word, and in the enjoyment of other ordinances, without tasting in and by them that the Lord is gracious, they will grow weary of it and them. Wherefore prayer is the way of his appointment for the application of our souls to him, to obtain a participation of all needful grace, which, therefore, he has proposed to us in the promises of the covenant, that we may know what to ask, and how to plead for it. In the sacraments the same promises are sealed to us, and the grace represented in them effectually exhibited. Meditation confirms our souls in the exercise of faith about it, and is the especial opening of the heart to the reception of it. By these means, I say, doth God communicate all supplies of renewing, strengthening, and sanctifying grace to us, that we may live to him in all holy obedience, and be able to get the victory over our temptations. Under this apprehension, believers approach to God in the ordinances of his worship: they come to them as the means of God's communication to their souls; hence they cleave to them with delight, so far as their affections are renewed. So the spouse testifieth of herself—I sat down under his shadow with great delight. Cant. ii. 3. In these ordinances is the protecting, refreshing presence of Christ. This she rested in with great delight.

As they come to them with these designs and expectations, so they have experience of the spiritual benefits and advantages which they receive by them, which more and more engageth them to them in their affections and delight. All these things, those who have a change wrought in their affections, but not a spiritual renovation, are strangers to. They neither have the design before mentioned in coming to them, nor the experience of this efficacy now proposed in their attendance on them. But these benefits are great; as, for instance, when men find the worth and effect of the word preached on their souls, in its enlightening, refreshing, strengthening, transforming power; when they find their hearts warmed, their graces excited and strengthened, the love of God improved, their desponding spirits under trials and temptations relieved, their whole souls gradually more and more conformed to Christ; when they find themselves by it extricated out of snares, doubts, fears, temptations, and brought to satisfaction and rest; they cannot but delight in the dispensation of it, and rejoice in it as the food of their souls. And it is a great hinderance to the increase of spiritual life, and obstruction to fruitfulness, thankfulness, and consolation, when we are negligent in our meditation about the benefits that we receive by the word, and the advantages which we have thereby. For whilst it is so with us, we can neither value the grace of God, in granting us this inestimable privilege, nor perform any duty with respect to it, in a right manner. This renders it an especial object of our affections as spiritually renewed. That secret love to, and heavenly delight in, the statutes and testimonies of God, which David expresseth, (Psal. cxix,) arose from the spiritual benefit and advantage which he received by them, as he constantly declares. And the sole reason, on the one hand, why men grow so careless, negligent, and cold, in their attendance to the preaching of the word, is because they have no experience of any spiritual benefit or advantage by it. They have been brought to it by one means or another, mostly by conviction of their duty. Their minds have been variously affected with it, to a joy in the hearing of it, and readiness to sundry duties of obedience: but after a while, when a sense of those temporary impressions is worn off, finding no real spiritual benefit by it, they lose all delight in it, and become very indifferent as to its enjoyment. The frame which such persons at length arrive to is described, Mal. i. 13, and iii. 14. And none can give any greater evidence of the decay of all manner of grace in them, or of their being destitute of all saving grace, than when they apostatize from some degree of zeal for, and delight in, the dispensation of the word of God, with such a cursed indifferency, as many are overtaken with. It cannot be otherwise. For seeing this is a way and means of the exercise of all grace, it will not be neglected, but where there is a decay of all grace; however men may please themselves with other pretences. And when they are thus ensnared, every foolish prejudice, every provocation, every wanton opinion and imagination will confirm them in, and increase their gradual backsliding.

And as it is with believers, as to the hearing of the word in general, so it is as to the degrees of advantage which they find by it. When men have enjoyed the dispensation of the word in a peculiar manner, spiritual and effectual; if they can be content to forego it, for that which is more cold and lifeless, provided it possesseth the same time and outward form with the other, it is no great evidence that their souls prosper. It is therefore those alone, who, having a sense of the efficacy of the word on their souls and consciences to all the holy ends of it, who cleave to it with spiritual love and delight. They continually remember what holy impressions it hath made on them, what engagements it hath brought their souls into, what encouragements to faith and obedience it hath furnished them with, and long after a renewed sense of its enjoyments. When we do not find in ourselves this foundation of spiritual delight in the dispensation of the gospel, we can have no great evidence that our affections are renewed.

So also it is in the duties of prayer and meditation. When the soul of a believer hath had experience of the communion which it hath had with God in them, or either of them; of the spiritual refreshment which it hath had from them; of the benefits and mercies which are obtained by them, in recovery from temptations, snares, despondencies, in victory over sin and Satan, in spiritual impressions, working it to a holy watchful frame, which hath abode with it in other ways and occasions, with the like advantages wherewith fervent and effectual prayer, and sincere heavenly meditation are accompanied, it cannot but have love to them, and delight in them; but if, indeed, we have no experience of these things, if we find not these advantages in and by these duties, they cannot but be a burden to us, nor do serve to any other end but to satisfy convictions. He who had the benefit of a serene and wholesome air in a recovery from many diseases and distempers, with the preservation of his health so obtained, will love it and prize it; and so will he these duties, who hath been partaker of any of these saving mercies and privileges wherewith they are accompanied. Some have been delivered from the worst of temptations, and the nearest approach of their prevalency (as to destroy themselves,) by a sudden remembrance of the frame of their souls, and the intimations of God's love in such, or such a prayer, at such a time. Some have had the same deliverance from temptations to sin; when they had been carried away under the power of their corruptions, and all circumstances had concurred under the apprehensions of it, a sudden thought of such a prayer or meditation, with the engagement they made of themselves therein to God, hath caused all the weapons of sin to fall out of its hands, and all the beauties of its allurements to disappear.

When others have been under the power of such despondencies and disconsolations, as that no present tenders of relief can approach to them, they have been suddenly raised and refreshed by the remembrance of the intimate love and kindness between Christ and their souls, that has evidenced itself in former duties. Multitudes in fears, distresses, and temptations, have found relief to their spirits, and encouragement to their faith, in the remembrance of the returns they have had to former supplications in the like distresses. These are grounds of spiritual delight in these duties.

Heartless, lifeless, wordy prayer, the fruit of convictions and gifts, or of custom and outward occasions, however multiplied, and whatever devotion they seem to be accompanied with, will never engage spiritual affections to them. When these things are absent, when the soul hath not experience of them, prayer is but a lifeless form, a dead carcass, which it would be a torment to a soul spiritually alive to be tied to. There may be a season, indeed, when God will seem to hide himself from believers in their prayers, so as they shall neither find that life in themselves which they have done formerly, nor be sensible of any gracious communications from him; but this is done only for a time, and principally to stir them up to that fervency and perseverance in prayer, as may recover them into their former, or a better estate than yet they have attained to. The like may be said concerning all other duties of religion, or ordinances of divine worship.

Fourthly. Believers, whose affections are spiritually renewed, delight greatly in the duties of divine worship, because they are the great instituted way whereby they may give glory to God. This is the first and principal end of all duties of religion, as they respect divine appointment, namely, to ascribe and give to God the glory that is his due; for in them acknowledgment is made of all the glorious excellencies of the divine nature, our dependence on him, and relation to him. And this is that which, in the first place, believers design in all the duties of divine worship. And the pattern set us by our blessed Saviour, in the prayer he taught his disciples, directs us thereto. All the first requests of it concern immediately the glory of God, and the advancement thereof. For therein also all the blessedness and safety of the church is included. Those who fail in this design, err in all that they do; they never tend to the mark proposed to them. But this is that which principally animates the souls of them that believe in all their duties; this, their universal relation to him, and love in that relation, makes necessary. Wherefore, that way and means whereby they may directly and solemnly ascribe and give glory to God, is precious and delightful to them: and such are all the duties of divine worship. These are some of the things wherein the respect of affections spiritually renewed, to ordinances and duties of divine worship, doth differ from the actings of affection towards the same object, which are not so sanctified and renewed.

There are yet other things accompanied with the same evidence of the difference between affections spiritually renewed, and those which have only a general change wrought in them by convictions, and some outward occasions, which must, in one or two instances more, be insisted on, with the consideration of such cases as derive from them. For my design herein is not only to declare when our minds are spiritually renewed, but also what is the nature and operation of our affections, whereby we are consituted and denominated spiritually minded, which is the subject of our whole inquiry. Herein then we shall proceed.

CHAPTER XVI.

Assimilation to things heavenly and spiritual in affections spiritually renewed. This assimilation the work of faith. How, and whereby. Reasons of the want of growth in our spiritual affections, as to this assimilation.

WHEN affections are spiritually renewed in their exercise, or fixing of themselves on spiritual things; there is an assimilation wrought in them, and in the whole soul, to those spiritual and heavenly things by faith. But when there is a change in them only, from other causes and occasions, and not from renewing grace, there is an assimilation effected of spiritual and heavenly things to themselves, to those affections, by imagination.

This must somewhat at large be spoken to, as that which gives the most eminent distinction between the frames of mind, whose difference we inquire into. And to that end we shall cast our consideration of it into the ensuing observations.

First. Affections spiritually renewed are, in all their actings, in the whole exercise, under the guidance and conduct of faith. It is faith which, in its spiritual light, hath the leading of the soul in the whole life of God; we live here by faith, as we do hereafter by sight. If our affections deviate or decline in the least from the guidance of faith, they degenerate from their spirituality, and give up themselves to the service of superstition. Next to corrupt, secular interest, in the management of crafty, selfish seducers, this hath been the great inlet of superstition and false worship in the world. Blind affections, groping in the dark after spiritual things, having not the saving light of faith to conduct them, have seduced the minds of men into all manner of superstitions, imaginations, and practices continuing to do so at this day. And wherever they will lead the way, when faith goeth not before them to discover both way and end, they that lead, and the mind that is led, must fall into one snare and pit or another.

Wherefore, affections that are spiritually renewed, move not, act not, but as faith discovers their object, and directs them to it. It is faith that works by love; we can love nothing sincerely with divine love, but what we believe savingly with divine faith. Let our affections to any spiritual things be never so vehement, if they spring not from faith, if they are not guided by it, they are neither accepted with God, nor will promote the interest of spirituality and holiness to our own souls. Heb. xi. 6. Mat. vi. 22, 23. And this is the reason whence we ofttimes see great and plausible appearances of spiritual affections, which yet endure only for a season. They have been awakened, excited, acted by one means or another, outward or inward; but not having the light of faith to guide them to their proper object, they either wither and die, as to any appearing of spiritual motions, or else keep the mind tossed up and down in perpetual disquietment, without rest or peace. The foolish man wearieth himself, because he cannot find the way to the city. So was it with them, who, on account of their attendance to the doctrine of Christ, are called his disciples. John vi. Having preached to them about the bread which came down from heaven, and giveth life to them that feed, they were greatly affected with it, and cried out, Lord, evermore give us of this bread, v. 34. But when he proceeded to declare the mystery of it, they having not faith to discern and apprehend it, their affections immediately decayed, and they forsook both him and his doctrine, ver. 66.

We may consider one especial instance of this nature. Persons every day fall under great and effectual convictions of sin, and of their danger or certain misery thereby. This stirs up and acts all their affections, especially their fears, hopes, desires, sorrow, self-revenge, according as their condition calls for them. Hence sometimes they grow restless in their complaints, and turn themselves every way for relief, like men that are out of the way and bewildered in the night. But in this state and condition, tell them of the only proper ways and means of their relief, which let the world say what it will, is Christ and his righteousness alone, with the grace of God in him, and they quickly discover that they are strange things to them, such as they do not understand, nor indeed approve. They cannot see them, they cannot discern them, nor any beauty in them, for which they should be desired.

Wherefore, after their affections have been tossed up and down for a season, under the power and torment of this conviction, they come to one or other of these issues with them. For either they utterly decay, and the mind loseth all sense of any impressions from them, so as that they wonder in themselves, whence they were so foolish as to be tossed and troubled with such melancholy fancies, and so commonly prove as bad a sort of men as live upon the earth; or they take up in a formal legal profession, wherein they never attain to be spiritually minded. This is the best end that our affections towards spiritual things, not guided by the light of faith, come to.

Secondly. Faith hath a clear prospect into, and apprehension of, spiritual things, as they are in themselves, and in their own nature. It is true, the light of it cannot fully comprehend the nature of all those things which are the objects of its affections: for they are infinite and incomprehensible, such as are the nature of God, and the person of Christ; and some of them, as future glory, are not yet clearly revealed: but it discerns them all in a due manner, so as that they may in themselves, and not in any corrupt representation, or imagination of them, be the object of our affections. They are, as the apostle speaks, spiritually discerned, 1 Cor. ii. 14, which is the reason why the natural man cannot receive them, namely, because he hath not ability spiritually to discern them. And this is the principal end of the renovation of our minds, the principal quality and effect of faith, namely, the communication to our minds, and the acting in us, of a spiritual saving light, whereby we may see and discern spiritual things as they are in their own nature, kind, and proper use. See Eph. i. 17—19. 'That the God of our Lord Jesus Christ, the Father of Glory, may give to you the spirit of wisdom and revelation in the knowledge of him. The eyes of your understanding being enlightened; that ye may know what is the hope of his calling, and what the riches of the glory of his inheritance in the saints, and what is the exceeding greatness of his power to us-ward who believe, according to the working of his mighty power.' 2 Cor. iv. 6. 'God shines in our hearts, to give the light of the knowledge of his glory in the face of Jesus Christ.' The end God designs, is to draw our hearts and affections to himself. And to this end, he gives to us a glorious internal light, whereby we may be enabled to discern the true nature of the things that we are to cleave to with love and delight. Without this we have nothing but false images of spiritual things in our minds; not always as to the truth or doctrine concerning them, but as to their reality, power, and efficacy. This is one of the principal effects of faith, as it is the principal part of the renovation of our minds, namely, to discover in the soul, and represent to the affections, things spiritual and heavenly, in their nature, beauty, and genuine excellency. This attracts them, if they are spiritually renewed, and causeth them to cleave with delight to what is so proposed to them. He that believes in Christ in a due manner, who thereon discovers the excellency of his person, and the glory of his mediation, will both love him, and on his believing, rejoice with joy unspeakable and full of glory. So is it in all other instances; the more steady is our view by faith of spiritual things, the more firm and constant will our affections be in cleaving to them. And wherever the mind is darkened about them by temptation or seduction from the truth, there the affections will be quickly weakened and impaired. Wherefore,

Thirdly. Affections thus led to, and fixed on, spiritual and heavenly things, under the light and conduct of faith, are more and more renewed, or made in themselves more spiritual and heavenly. They are, in their cleaving to them, and delight in them, continually changed and assimilated to the things themselves; becoming more and more to be what they are, namely, spiritual and heavenly.

This transformation is wrought by faith, and is one of the most excellent faculties and operations; see 2 Cor. iii. 18; and the means whereby it works herein, are our affections. In them, as we are carnal, we are conformed to this world: and by them, as sanctified, are we transformed in the renewing of our minds, Rom. xii. 2. And this transformation is the introduction of a new form or nature into our souls, diverse from that wherewith we were before endued. So is it described, Isaiah xi. 6—9. A spiritual nature they were changed into. And it is two-fold.

First. Original and radical as to the substance or essence of it, which is the effect of the first act of divine grace upon our souls, when we are made new creatures. Herein our affections are passive, they do not transform us, but are transformed.

Secondly. Gradual as to its increase; and therein faith works in and by the affections.

Whenever the affections cleave intensely to any object, they receive an impression from it, as the wax doth from the seal when applied to it, which changeth them into its own likeness. So the apostle affirms of sensual unclean persons; they have eyes full of adultery, 2 Pet. ii. 14. Their affections are so wholly possessed and filled with their lustful objects, as that they have brought forth their own likeness upon their imaginations. That blots out all others, and leaves them no inclinations but what they stir up in them. When men are filled with the love of this world, which carries along with it all their other affections, their hopes, fears, and desires, to a constant exercise about the same object, they become earthly minded. Their minds are so changed into the image of the things themselves, by the effectual working of the corrupt principles of sin, self-love, and lust, as if they were made up of the earth, and therefore have no savor of any thing else.

In like manner, when by faith men come to embrace heavenly things, through the effectual working of a principle of spiritual life and grace in them, they are every day more and more made heavenly. The inward man is renewed day by day. Love is more sincere and ardent, delight is more ravishing and sensible, desires are more enlarged and intense, and by all a taste and relish of heavenly things is heightened into refreshing experience. See Rom. v. 2—5.

This is the way whereby one grace is added to another, 2 Pet. i. 5, 6, in degrees. Great is the assimilation between renewed affections and their spiritual objects, that by this means may be attained.

The mind hereby becomes the temple of God, wherein he dwells by the Spirit; Christ also dwelleth in believers, and they in him. God is love, and he that 'dwelleth in love, dwelleth in God, and God in him.' 1 John iv. 16.

Love, in its proper exercise, gives a mutual inhabitation to God and believers. In brief, he whose affections are set upon heavenly things in a due manner, will be heavenly minded. And in the due exercise of them, will that heavenly mindedness be increased. The transformation and assimilation that is wrought, is not in the object, or spiritual things themselves; they are not changed, neither in themselves, nor in the representation made of them to our minds; but the change is in our affections, which are made like to them.

Two cases deriving from this principle and consideration, may be here spoken to, and shall be so: the first in this, and the other in the following chapter. The one is concerning the slowness and imperceptibility of the growth of our affections in their assimilation to heavenly things, with the causes and reasons of it. The other is, the decays that frequently befall men in their affections to spiritual things, instead of growing and thriving in them, with the reasons and causes thereof.

First. This progress and growth of our affections into spirituality and heavenliness, into conformity to the things they are set upon, is oft-times very slow, and sometimes imperceptible. Yea, for the most part, it is a hard thing to find it satisfactorily in ourselves or others. Our affections stand like shrubs in the wilderness, which see not when good cometh, and are not like plants in a garden enclosed, which are watered every day. But it is not so without our folly and our sin.

The folly that keeps many in this condition, consists herein: the generality of Christians are contented with their present measures, and design little more, than not to lose the ground they have gained. And a pernicious folly it is, that both ruins the glory of religion, and deprives the souls of men of peace and consolation. But so it is, men have some grounds of persuasion, or at least they hope, and suppose they have such grounds, that they are passed from death to life, that they are in a state of grace and acceptance with God. This state they will endeavor to preserve by a diligent performance of the duties it requireth, and the avoidance of such sins whereby they might make a forfeiture of it. But as for earnest watchful endeavors and diligence, to thrive in this state, to grow in grace, to be changed from glory to glory into the image of Christ, to press forward towards the mark of the high calling, and after perfection to lay hold on eternal life, to be more holy, more humble, more righteous, more spiritually minded; to have their affections more and more transformed into the likeness of things above. They are but few, that sincerely and diligently apply themselves to it, or to the means of these things. The measures which they have attained to, give satisfaction to the church, and reputation in the world, that they are professors, and some so speak peace to their own souls. To be more holy and heavenly, to have their affections more taken up with the things above, they suppose somewhat inconsistent with their present occasions and affairs. By this means hath religion lost much of its glory, and the souls of men have been deprived of the principal advantages of it in this world.

Such persons are like to men who live in a country wherin they are not only pressed with poverty, and all sorts of misery; but are also obnoxious to grievous punishments, and death itself, if they are taken in it. In this condition they are told and assured of another country, wherein, so soon as they arrive, they shall be freed from all fear of danger of punishment, and if they pass further into it, they shall meet with riches, plenty, and a fair inheritance provided for them. Hereon they betake themselves to their voyage to obtain an entrance into it, and possession of it. But no sooner do they come within the borders, and so are free from danger, or fear of punishment and death, but they sit down, and will go no further, to enjoy the good things of the country whereto they are come. And it falls out with many of them, that through their sloth, negligence, and ignorance, they take up short of the true bounds and limits of the country of liberty and peace which they aimed at, whereby danger and death surprise them unawares. This ruin could not have befallen them, had they industriously endeavored to enter into the heart of the country, and have possessed the good things thereof. At best, being only in the borders, they lead a poor life all their days, exposed to wants and danger.

So it is in this case. Men falling under the power of convictions, and those restless fears wherewith they are accompanied, will stir up themselves, and inquire how they may fly from the wrath to come, how they may be delivered from the state of sin, and the eternal misery which will ensue thereon.

In the gospel, not only mercy and pardon are proposed to them, on their believing, which is the first entrance into the heavenly country; but peace, and joy, and spiritual strength, upon their admission into it, and a progress made in it by faith and obedience. But many, when they have attained so far, as that they have some hopes of pardon and freedom from the curse, so as to deliver them from their tormenting fears, will endeavor to preserve those hopes, and keep that state; but will not pass on to a full enjoyment of the precious things of the gospel, by growth in grace and spiritual affections. But how many of them fall under woful mistakes! For supposing themselves to be in a gospel state, it proves in the issue, that they never entered into it. They were not, it may be, far from the kingdom of heaven, in the same sense as it was spoken of him who never came thither. There is no way to secure an interest in the gospel, as to pardon and mercy, safety and deliverance, but by a growth in grace, holiness, and spirituality, which gives an entrance in the choicest mercies and privileges of it.

This folly of men in taking up with their measures, endeavoring only to maintain that state and condition which they hope they have attained, is the great reason why their affections do not daily grow up into spirituality, through an assimilation to heavenly things. And a folly it is, attended with innumerable aggravations. As for instance:

First. It is contrary and destructive to the genuine and principal property of gospel grace. For it is every where compared by our Saviour to things which, from small seeds and beginnings, do grow up by a continual increase to large measures, as to a grain of mustard seed, a little leaven, and the like.

That grace in whose nature it is not to thrive and

grow, may justly be suspected, and ought diligently to be examined by them who take care of their own souls, and would not be eternally deceived.

Secondly. It is contrary to the most excellent or invariably evangelical promises recorded in the Old Testament and the New; and which are amongst the principal supportments of the faith, hope, and comfort of believers. God hath given them to us, to encourage us into an expectation of such supplies of grace, as shall cause us to thrive and grow against all opposition, to the utmost of our continuation in this world. And they are so multiplied as that there is no need to mention any of them in particular; God evidencing thereby how great is the grace, and how precious, which he so often promiseth, and of what consideration it is of to ourselves. See Psal. xcii. 13—15. Isa. xl. 28—31. Wherefore the folly of taking up with present measures of grace, holiness, and spirituality, is attended with two unspeakable evils.

First. A signal contempt of the love, grace, faithfulness, and wisdom of God, in giving us such promises of grace, to make us increase, thrive, and grow. How can it be done more effectually, than by such a neglect of his promised grace?

Secondly. An evidence that such persons love not, care not, for grace or holiness for their own souls, but merely to serve their turn at present, as they suppose, nor to desire the least of grace or privilege by Christ, without which they can have no hopes to get to heaven. This sufficiently discovers men to be wholly under the power of self love, and to centre therein; for if they may have so much grace and mercy as may save them, they care for no more.

Thirdly. It is repugnant to the honor of gospel

grace, as though it would carry us so far, and no further, in the way to glory. For it must be known, that this sort of persons who sit down in their present measures and attainments, either really have no grace at all, or that which is of the lowest, meanest, and most imperceptible size and degree. For if any one hath attained any considerable growth in faith and love, in the mortification of sin, in heavenly mindedness, it is utterly impossible but that ordinarily he will be pressing forward towards further attainments, and further degrees of spiritual strength in the life of God. So the apostle declares it in his own example. Phil. iii. 10—14. What thoughts can these persons have concerning the glory, power, and efficacy of gospel grace which they suppose they have received? If they measure them by the effects which they find in themselves, either as to the mortification of sin, or strength to, and delight in, duties of holiness, or as to spiritual consolation, they can see no excellency nor beauty in them: for they do not manifest themselves but in their success, as they transform the soul daily into the image of Christ.

Fourthly. It is that which hath lost the reputation and glory of religion in the world, and therein the honor of the gospel itself; for the most part of professors do take up with such lustre upon it, as gives no commendation to the religion they profess; for their measures allow them such a conformity to the world, in their ways, words, and actions, in their gestures, apparel, and attire, as that they are no way visibly to be distinguished from it. Yea, the ground and reason why the most do rest in their present measures is, because they will not be further differenced from the world. This hath greatly lost the glory, honor, and reputation of religion amongst us: and, on the other side, if all visible professors would endeavor continually to grow and thrive in spirituality of mind, and heavenliness of affections, with fruits suitable thereto, it would bring a conviction on the world, that there is a secret invisible power accompanying the religion they profess, transforming them daily into the image and likeness of God.

Fifthly. Whatever is pretended to the contrary, it is inconsistent with all solid peace of conscience; for no such thing is promised to any who live in such a contempt of divine promises; nor is it attainable, but by the diligent exercise of all those graces which lie neglected under this frame. Few men are able to judge whether they have real, eternal, abiding peace, or not, unless it be in case of trials and temptations. At other seasons, general hopes and confidences do or may supply the want of it in their minds; but when any fear, danger, trial, or word of conviction befalls them, they cannot but inquire and examine how it is with them. And if they find their affections cold, dead, earthly, carnal, withering, not spiritual or heavenly, there will be an end of their supposed peace, and they will fall into woful disquietments; and they will then find that the root of all this evil lies in this frame and disposition. They have been so far satisfied with their present measures or attainments in religion, as that the utmost of their endeavors have been but to preserve their station, or not to forfeit it by open sins, to keep their souls alive from the severe reflections of the word, and their reputation fair in the church of God. Spiritually to thrive, to prosper in their souls, to wax fat and flourishing in the inward man, to bring forth more fruit as age increaseth, to press towards perfection, are things they have not designed nor pursued.

Hence it is that so many among us are visibly at an unthrifty stand in the world: that where they were one year, there they are another, like shrubs in the wilderness, not like the plants in the garden of God, not as vines planted in a very fruitful hill. Yea, though many are sensible themselves that they are cold, lifeless, and fruitless, yet will they not be convinced that there is a necessity of making a daily progress in spirituality and heavenly mindedness, whereby the inward man may be renewed day by day, and grace augmented with the increase of God. This is a work, as they suppose, for them who have nothing else to do; not consistent with their business, callings, and occasions; not necessary, as they hope, to their salvation, nor, it may be, to be attained by them if they should set themselves about it. This apprehension or imagination, upon the beginning of the declension and decay of Christian religion in the many, cast off all holiness and devotion to a sort of men who undertook to retire themselves utterly out of the world; amongst whom also the substance of religion was quickly lost, and a cloud, or meteor of superstition, embraced in the room of it. But this folly is ominous to the souls of men.

Those who have made the greatest progress in the conformity of their affections to things spiritual and heavenly, know most of its necessity, excellency, and desirableness; yea, without some progress in it, these things will not be known. Such will testify, that the more they attain herein, the more they see is yet to be attained, and the more they desire to attain what is behind. 'Forgetting those things which are behind, they reach forth unto the things that are yet before them; like men running in a race, whose prize and reward is yet before them.' Phil. iii. 13, 14. It is a comely thing to see a Christian weaned from the world, minding heavenly things, green and flourishing in spiritual affection. And it is the more lovely because it is so rare. The generality of them take up with those measures which neither glorify God, nor bring durable peace to their own souls.

That which men pretend and complain of herein, is the difficulty of the work. They can, as they suppose, preserve their present station; but to press forward, to grow in grace, to thrive in their affections, this is too hard for them. But this complaint is unequal and unjust, and adds to the guilt of their sloth. It reflects upon the words of our Saviour, that his yoke is easy, and his burden light, that his commandments are not grievous. It expresseth unbelief in the promises of God, tendering such supplies of grace, as to render all the ways of wisdom easy, yea, mercy and peace. It is contrary to the experience of all who have, with any sincerity and diligence, engaged in the ways of gospel obedience; and the whole cause of the pretended difficulty lies in themselves alone, which may be reduced to these two heads.

First. A desire to retain some thing, or things, that is, or are, inconsistent with such a progress: for unless the heart be ready on all occasions to esteem every thing as loss and dung, so as we may win Christ, the work will be accompanied with insuperable difficulties. This is the first principle of religion, of gospel obedience, that all things are to be despised for Christ. But this difficulty ariseth not from the thing itself, but from our indisposition to it, and unfitness for it. That which is an easy, pleasant walk to a sound and healthy man, is a toilsome journey to him that is diseased and infirm. In particular, whilst men will retain an inordinate respect to the world, the vanities, the pleasures, the profits, the contentments of it; whilst self-love, putting an undue valuation on our persons, our relations, our enjoyments, our reputations, doth cleave to us, we shall labor in the fire when we engage in this duty, or, rather, we shall not at all sincerely engage in it; wherefore the apostle tells us that, in this case, we must cast off every weight, and the sin that doth so easily beset us, if we intend to run with joy the race that is set before us. Heb. xii. 1.

Secondly. It is because men dwell continually upon the entrances of religion, in the first and lowest exercise of grace, some are always beginning at religion, and the beginning of things is always difficult. They design not to be complete in the whole will of God, nor to give all graces their perfect work. They do not, with use, habituate grace to a readiness in all the actings of it, which the apostle commends in them that are perfect and complete. Heb. v. 14. Hence he calls such persons babes and carnal, comparatively to them that are strong men and spiritual. Such persons do not oblige themselves to the whole work, and all the duties of religion, but only what they judge necessary to them in their present circumstances. In particular, they do not attempt a thorough work in the mortification of any sin, but are hewing and hacking at it, as their convictions are urgent, or abate the wounds whereof in the body of sin, are quickly healed. They give not any grace its perfect work, but are always making essays, and so give over.

Whilst it is thus with any, they shall always be

deluded with the apprehensions of insuperable difficulties, as to the growth of their affections in spirituality and heavenliness. Remove these things out of the way, as they ought to be removed, and we shall find all the paths wherein we are to walk towards God to be pleasantness and peace.

This is the first cause whence it is, that there may be affections truly spiritual and graciously renewed in some persons, who yet do not thrive in an assimilation and conformity to heavenly things. Men take up with their present measures, and thereon pretend either necessary occasion, or discouragement from difficulties, in attempting spiritual growth in the inward man. But they may thank themselves, if, as they bring no honor to Christ, so they have no solid peace in their own souls.

Secondly. As the evil proceedeth from folly, so it is always the consequent of sin, of many sins, of various sorts. Let us not dwell on heartless complaints that we do not find our affections lively and heavenly, that we do not find the inward man to thrive or grow. Let us not hearken after this or that relief or comfort, under this consideration, as many things are usually insisted on to that purpose. They may be of use when persons are under temptations, and not able to make a right judgment of themselves, but in the course of our ordinary walking with God, they are not to be attended or retired to. The general reason of this evil state, is our own sinful carelessness, negligence, and sloth, with, perhaps, an indulgence to some known lust or corruption. And we do in vain seek after refreshing cordials, as though we were only spiritually faint, when we stand in need of lancings and burnings, as nigh to a lethargy: it would be too long to give instances of these sins, which fail not effectually to obstruct the thriving of spiritual affections. But in general, when men are careless as to that continual watch which they ought to keep over their hearts; whilst they are negligent in holy duties, either as to the seasons of them, or in the manner of their performance; when they are strangers to holy meditation and self-examination; whilst they inordinately pursue the things of the world, or are so tender and delicate as that they will not undergo the hardship of an heavenly life, either as to the inward or outward man; much more when they are vain in their conversation, corrupt in their communication, especially if under the predominant influence of any particular lust; it is in vain to think of thriving in spiritual affections. And yet thus it is with all who ordinarily, and in their constant course, are thriftless herein.

CHAPTER XVII.

Decays in spiritual affections, with the causes and danger of them. Advice to them who are sensible of the evil of spiritual decays.

It must be acknowledged, that there is yet that which is worse than what we have yet insisted on, and more opposite to the growth of affections in conformity to heavenly things, which is the proper character of those that are spiritually renewed. And this is their spiritual decay, manifesting itself in sensible and visible effects.

Some there are, yea, many, who, upon the beginning of a profession of their conversion to God, have made a great appearance of vigorous, active, spiritual affections; yea, it is so with most, it may be all, who are really so converted. God takes notice of the love of the youth in his people, of the love of their espousals.

In some, this vigor of spiritual affections is from the real power of grace, exerting its efficacy on their hearts and in their minds. In others, it is from other causes, as for instance, relief from conviction, by spiritual illumination, will produce this effect. And this falls out to the advantage of such persons, that generally a change is wrought in their younger days. For then their affections, in their natural powers, are active, and bear great sway in the whole soul. Wherefore the change that is made, is most eminent in them, be it what it will. But as men increase in age, and thereon grow up in carnal wisdom, and a great valuation of earthly things, with their care about them, and converse in them, they abate and decay in their spiritual affections every day. They will abide in their profession, but have lost their first love.

It is a shame and folly unutterable, that it should be so with any who make profession of that religion, wherein there are so many incomparable excellencies to endear and engage them to it more and more; but why should we hide what experience makes manifest in the sight of the sun; and what multitudes proclaim concerning themselves? Wherefore, I look upon it as a great evidence, if not absolutely of the sincerity of grace, yet of the life and growth of it, when men, as they grow up in age, grow in an undervaluation of present things, in contempt of the world, in duties of charity and bounty, and decay not in any of them. But I say, it is usual that the entrances of men's profession of religion and conversion to God, are attended with vigorous active affections towards spiritual things.

Of them, who really and sincerely believed, it is said, that on their believing, they rejoiced with joy unspeakable and full of glory. And of those who only had a work of conviction on them, improved by temporary faith, that they received the word with joy, and did many things gladly.

In this state do many abide and thrive, until their affections be wholly transformed into the image and likeness of things above. But with many of all sorts it is not so; they fall into woful decays as to their affections about spiritual things, and consequently in their whole profession and conversation, their moisture becomes as the drought in summer. They have no experience of the life and actings of them in themselves, nor any comfort, or refreshment from them; they honor not the gospel with any fruits of love, zeal, or delight, nor are useful any way to others by their example. Some of them have had seeming recoveries, and are yet again taken into a lifeless frame: warnings, afflictions, sicknesses, the word, have awakened them, but they are fallen again into a dead sleep; so as that they seem to be trees whose fruit withereth; without fruit; twice dead; plucked up by the roots.

Some things must be spoken to this woful condition in general, as that which is directly opposite to the grace and duty of being spiritually minded; and contrary to, and obstructive of, the growth of spiritual affections in an assimilation unto heavenly things. And what shall be spoken, may be applied to all the degrees of these decays, though all of them are not alike dangerous or perilous.

First. There may be a time of temptation, wherein a soul may apprehend in itself not only decay in, but an utter loss of, all spiritual affections, when yet it is not so. As believers may apprehend and judge, that the 'Lord hath forsaken and forgotten them, when he hath not done so,' Isaiah xlix. 14, 15; so they may, under temptations, apprehend that they have forsaken God, when they have not done so: as a man in the night may apprehend he hath lost his way, and be in great distress, when he is in his proper road. For temptation brings darkness and amazement, and leads into mistakes and a false judgment in all things. They find not, it may be, grace working in love, joy, and delight, as formerly, nor that activity of heart and mind in holy duties, which spiritual affections gave to them. But yet it may be, the same grace works in godly sorrow by mourning, humiliation, and self-abasement, no less effectually, nor less acceptably to God. Such as these I separate from the present consideration.

Secondly. There may be a decay in affections themselves, as to their actings towards any objects whatever; at least as to the outward symptoms and effects of them, and on this ground, their operations towards spiritual things may be less sensible. So men in their younger days may be more ready to express their sorrow by tears, and their joy by sensible exaltation and motion of their spirits, than in riper years. And this may be so, when there is no decay of grace in the affections as renewed. But,

(1.) When it is so, it is a burthen to them in whom it is. They cannot but mourn and have a godly jealousy over themselves, lest the decays they find, should not be in the outward, but in the inward, not in the natural, but the spiritual, man. And they will labor, that in all duties, and at all times, it may be with them as in days of old, although they cannot attain strength in them, that vigor of spirit, that life, joy, peace, and comfort, which any have had experience of.

Secondly. There will be in such persons, no decays in holiness of life, nor as to diligence in all religious duties. If the decay be really of grace in the affections, it will be accompanied with a proportionable decay in all other things, wherein the life of God is concerned. But if it be only as to the sensible actings of natural affections, no such decay will ensue.

Thirdly. Grace will, in this case, more vigorously act itself in the other faculties and powers of the soul, as the judgment and the will in their approbation of and firm adherence to spiritual things. But,

Fourthly. When men find, or may find, their affections yet quick, active, and intent on other things, as the lawful enjoyments and comforts of this life; it is in vain for them to relieve themselves, that the decays they find are in their affections as natural, and not as they ought to conclude, as gracious If we see a man in his old age grow more in love with the things of this world, and less in love with the things of God, it is not through the weakness of nature, but through the strength of sin.

On these, and it may be, some other the like occasions, there may be an apprehension of a decay in spiritual affections, when it may not be so, at least not to the degree that is apprehended. But when it is so really, as it is evidently with many, I had almost said with the most in these days, it is a woful frame of heart, and never enough to be lamented. It is that which lies in direct contradiction to that spiritual mindedness which is life and peace. It is a consumption of the soul which threatens it with death every day.

It belongs not to my design to treat of it in particular; yet I cannot let it pass without some remarks upon it, it being an evil almost epidemical among professors, and prevalent in some to such a degree, as that they seem to be utterly forsaken of all powers of spiritual life.

Now, besides all that folly and sin, which we before discovered as the causes of the want of the growth of our affections in spirituality and heavenliness, which in this case of their decay are more abominable, there is a multiplication of evils wherewith this state of heart and mind is accompanied. For,

First. It is that which of all things the Lord Christ is most displeased with in churches or professors. He pities them in their temptations, he suffers with them in their persecution, he intercedes for them on their surprisal, but threatens them under their spiritual decays. Rev. ii. 4, 5, and iii. 2. This he cannot bear with, as that which both reflects dishonor upon himself, and which he knows to be ruinous to those in whom it is. He will longer bear with them who are utterly dead, than with those who abide under these decays. Rev. iii. 15, 16. This is the only case wherein he threatens to reject and cast off a professing church; to take away his candlestick from it, unless it be that of false worship and idolatry. He that spake thus to the churches of old, speaks now the same to us; for he lives forever, and is always the same, and his word is living and unchangeable. There is not one of us who are under this frame, but the Lord Christ, by his word and Spirit, testifieth his displeasure against us; and if he be against us, who shall plead for us? Consider what he says in this case, Rev. ii. 5, and iii. 8. O, who can stand before these dreadful intimations of his displeasure! the Lord help us to mind it, lest he in whom we profess to place our only trust, be in our trial found our greatest enemy. Take heed of such sins as Christ himself, our only advocate, hath put a mark upon as those which he will not save us in.

Secondly. It is that wherewith above all things the Holy Spirit is grieved. His work it is to give an increase and progress in our souls. He begins it, and carries it on. And there can be no greater grief to a wise and gracious workman, than to have his work decay and go backward under his hand. This is the occasion of those complaints of God which we find in the scripture, of the unprofitableness and backsliding of men, after the use of means and remedies for their fruitfulness and cure. 'What,' saith he, 'could I have done more for my vineyard than I have done? Why then, when I looked for grapes, did it bring forth wild grapes?' Can any thing be apprehended to be such a just matter of grief and complaint to the Holy Spirit, as to see and find those whom he had once raised up to holy and heavenly affections, so as that their delights were in, and their thoughts much upon, the things that are above, to become earthly or sensual, to have no sensible actings of any of his graces in them, which is the state of them who are under the power of spiritual decays? And this is the only cause wherein God speaks to men in the way of complaint and expostulation; and useth all sorts of arguments to convince them of their folly herein.

Wherein a wise, tender, and careful parent, hath been diligent in the use of all means for the education of his child, and he for some time hath given good hopes of himself, finds him to slacken in his diligence, to be careless in his calling, to delight in evil company; how solicitous is his heart about him, how much is he grieved and affected with his miscarriage! The heart of the Spirit of God is infinitely more tender towards us, than that of the most affectionate parent can be towards an only child. And when he with cost and care hath nourished, and brought us up to some growth and progress in spiritual affections, wherein all his concerns in us lie, for us to grow cold, dull, earthly minded, to cleave to the pleasures or lusts of this world, how is he grieved, how is he provoked! It may be this consideration of grieving the Holy Spirit, is of no great weight with some; they should have little concernment herein, if they could well free themselves in other respects; but let such persons know, it is impossible for them to give a greater evidence of a profligate hardness in sin.

Thirdly. This is that which in an especial manner provoketh the judgments of God against any church, as was intimated before: When, in the order of profession and worship, any church hath a name to live, but as to the power of grace acting in the affections, is dead; when it is not so cold as to forsake the external institutions of worship, nor so hot as to enliven their duties with spiritual affections, the Lord Christ will not long bear with them; yea, judgment will suddenly break out towards such a house of God.

Fourthly. It is absolutely inconsistent with all comfortable assurance of the love of God. Whatever persons, under the power of such a frame, pretend to of that kind, it is sinful security, not gracious assurance or peace; and constantly, as professors grow old and decay in their spiritual affections, stupidity of conscience and security of mind grow also upon them.

It is so, I say, unless they are sometimes surprised or overtaken with some greater sin, which reflects severely on their consciences, and casts them for a time under troubles and distresses. But that peace with God, and a comfortable assurance of salvation, should be consistent with a habitual decay in grace, especially in those graces which should act themselves in our affections; is contrary to the whole tenor and testimony of the scripture: and the supposition of it would be the bane and poison of religion. I do not say that our assurance and peace with God, arise wholly from the actings of grace in us; there are other causes of them, whereto they are principally resolved: but this I say, under a habitual declension, or decay of grace in the spirituality of our affections, no man can keep or maintain a gracious sense of the love of God, or of peace with him. And therefore there is no duty more severely to be pressed on all at this day, than a diligent examination and trial of the grounds of their peace; lest it should be with any of them as it was with Laodicea, who was satisfied in her good state and condition, when it was most miserable, and almost desperate. Yea, I must say that it is impossible that many professors, whom we see and converse with, should have any solid peace with God. Do men gather figs from thorns, or grapes from thistles? It is a fruit that will not grow on a vain, earthly, selfish frame of mind and conversation: and therefore such persons, whatever they pretend, are either asleep in a sinful security, or live on most uncertain hopes, which probably may deceive them. Nothing can be so ruinous to our profession, as once to suppose it is an easy matter, a thing of course, to maintain our peace with God. God forbid that our utmost diligence, and continued endeavors to thrive in every grace, should not be required thereto. The whole beauty and glory of our religion depends hereon. To be spiritually minded is life and peace.

Fifthly. Such a decay as that described, is a dangerous symptom of an evil state and condition, and that those in whom it is, will at last be found to be but hypocrites. I know such persons will or may have pretended evidences to the contrary, and are well enough satisfied of, and with, their own sincerity, in many things; so as that it is impossible to fix upon them the sense and conviction of being but hypocrites. But this apprehension ariseth from a false notion of hypocrisy. No man they suppose is a hypocrite, but he that generally or universally pretends himself in religion to be what he is not, and what he knows himself not to be, or at least, might easily know. And it is true that this is the broadest notion of Pharisaical hypocrisy. But take a hypocrite for him who under light, profession, gifts, duties, doth habitually and willingly fail in any point of sincerity, he is no less a perishing hypocrite than the former, and it may alter the case with them. I do not say that every one in whom there is this prevalent decay in spiritual affections, is a hypocrite; God forbid: I only say that where it continues without remedy, it is such a symptom of hypocrisy, as that he who is wise, and hath a care of his soul, will not rest until he hath searched it to the bottom. For it seems as if it were thus with such persons, they have had a false or imperfect work in that conversion unto God which they have professed. Conviction of sin, communication of spiritual light and gifts, alteration upon the affections, change of society and conversation, have made it up. Now it is the nature of such a work greatly to flourish for a season, in all the principal parts and duties of profession: but it is in its nature also gradually to decay, until it be quite withered away: in some, it is lost by the power of some vigorous temptations, and particular lusts indulged to, ending in worldliness and sensuality; but in the most, it decays gradually, until it hath lost all its savor and sap. See Job xv. 3. Wherefore, whilst men find this decay in themselves, unless they are fallen under the power of a destructive security, unless they are hardened through the deceitfulness of sin, they cannot but think it their duty to examine how things stand with them, whether they ever effectually closed with Christ, and had the faith of God's elect, which works by love; seeing it is with them, as though they had only a work of another nature. For a saving work in its own nature, and in the diligent use of means, thrives and grows, as the whole scripture testifieth; but it is this false and imperfect working that hath no root, and is thus subject to withering.

Sixthly. Persons in such an estate are apt to deceive themselves with false hopes and notions, whereby the deceitfulness of sin doth put forth its power, to harden them to their ruin. Two ways there are whereby this pernicious effect is produced. The one by the prevalency of a particular lust or sin, the other by a neglect of spiritual duties, and a vain conversation in the world, under which the soul pines away and consumes.

As to the first of these, there are three false notions, whereby the deceitfulness of sin deludes the souls of men.

The first is, that it is that one sin alone wherein they would be indulged. Let them be spared in this one thing, and in all others they will be exact enough.

This is the composition that Naaman would have made in the matters of religion, 2 Kings v. 18. And it is that which many trust to. Hence it hath by the event been made to appear, that some persons have lived long in the practice of some gross sins, and yet all the while used a semblance of great diligence in other duties of religion. This is a false notion whereby poor sinners delude their own souls. For suppose it possible that a man should give himself up to any lust, or be under the power of it, and yet be observant of all other duties, yet this would give him no relief as to the eternal condition of his soul. The rule is peremptory to this purpose. Jam. ii. 10, 11. One sin willingly lived in, is as able to destroy a man's soul, as a thousand. Besides, it is practically false. There is no man that lives in any one known sin, but he really lives in more, though that only bears the chiefest sway. With some such persons, these sins appear to others, who observe their frame and spirit, though they appear not to themselves: in some they are manifest in themselves, although they are hidden from others. 1 Tim. v. 24. But let no man relieve himself with thoughts that it is but one sin, whilst that one sin keeps him in a constant neglect of God. Hence,

Secondly. They deceive themselves hereby; for they judge, that although they cannot as yet shake off their sin, yet they will continue still to love God, and abound in the duties of his worship. They will not become haters of God and his ways, and persecutors, for all the world; and therefore hope that, notwithstanding this one Zoar, this lesser sin, which their constitution and their circumstances engage them in, that it may be well with them at the last. This, also, is a false notion, a mere instrument in the hand of sin to act its deceit by: for no man that willingly liveth in any sins can love God at all; as is evident in that rule, 1 John ii. 15. It is but a false pretence of love to God that any man hath, who liveth in any known sin. Where God is not loved above all, he is not loved at all: and he is not so, where men will not part with one cursed lust for his sake. Let not your light deceive you, nor your gifts, nor your duties, nor your profession; if you live in sin, you love not God.

Thirdly. They determine, that at such or such a season or time, after such satisfaction given to their lusts or pleasures, they will utterly give over, so as that iniquity shall not be their ruin. But this is a false notion also, an effectual instrument of the deceitfulness of sin. He that will not now give over, who will not immediately upon the discovery of the prevalency of any sin, and warning about it, endeavor sincerely and constantly its relinquishment, say what he will, and pretend what he will, he never intends to give over; nor is it probable in an ordinary way that ever he will do so. When men's decays are from the prevalency of particular sins, by these and the like false notions they harden themselves to ruin.

For those who are pining away under a hectical consumption, a general decay of the vital spirits of religion, they have also false notions whereby they deceive themselves. As,

First. That although they have some cause to mistrust themselves, yet indeed their condition is not so bad as some may apprehend it, or as they are warned it is. And this ariseth from hence, that they have not as yet been overtaken with any enormous sin which hath filled their consciences with terror and disquietment. But this is a false notion also; for every decay is dangerous, especially such as the mind is ready to plead for, and to countenance itself in.

Secondly. They are prone to suppose that this decay doth not arise from themselves, and the evil of their own hearts, but from their circumstances, business, present occasion, and state of life, which when they are freed from, they will at least return to their former love and delight in spiritual things. But this is a false notion also, by virtue of that rule, Heb. iii. 12. Let men's circumstances and occasions of life be what they will, all their departures from God are from an evil heart of unbelief.

Thirdly. They judge it no hard matter to retrieve themselves out of this state, but that which they can easily do, when there is an absolute necessity for it. But this is a false notion also. Recovery from backsliding is the hardest task in the Christian religion, and which few make either comfortable or honorable work of.

In this state, I say, men are apt by such false reasonings to deceive themselves to their eternal ruin, which makes the consideration of it the more necessary.

Wherefore I say, lastly, upon the whole, that whoso find themselves under the power of this wretched frame, who are sensible in themselves, or at least make it evident to others, that they are under a decay in their spiritual condition; if they rest in that state, without groaning, laboring, endeavoring for deliverance from it, they can have no well grounded hopes in themselves of life and immortality; yea, they are in those paths which go down to the chambers of death.

I cannot let this pass, without something of advice to them who find themselves under such decays, who are sensible of them, and would be delivered from them; and I shall give it in a few words.

First. Remember former things: call to mind how it was with you in the spring and vigor of your affections, and compare your present state, enjoyment, peace, and quiet, with what they were then. This will be a great principle of return to God. Hos. ii. 7. And to put a little weight upon it, we may consider,

First. God himself makes it, on his part, a ground and reason of his return to us in a way of mercy, and of the continuance of his love. Jer. ii. 2. Even when a people are under manifold decays, whilst yet they are within the bounds of God's covenant and mercy, he will remember their first love, with the fruits and actings of it in trials and temptations, which moves his compassion towards them. And the way to have God thus remember it, is for us to remember our former experience with delight, and longing of soul that it were with us as in those days of old, when we had the love of espousals of God in Christ, Jer. xxxi. 18—20.

Secondly. It is the way whereby the saints of old have refreshed and encouraged themselves under their greatest despondencies. So doth the Psalmist in many places, as for instance, Ps. xlii. 6. 'O my God, my soul is cast down within me: therefore will I remember thee from the land of Jordan, and of the Hermonites, from the hill Mizar.' David, in the time of his persecution by Saul, when he wandered up and down in deserts, wildernesses, and solitudes, had, under his fears, distresses, and exercise, great, holy, spiritual communion with God, as many of his psalms composed on such occasions testify. And the greater his distresses were, the more fervent were his affections in all his addresses to God. And he was never in greater, than when he escaped out of the cave at Adullam, and went thence unto Mizpeh of Moab, to get shelter for his parents, 1 Sam. xxii. 13. Then was he in the land of the Hermonites, the hill Hermon being the boundary eastward of the Israelites' possession, next to Moab, Deut. iii. 8, 9. There, no doubt, David had a blessed exercise of his faith, and of all his affections towards God, wherein his soul found great refreshment. Being now in great distress and disconsolation of spirit, among other things, under a sense that God had forgotten him, ver. 9, he calls to mind the blessed experience he had of communion with God in the land of the Hermonites, wherein he now found support and refreshment. So at other times he called to remembrance the days of old, and in them his song in the night, or the sweet refreshment he had in spiritual converse with God in former times. I have known one in the depth of distress and darkness of mind, who, going through temptation to destroy himself, was relieved and delivered in the instant of ruin, by a sudden remembrance that at such a time, and in such a place, he had prayed fervently with the engagement of all his affections to God.

Wherefore, you that are sensible of these decays or ought so to be, take the advice of our Saviour, remember whence you are fallen; call to mind the former days; consider if it were not better with you than now: when, in your lying down and your rising up, you had many thoughts of God, and of the things of God, and they were sweet and precious to your souls; when you rejoiced at the remembrance of his holiness; when you had zeal for his glory, delight in his worship, and were glad when they said, 'Let us go to the house of God together;' when you poured forth your souls with freedom and enlarged affections before him, and were sensible of the visits and refreshments of his love: remember what peace, what tranquility of mind, what joy you had whilst it was so with you; and consider what you have gotten since you have forsaken God, in any measure or degree. Dare to deal plainly with yourselves. Is not all wherein you have to do with God, either from custom and selfishness, or attended with trouble, disquietment, and fears? Do you truly know either how to live or how to die? Are you not sometimes a terror to yourselves? It must be so, unless you are hardened through the deceitfulness of sin. What have all your lovers done for you, that you have entertained in the room of God in Christ, and spiritual things? Speak plainly; have they not defiled you, wounded you, weakened you, and brought you into that condition, that you know not what you are, nor to whom ye do belong? What are your thoughts when your are most awake, when you are most yourselves? Do you not sometimes pant within yourselves, and say, O that it were with us as in former days?

And if you can be no way affected with the remembrance of former things, then one of these two great evils you are certainly under: Either, (1.) You never had a true and real work on your souls, whatever you professed; and so never had true and real communion with God in any duties: you had only a temporary work, which excited your affections for a season, which, now it is worn off, leaves no sweet remembrance of it upon your minds; for had your faith and love been sincere in what you did, it were impossible but that the remembrance of their actings in some especial instances, should be sweet and refreshing to you. Or else,

(2.) You are hardened through the deceitfulness of sin, and there is no way left to give a sense or impression of spiritual things upon your minds. You have truly nothing left in religion, but the fear of hell and trouble of duties. I speak not to such at present.

As to those to whom this frame is a burden, there is no more effectual means to stir them to endeavors for deliverance, than a continual remembrance of former things, and experiences they have had of holy intercourse and communion with God. This will revive, quicken, and strengthen the things that are ready to die, and beget a self-abhorrency in them, in consideration of that woful frame and temper of mind, which by their sins and negligence they have brought themselves into.

2dly. Consider, that as there are many things dreadfully pronounced in the Scripture against backsliding and backsliders in heart, as it is with you; yet also there are especial calls and promises given and made to those in your condition. And know assuredly, that upon your compliance or non-compliance with them, depends your everlasting blessedness or wo.

Consider both call and promise in that word of God's grace, Jer. iii. 12—14. 'Go and proclaim these words towards the north, and say, Return, thou backsliding Israel, saith the Lord, and I will not cause mine anger to fall upon you: for I am merciful, saith the Lord, and I will not keep anger for ever. Only acknowledge thine iniquity, that thou hast transgressed against the Lord thy God, and hast scattered thy ways to the strangers under every green tree, and ye have not obeyed my voice, saith the Lord. Turn, O backsliding children, saith the Lord, for I am married unto you: and I will take you one of a city, and two of a family, and I will bring you to Zion.' Add thereto this blessed promise, Hos. xiv. 14. 'I will heal their backslidings, I will love them freely: for mine anger is turned away from them.' If you design to live and not die, it must be by yielding obedience to this call, and pleading this promise before God, mixing it with faith. Your return must be by the word, Isa. lvii. 18, 19. Here lies your great encouragement and direction; herein lieth your only relief. As you value your souls, defer not the duty you are called to one moment. You know not how soon you may be without the reach of calls and promises. And he that can hear them without stirring up himself in sincerity to comply with them, hath made already a great progress towards that length.

(3.) As to those who, on these and the like considerations, do not only desire, but will endeavor also to retrieve themselves from this condition, I shall give no advice at present but this: be in good earnest. As the prophet speaks in another case; if you will return, return and come, make thorough work of it. You must do so at one time or another, or you will perish. Why not now? Why is not this the best season? Who knows but it may be the only time you will have for it? It were easy to multiply all sorts of arguments to this purpose. Trifling endeavors, occasional resolutions and attempts, like the early cloud, and morning dew, shifting with warnings and convictions by renewed duties, until their impressions are worn out, will ruin your souls. Unless there be universal diligence and permanency in your endeavors, you are undone. Then shall ye know the Lord, if you follow on to know him.

But now to return. These things I say, through our sloth, negligence, and sin, may befall us as to our spiritually renewed affections. Their progress, in conformity to spiritual and heavenly things, may be slow, imperceptible, yea, totally obstructed, for a season; and not only so, but they may fall under decays, and the soul therein be guilty of backsliding from God. But this is that which they are capacitated for by their renovation; this is that whereby the grace wherewith they are renewed leads to; this is that which, in the diligent use of means, they will grow up to, whereon our comfort and peace depend; namely, a holy assimilation to those spiritual and heavenly things which they are set and fixed on, wherein they are renewed and made more spiritual and heavenly every day.

CHAPTER XVIII.

It remains only as to this head now spoken to, that we briefly consider what is the state of spiritual affections thus daily exercised and improved. And this we shall do by showing,

(1.) What is their pattern.

(2.) What is their rule.

(3.) What is their measure, or whereto they may attain.

First. The pattern which we ought continually to bear in our eyes, whereto our affections ought to be conformed, is Jesus Christ, and the affections of his holy soul. The mind is the seat of all our affections; and this is that which we ought continually to design and endeavor, namely, that the same mind be in us that was in Christ Jesus, Phil. ii. 5. To have our minds so affected with spiritual things as was the mind of Christ, is the principal part of our duty and grace. Nor do I think that any man can attain any considerable degree in spiritual mindedness, who is not much in the contemplation of the same mind that was in Christ, 2 Cor. iii. 18. To this purpose, ought we to furnish our minds with instances of the holy affections that were in Christ, and their blessed exercise on all occasions. The scripture makes a full representation of them to us, and we ought to be conversant in our meditations on them. What glorious things are spoken of his love to God, and his delight in him, whence also he delighteth to do his will, and his law was in the midst of his bowels, Psal. xl. 8, seated in the throne of his affections! What pity and compassion had he for the souls of men, yea, for the whole human kind, in all their sufferings, pains and distresses! How were all his affections always in perfection of order, under the conduct of the spirit of his mind! Thence was his self-denial, his contempt of the world, his readiness for the cross, to do or suffer according to the will of God. If this pattern be continually before us, it will put forth a transforming efficacy to change us into the same image. When we find our minds liable to any disorders, cleaving inordinately to the things of this world, moved with intemperate passions, vain and frothy in conversation, darkened or disturbed by the fumes of distempered lusts, let us call things to an account, and ask of ourselves, whether this be the frame of mind that was in Christ Jesus? This, therefore, is an evidence that our affections are spiritually renewed, and that they have received some progress in an assimilation to heavenly things: namely, when the soul is delighted in making Christ their pattern in all things.

Secondly. The rule of our affections in their utmost spiritual improvements, is the scripture. And two things are respected in them:

(1.) Their internal actings.

(2.) Their exercise in outward ways and means whereby they are expressed. Of them both, the scripture is the entire rule. And with respect to the former, it gives us one general law, or rule, that is comprehensive of all others; namely, that we love the Lord our God with all our hearts, souls, minds, and strength. The actings of all our affections towards God, in the utmost degree of perfection, is required of us; that in all instances we prefer and value him above all things; that we inseparably cleave to him, and do nothing whatever, at any time, that is not influenced and directed by the love of God. This perfection, as we shall see immediately, is not attainable absolutely in this life; but it is proposed to us as that which the excellency of God's nature requires, which the powers and faculties of our nature were created for, and which we ought in all things to design and aim at. But the indispensable obligation of this rule is, that we should always be in a sincere endeavor to cleave to God continually in all things, to prefer him above all, and delight in him as our chiefest good. When this frame and disposition is habitually fixed in our minds, it will declare and act itself in all instances of duties, on all occasions of trial, when other things put in for a predominant interest in our affections, as they do every day. And if it be not so with us, we shall be at a continual loss in all our ways. This is that which makes us lifeless and heartless in duties, careless in temptations or occasions of them, forgetful of God, when it is impossible we should be preserved from sin without a due remembrance of his holiness. In brief, the want of a predominant love to God, kept in continual exercise, is the spring of all that unprofitable profession of religion that the world is filled with.

Secondly. There are outward ways and duties whereby our spiritual affections are expressed. The rule of them also is the scripture. The way marked out therein, is the only channel wherein the stream of our spiritual affections takes its course to God. The graces required therein, are to act themselves by this rule: the duties it prescribes, are those which they stir up and enliven; the religious worship which it appoints, is that wherein they have their exercise. Where this rule hath been neglected, men's religious affections have grown irregular, yea, wild and ungovernable. All the superstitions that the world is filled with, owe their original principally to men's affections set loose from the rule of the word. There is nothing so fond, absurd, and foolish, but they have imbondaged the souls of men to; nothing so horrid and difficult but they have engaged them in. And having once taken to themselves this liberty, the corrupt minds of men are a thousand times more satisfied than in the regular exercise of them according to the word of God. Hence they will rejoice in such penances as are not without their austerities; in such outward duties of devotion as are troublesome and chargeable; in every thing that hath a show of wisdom in will worship, and humility and neglect of the body. Hence will all their affections be more sensibly moved by images and pictures, and a melting devotion be stirred up in them, than by all the motives and incentives which God proposeth to them to draw their affections to himself. Nothing is more extravagant than the affections of men, tinctured with some devotion, if they forsake the rule of the scripture.

Thirdly. There is considerable concerning them, the measure of their attainments, or what, through due exercise and holy diligence, they may be raised to. Now this is not absolute perfection. 'Not as though I had already attained, or were already perfect, but I follow after,' as the apostle speaks, Phil. iii. 12. But there is that attainable, which those who pretend highly to perfection seem to be strangers to. And the state of our affections under a due exercise on heavenly things, and in their assimilation to them, may be fixed in these three things:

(1.) An habitual suitableness to spiritual things upon the proposal of them. The ways whereby spiritual things are proposed to our minds are various. They are so, directly, in all ordinances of divine worship; they are so, indirectly, and in just consequence, by all the especial providences wherein we are concerned by our own thoughts and stated meditations; they are so by the motions of the Holy Spirit, when he causeth us to hear a word behind us, saying, this is the way, walk in it; by holy converse with others; by all sorts of occurrences. And as the ways of their proposal are various, so the times and seasons wherein a representation of them is made to us, are comprehensive of all, at least are not exclusive of any, times and seasons of our lives. Be the way of their proposal what it will, and whenever be the season of it, if our affections are duly improved by spiritual exercises, they are suited to them, and will be ready to give them entertainment. Hence, or for want hereof, on the other hand, are tergiversations and shiftings in duties, proneness to comply with diversion, all to keep off the mind from closing with, and receiving of, those spiritual things which it is not suited to. Wherefore, as to the solemn way of proposing spiritual things to our minds which is in and by the ordinances of divine worship, when men have a prevalent loathness to engage in them, or when they are satisfied with an outward attendance on them, but are not enabled to a vigorous stirring up of the inward man, to an holy affectionate converse with spiritual and heavenly things, it is because they are carnal. When men can receive the fiery darts of Satan in his temptations into their bosoms, and suffer them to abide there, yea, foster and cherish them in thoughts of the lusts that they kindle, but quickly quench the motions of the Spirit, stirring them up to the embracing of heavenly things; they are carnal, and carnally minded. When providences of concernment in afflictions, trials, deliverances, do not engage the mind in thoughts of spiritual things, and excite the affections to the attainment of them, men are carnal and earthly. When every lust, corruption, or passion—as anger, envy, displeasure at this or that person or thing, can divert the mind from compliance with the proposal of spiritual things that is made to it, we are carnal.

It is otherwise, when our affections are conformed to things spiritual and heavenly. Upon every proposal of this, the mind finds a suitableness to itself, like that which a well disposed appetite finds to savory meat. As the full soul loathes the honey comb, so a mind under the power of carnal affections, hath an aversion to all spiritual sweetness. But spiritualized affections desire them, have an appetite to them, readily receive them on all occasions, as those which are natural to them, as milk is to new born babes.

(2.) Affections so disposed, constantly find a gust, a pleasant taste, a relish, in spiritual things. They do in them taste that the Lord is gracious, 1 Pet. ii. 3. To taste of God's goodness, is to have an experience of a savory relish and sweetness, in converse and communion with him. And persons whose affections are thus renewed and thus improved, do taste a sweet savor in all spiritual things. Some of them, as a sense of the love of Christ, are sometimes as it were too hard for them, and overpower them, until they are sick of love, and rejoice with joy unspeakable and full of glory. Neither is there any of them, however conflicted with afflictions or mortifications, but is sweet to them, Prov. xxvii. 7. Every thing that is wholesome food, that is good nourishment, though it be but bitter herbs, is sweet to him that is hungry. And when by our affections we have raised up in us a spiritual appetite to heavenly things, however any of them in their own nature, or in their dispensation, may be bitter to flesh and blood, as are all the doctrines of the cross, they are all sweet to us, and we can taste how gracious the Lord is in them. When the soul is filled with earthly things, the love of this world, or when the appetite is lost by spiritual sickness, or vitiated and corrupted by any prevalent sin, heavenly things are unsavory and sapless, or, as Job speaks, like the white of an egg, wherein there is no taste. There may be in the dispensation of the word a taste, or pleasing relish, given to the fancy; there may be so to the notional understanding, when the affections find no complacency in the things themselves. But to them who are spiritually minded to the degree intended, they are all sweet, savory, pleasant; the affections taste them immediately, as the palate doth meat.

(3.) They are a just repository of all graces, and therein the treasury of the soul. There are graces of the spirit, whose formal direct residence is in the understanding and the will, as faith itself. And therein are all other graces radically comprised; they grow from that root. Howbeit the most of them have their principal residence in the affections. In them are they preserved secure and ready for exercise, on all occasions: and when they are duly spiritual, there is nothing that tends to their growth or improvement, to their cherishing or quickening, which they stand in need of continually, and which God hath made provision for in his word, but they readily receive it, lay it up, keep and preserve it. Hereby they come to be filled with grace, with all graces; for there is room in them for all the graces of the spirit to inhabit; and they readily comply with the light and direction of faith to their exercise. When faith discerns and determines that there is any thing to be done or suffered in a way of duty to the glory of God, the affections thus disposed do not shut up or stifle the graces that are in them, but cheerfully offer them to their proper exercise.

These are some of those things, which our affections, conformed to heavenly things, will attain to. And thus it is with affections spiritually renewed; by being fixed on things spiritual and heavenly, they are more and more conformed to them, made like them, and become more spiritual and heavenly themselves.

It is not thus with them whose affections have only an occasional change wrought upon them by the means before described, but are not spiritually renewed; yea, on the contrary, such persons design to debate spiritual things, to bring down heavenly things into a conformity with their affections, which, however changed, are not spiritual, but carnal. To evince this, we may observe,

(1.) These affections are under the light and conduct of such notions in the mind and understanding, as do not give a clear distinct representation of them in their own nature to them. For where they are not themselves spiritually renewed, there the mind itself is carnal and unrenewed. And such a mind discerneth not the things of God, nor can do so, because they are spiritually discerned. They cannot be discerned aright in their own beauty and glory, but in and by a spiritual saving light, which the mind is devoid of. And where they are not thus represented, the affections cannot receive, or cleave to them as they ought, nor will ever be conformed to them.

(2.) Those notions in such persons are ofttimes variously influenced and corrupted by fancy and imagination. They are merely puffed up in their fleshly minds; that is, they are filled with vain, foolish, proud imaginations, about spiritual things, as the apostle declares, Col. ii. 18, 19. And the work of fancy in a fleshly mind, is to raise up such images of spiritual things as may render them suitable to natural unrenewed affections.

(3.) This in the progress of it produceth superstition, false worship, and idolatry. For they are all of them an attempt to represent spiritual things in a way suited to carnal unrenewed affections; hence men suppose themselves to be excited by them to love, joy, fear, delight, in the things themselves, when they all respect that false representation of them, whereby they are suited to them as carnal. These have been the spring of all false worship and idolatry in the Christian world.

First. The mind and affections have been changed and tinctured with devotion by some of the means we have before insisted on. Herein they will one way or other be exercised about spiritual things, and are ready to receive impressions from any thing that superstition can impose upon them.

Secondly. They are, by error and false information, set at liberty from the only rule of their actings and exercise, that is, the word of God. Men satisfied themselves that so their affections were engaged about things spiritual and heavenly, it was no matter at all, whether the way of their exercise was directed by the scripture or not. Having thus lost their guide and their way, every *ignis fatuus*, every wandering meteor, allures them to follow its conduct into foolish superstitions. Nothing almost is so ridiculous, nothing so horrid and difficult, that they will not embrace under the notion of things spiritual and heavenly.

Thirdly. The carnal minds of men, having no proper distinct apprehensions and notions of spiritual things in their own nature, endeavor to represent them under such notions and images as may suit their carnal unrenewed affections. For it is implanted almost indelibly upon them, that the end of all knowledge of spiritual things is to propose them to the embraces of the affections. It were easy to manifest, that from these three corrupt springs, arose that flood of idolatry and false worship which spread itself over the church of Rome, and with whose machinations the minds of men are yet too much replenished.

Fourthly. Where it is not thus, yet carnal affections variously debase spiritual things, to bring them into a conformity with themselves. And this may proceed so far, until men think wickedly, that God is altogether like to them. But I shall not insist on these things any further.

Lastly. Where affections are spiritually renewed, the person of Christ is the centre of them; but where they are changed only, they tend to an end in self. Where the new man is put on, Christ is all in all, Col. iii. 10, 11. He is the spring, by his Spirit, that gives them life, light, and being; and he is the ocean that receives all their streams. God, even the Father, presents not himself in his beauty and amiableness as the object of our affections, but as he is in Christ, acting his love in him, 1 John iv. 8, 9. And as to all other spiritual things, renewed affections cleave to them, according as they derive from Christ and lead to him; for he is to them all and in all. It is he whom the souls of his saints love for himself, for his own sake, and all other things of religion in and for him. The air is pleasant and useful, that without which we cannot live or breathe; but if the sun did not enlighten it, and warm it with its beams; if it were always one perpetual night, and cold, what refreshment could be received by it? Christ is the sun of righteousness, and if his beams did not quicken, animate, and enlighten the best, the most necessary duties of religion, nothing desirable would remain in them. This is the most certain character of affections spiritually renewed. They can rest in nothing but in Christ; they fix on nothing but what is amiable by a participation of his beauty; and in whatever he is, therein they find complacency. It is otherwise with them whose affections may be changed, but are not renewed. The truth is, and it may be made good by all sorts of instances, that Christ in the mystery of his person, and in the glory of his meditation, are the only things that they dislike in religion. False representations of him by images and pictures, they may embrace; and delight in false notions of his present glory, greatness, and power, may affect them; a worship of their own devising they may give to him, and please themselves in it; corrupt opinions concerning his office and grace, may possess their minds, and they may contend for them; but those who are not spiritually renewed, cannot love the Lord Jesus Christ in sincerity: yea, they have an inward secret aversion from the mystery of his person and his grace. It is self which all their affections centre in, the ways whereof are too long here to be declared.

This is the first thing that is required, to render our affections in such a state and condition, as that from and by them we may be spiritually minded, namely, that they themselves are spiritually and savingly renewed.

The things that remain will admit of a speedy dispatch, as I suppose.

CHAPTER XIX.

The second thing required that we may be spiritually minded, as to the interest of our affections therein, is the object of them about which they are conversant, and whereto they adhere. What this is materially, or what are the spiritual things which our affections are to be set upon, hath been declared already, under the consideration of the object of our thoughts and meditations, for they are the same. Yea, as hath been intimated, the fixing of our affections upon them is the spring and cause of our thoughts about them.

But that which we shall now inquire into, is the true notion and consideration of spiritual and heavenly things, which renders them the formal proper object of spiritual affections, and is the reason of their adherence to them. For, as was intimated before, men may have false notions of spiritual things, under which they may like them and embrace them with unrenewed affections. Wherefore we shall inquire into some of those considerations of heavenly things, under which affections, spiritually renewed, satisfactorily cleave to with delight and complacency.

(1.) And the first is, that as they comprehend God in Christ, and in all other things, as deriving from him, and tending to him, they have an infinite beauty, goodness, and amiableness in them, which are powerfully attractive of spiritual affections, and which alone are able to fill them, to satisfy them, to give them rest and acquiescency. Love is the most ruling and prevalent affection in the whole soul: but it cannot be fixed on any object without an apprehension, true or false, of an amiableness and desirableness in it, from a goodness suitable to all its desires.

And our fear, so far as it is spiritual, hath divine goodness for its object, Hos. iii 5. Unless this be that which draws our hearts to God, and the things of God, in all pretences of love to him, men do but frame idols to themselves, according to their own understanding, as the prophet speaks, Hos. viii. 2. Wherefore, that our affections may cleave to spiritual things in a due manner, three things are required.

(1.) That we apprehend, and do find a goodness, a beauty, and thence an amiableness and desirableness in them, Zech. ix. 17. Many pretend to love God and spiritual things, but they know not why. Why they love other things, they know well enough, but why they love God, they cannot tell. Many are afraid of him, and suppose they ought to love him, and therefore pretend so to do, though indeed they know they do not; they do but flatter him with their lips, when their hearts are far from him. Some are much affected with the benefits and mercies they receive from him, and suppose they love him on that account. But this love is no other but what the devil falsely charged Job with, chap. i. 8—11. Some have delight in the outward modes and rites of divine worship, wherewith they satisfy themselves that they love God and spiritual things, when they only please their own imaginations and carnal minds. Many have a traditional apprehension that they ought to love God; they know no reason why they should not; they know it will be ill for them if they do not, and these take it for granted that they do. How few are there, who have that spiritual discerning and apprehension of the divine excellencies, that view of the excellency of the goodness and love of God in Christ, as thereby alone to be drawn after him, and to delight in him! yet is this the ground of all sincere real love to God. Two things are required that we may apprehend an amiable goodness in any thing, and cleave to it with sincere affection.

First. A real worth, or excellency in itself.

Secondly. A suitableness therein to our condition, state, and desires after blessedness. The first of these is in God, from what he is in himself; the latter is from what he is to us in Christ; from both he is the only suitable object to our affections. Under this apprehension do we love God for himself, or for his own sake; not exclusively to our own advantage therein:

for a desire of union and enjoyment, which is our only advantage, is inseparable from this love.

It may be, some cannot say that a distinct apprehension of these things was the first foundation and cause of their love to God; yet are they satisfied that they do love him in sincerity with all their souls. And I say, it may be so. God sometimes casts the skirts of his own love over the heart of a poor sinner, and efficaciously draws it to himself, without a distinct apprehension of these things, by a mere sense of the love it hath received. So Elijah passed by Elisha, and cast his mantle upon him as a transient act. But there was such a communication of virtue thereby, that he ran after him, and would not be deferred, though Elijah said, Go back again, for what have I done to thee? 1 Kings xix. 19, 20. When God hath so cast his love on any soul, it follows after him with all its affections. And whereas God may seem, at some times, to say, Go back again, for what have I done to thee? its answer is, Lord, whither shall I go? I cannot leave thee, my heart is given up to thee, and shall never be taken from thee.

But I say to such, and to all others, that if we would have refreshing evidences of our love to God, that it is sincere, if we would have it thrive and flourish, be fervent and constant, we are to exercise ourselves to the contemplation of divine goodness, and the suitableness of it to our souls in and by Jesus Christ. Nor can we cleave to any spiritual things whatever, with sincere affections, but under these notions of it.

First. That it hath a real worth or excellency in itself.

Secondly. That it is suitable and desirable to us. And it is to be bewailed to see how many walk at random in profession, that know neither what they do nor where they go.

Secondly. As we must see a goodness and probableness in spiritual things absolutely, so that we may fix our affections on them in a due manner, so we must see it comparatively with respect to all other things, which gives them a preference in our affections before and above them all. The trial of love lies in the prevailing degree, on more or less. If we love other things, father, mother, houses, lands, possesions, more than Christ, we do not love him at all. Nor is there any equality allowed in this matter, that we may equally love temporal and spiritual things. If we love not Christ more than all these things, we love him not at all. Wherefore, that our affections may cleave to them in a due manner, we must see an excellency in things spiritual and heavenly, rendering them more desirable than all other things whatever.

With what loving countenances do men look upon their temporal enjoyments! with what tenacious embraces do they cleave to them! They see that in them which is amiable, which is desirable and suitable to their affections. Let them pretend what they please, if they see not a greater goodness, that which is more amiable, more desirable in spiritual things, they love them not in a due manner; it is temporal things that hath the rule of their affections. Our Psalmist prefers 'Jerusalem before his chiefest joy,' Ps. cxxxvii. 6. Another affirms, that the 'law of God's mouth was better to him than thousands of gold and silver,' Ps. cxix. 72. More to be desired are the 'statutes of the Lord than gold, yea, than much fine gold; sweeter also than honey, or the honey comb,' Ps. xix. 10. For 'wisdom is better than rubies, and all things that may be desired are not to be compared unto it,' Prov. viii. 11. This is the only stable foundation of all divine affections. A spiritual view and judgment of a goodness, an excellency in them, incomparably above whatever is in the most desirable things in this world, are required thereto. And if the affections of many pretending highly to them, should come to be weighed in this balance, I fear they would be found light and wanting. However, it is the duty of them who would not be deceived in this matter, which is of eternal importance, to examine what is that goodness and excellency which is in spiritual things, which they desire in them, upon the account whereof they sincerely value and esteem them above all things in this world whatever. And let not any deceive themselves with vain words and pretences, whilst their esteem and valuation of present enjoyments doth evidently engage all their affections, their care, their diligence, their industry, so as that a man of a discerning spirit may even feel them turned into self, whilst they are cold, formal, negligent, about spiritual things, we must say, how dwelleth the love of God in them? Much more, when we see men not only giving up the whole of their time and strength, with the vigor of their spirits, but sacrificing their consciences also, to the attaining of dignities, honors, preferments, wealth, and ease in the world, who know in their own hearts that they perform religious duties with respect to temporal advantages, I cannot conceive how it is possible they should discern and approve of a goodness and excellency in spiritual things above all others.

A due consideration is required hereto, that all spiritual things proceed from, and are resolved into, an infinite fountain of goodness, so as that our affections may absolutely come to rest and complacency, and find full assured satisfaction in them. It is otherwise as to all temporal things. Men would fain have them to be such as might give absolute rest and satisfaction to all their affections. But they are every one of them so far from it, that all of them together cannot compose their minds in rest and peace for one hour. They gain sometimes a transport of affections, and seem for a season to have filled the whole soul, so as it hath no liesure to consider their emptiness and vanity. But a little composure of men's thoughts, show that they are but a diversion in a journey or labor; they are no rest. Hence are they called broken cisterns, that will hold no water. Let a man prize them at the highest rate that it is possible for a rational creature to be seduced into the thoughts of, whereof there have been prodigious instances; let him possess them in abundance, beyond whatever any man enjoyed in this world, or his own imagination could beforehand reach to; let him be assured of the utmost peaceable continuance in the enjoyment of them that his and their natures are capable of: yet would he not dare to pretend, that all his affections were filled and satisfied with them, that they afforded him perfect rest and peace. Should he do so, the working of his mind every day, would convince him of his falsehood and folly.

But all spiritual things derive from, and lead to, that which is infinite, which is therefore able to fill all our affections, and to give them full satisfaction with rest and peace. They all lead us to the fountain of living waters, the eternal spring of goodness and blessedness.

I do not say that our affections do attain to this full rest and satisfaction in this life: but what they come short of therein, ariseth not from any defect in the things themselves to give this rest and satisfaction, as it is with the whole world; but from the weakness of our affections themselves, which are in part only renewed, and cannot take in the full measures of divine goodness, which in another world they will receive. But whilst we are here, the more we receive them into our minds and souls, the more firmly we adhere to them, the nearer approaches we make to our rest and centre.

Secondly. Spiritual things are to be considered as they are filled with divine wisdom. I speak not of himself, whose essential wisdom is one of the most amiable excellencies of his holy nature; but of all the effects of his will and grace by Jesus Christ. All spiritual truths, all spiritual and heavenly things, whereby God reveals and communicates himself to the souls of men, and all the ways and means of our approach to him in faith and obedience through Christ Jesus, I now intend. All these are filled with divine wisdom. See 1 Cor. ii. 7. Eph. i. 8, 9, and iii. 10. Now wisdom in itself, and in all the effects of it, is attractive of rational affections. Most men are brutish in them and their actings, for the most part pouring them out on things fleshly, sensual, and carnal. But where they are at all reduced under the conduct of reason, nothing is so attractive of them, so suited to them, which they delight in, as that which hath at least an appearance of wisdom. A wise and good man commands the affections of others, unless it be their interest to hate and oppose him, as commonly it is: and where there is true wisdom in the conduct of civil affairs, sober men cannot but approve of it, like it, delight in it; and men of understanding bewail the loss of it, since craft, falsehood, treachery, and all sorts of villany, have driven it out of the world. So is divine wisdom attractive of divine gracious affections. The Psalmist declares his admiration of, and delight in, the works of God, because 'he hath made them all in wisdom,' Ps. civ. 24. Those characters of divine wisdom which are upon them, which they are filled with, draw the souls of men into a delightful contemplation of them. But all the treasures, all the glory of this wisdom, are laid up, and laid forth, in the great spiritual things of the gospel in the mystery of God in Christ, and the dispensation of his grace and goodness to us by him The consideration hereof fills the souls of believers with holy admiration and delight, and thereon they cleave to them with all their affections. When we see there is light in them, and all other things are in darkness, that wisdom is in them, in them alone, and all other things are filled with vanity and folly, then are our souls truly affected with them, and rejoice in them with joy unspeakable and full of glory.

Unto the most, this wisdom of God is foolishness. It was so of old, as the apostle testifieth, 1 Cor. i. And so it continues yet to be. And therefore is the mystery of the gospel despised by them; they can see neither form nor comeliness in it, for which it should be desired. Nor will ever any man have sincere spiritual affections to spiritual things, who hath not a spiritual view of the wisdom of God in them.

This is that which attracts our souls by holy admiration to unspeakable delight. And the reason why men do so generally decline from any love to the gospel, and lose all satisfaction in the mystery of it is, because they are not able to discern that infinite wisdom which is the spring, life, and soul of it. When our minds are raised to the admiration of this wisdom in divine revelations, then will our affections cleave to the things that are revealed.

Thirdly. The acting of our affections in their adherence to spiritual things, is perfective of our present state and condition. That which of all other things doth most debase the nature of man; wherein it makes the nearest approaches to brutality; yea, whereby it becomes in some respects more vile than the nature of beasts, is the giving up of the affections to things sensual, unclean, base, and unworthy of its more noble principles. Hence are men said to debase themselves unto hell, Isa. lvii. 9. And their affections become vile; so as that their being under the power of them, is an effect of revenging justice punishing men for the worst of sins, Rom. i. 26. There is nothing more vile, nothing more contemptible, nothing more like to beasts in baseness, and to hell in punishment, than is the condition of them who have enslaved their nature to brutish sensual affections. I say vile affections fixed on, and cleaving to, sensual objects, debase the nature of man, and both corrupt and enslave all the more noble faculties of it; the very consciences and minds of men are defiled by them. If you see a man whose affections are set inordinately on any thing here below, it is easy to discern how he goes off from his native worth, and debaseth himself therein.

But the fixing of spiritual affections on spiritual objects, is perfective of our present state and condition. Not that we can attain perfection by it; but that therein our souls are in a progress towards perfection.

This may be granted; look how much vile affections fixed on, and furiously pursuing things carnal and sensual, debase our nature beneath its rational constitution, and make it degenerate into bestiality: so much spiritual affections fixed on, and cleaving to things spiritual and heavenly, exalt our nature above its mere natural capacity, making an approach to the state of angels, and of just men made perfect. And as brutish affections, when they have the reins, as they say, on their necks, and are pursued with delight and greediness, darken the mind, and disturb all the rational powers of the soul, (for whoredom, and wine, and new wine, do take away the heart, as the prophet speaks, and wickedness altereth the understanding;) so holy affections fixed on spiritual things, elevate, enlarge and enlighten the mind with true wisdom and understanding. For the fear of the Lord, that is wisdom; and to depart from iniquity, that is understanding. And again, as the power of vile affections fills the soul and conscience with tumult, disorder, fear, and shame, where men are not utterly profligate, so as that the minds, thoughts, and consciences of persons under their power, is a very hell for confusion and troubles; so spiritual affections, duly exercised on their proper objects, preserve all things in order in the whole soul, they are life and peace. All things are quiet and secure in the mind; there is order and peace in the whole soul, in all its faculties, and all their operations; whilst the affections are in a due prevailing manner fixed upon the things that are above. Hence many persons, after great turmoilings in the world, after they have endeavored by all means to come to rest and satisfaction therein, have utterly renounced all concernments in earthly things, and betaken themselves to the contemplation of things above, and that only. Many, I confess, of them, were mistaken as to the practical part of their devotions, having various superstitions imposed on their minds by the craft of others; but they missed it not in the principle, that tranquility of mind was attainable only in setting our affections upon things above. Jam. iv. 1. 'From whence come wars and fightings among you? come they not hence, even of your lusts that war in your members?' Whence are all the disorders in your minds, your vexations and disquietments, your passions breaking forth sometimes into unseemly brawlings? are they not from hence? The question is put to yourselves and your own consciences, namely, from your lusts, that is, the disorderly affections that tumultuate in you. Do but search yourselves, and you will quickly see whence all your troubles and disquietments arise. Your lusts, or corrupt and inordinate affections, war in you, continually inclining you to things earthly or sensual. Hence many are best and most at quiet when they are in the world, worst when at home in their families; but never are they in such confusion, as when they are forced to retire into themselves.

The due exercise of our affections on heavenly things, hath quite another tendency and effect. It so unites the mind to them, it so bringeth them to it, and gives them such a substance in it, as that all the powers and faculties of it are in a progress towards their perfection. See 2 Cor. vii. 1. True wisdom and understanding, with soundness of judgment, in eternal things, in the mind, holiness in the affections themselves, liberty in the will, power in the heart, and peace in the conscience, do in their measures all ensue hereon. Whatever tastes we may have of these things, whatever temporary experience we have of them, they will not flourish in us, they will not abide with us in any constancy, unless we are thus spiritually minded.

Fourthly. In the future enjoyment of the present object of our spiritual affections, our eternal blessedness consists. All men who are convinced of a future eternal condition, desire, when they depart hence, to enter into blessedness and glory. Howbeit, what that blessedness, even as to the general nature of it is, they know nothing at all; and if they did, they would not know how to desire it. For heaven or blessedness is nothing but the full enjoyment of what we are here to love and delight in above all of that which is the object of our affections as spiritually renewed. Herein have they neither interest nor concern; but this is that which giveth life to the affections of believers; they know that in the enjoyment of God in Christ their eternal blessedness doth consist. How this is their happiness and glory, how it will give them an everlasting overflowing satisfaction and rest, they understand in the first fruits of it which they here receive. And this is the ultimate object of their affections in this world, and they go forth to all other spiritual things in order thereto. The more, therefore, their affections are fixed on them, the more they are kept up to that due exercise, the nearer approaches they make to this blessed state. When their minds are possessed with this persuasion, when it is confirmed in them by daily experience of that sweetness, rest, and satisfaction, which they find in cleaving to God with fervent love and delight, in vain shall any other objects rise up in competition to draw them off to themselves. The more we love God, the more like we are to him, and the more near the enjoyment of him.

CHAPTER XX.

Having considered the nature of spiritual affections as renewed by grace, and those notions of their objects under which they cleave to them, it remains only that we inquire into the way of the soul's application of self to those objects by its affections, which belong also to our being spiritually minded. And I shall give an account hereof in some few particulars, with brief observations on them.

First. It is required that our adherence to all spiritual things, with love and delight, be firm and stable. The affections are the powers and instruments of the soul, whereby it makes application to any thing without itself and cleaves to it. This is their nature and use with reference to things spiritual. Transient thoughts of spiritual things, with vanishing desires, may rise out of present convictions, as they did with them who cried out to our Savior, Lord, give us evermore of this bread, and immediately left him. Such occasional thoughts and desires are common to all sorts of men, yea, the worst of them; let me die the death of the righteous, and let my end be as his. Fading satisfaction, with joy and delight, often befall men in their attendance on the word, who yet never come to have it rooted in their hearts.

There are sundry things wanting to the sincerity of these affections.

(1.) Those in whom they are, never had a clear spiritual view of the things themselves in their own nature, which they pretend to be affected with

(2.) They have not a sincere love to them, and

delight in them, for their own sakes, but are only affected with some outward circumstances and concernments of them.

(3.) They find not a suitableness in them to the ruling principles of their minds. They do not practically, they cannot truly say, the yoke of Christ is easy and his burden is light; his commandments are not grievous; or, with the Psalmist, Oh! how do I love thy law.

(4.) Their affections are transient, unstable, vanishing, as to their exercise and operations. They are on and off, now pleased, and anon displeased; earnest for a little while, and then cold and indifferent. Hence the things which they seem to effect, have no transforming efficacy upon their souls; they dwell not in them, in their power.

But where our affections to spiritual things are sincere, where they are the true genuine application of the soul, and adherence to them, they are firm and stable; love and delight are kept up to such a constant exercise, as renders them immovable; this is that which we are exhorted to, 1 Cor. xv. 58. Therefore, my beloved brethren, be ye steadfast, unmovable, always abounding in the work of the Lord, forasmuch as ye know that your labor is not in vain in the Lord. Transient affections, with their occasional operations, deceive multitudes: ofttimes they are pregnant in their actings, as those that are most sincere: and many effects in joys, in mournings, in complaints, they will produce, especially when excited by any outward affliction, sickness, and the like. But their goodness is like the early cloud, or morning dew. Let none, therefore, please themselves with the operations of transient affections with respect to spiritual things, be they never so urgent, or so pleasant, or so frequent in their returns; those that are sincere, are at all times firm and stable.

2. That the soul do find a spiritual relish and savor in the things which it so adheres to. The affections are the palate of the soul, whereby it tastes of all things which it receiveth or refuseth; and it will not long cleave to any thing which they find not a savor and relish in. Something was spoken before of that sweetness which is in spiritual things; and the taste of them consists in a gracious sense of their suitableness to the affections, inclinations, and dispositions of the mind. Hence they have no relish to men of carnal minds. Whoever, therefore, would know whether his affections do sincerely adhere to spiritual things, let him examine what relish, what sweetness, what savor he findeth in them. When he is pleased with them, as the palate with suitable and proper food, when he finds that he receives nourishment by them in the inward man, then doth he adhere to them in a due manner.

The spiritual taste is the ground of all experience; it is not what we have heard or understood only, but what we have tried and tasted, whereof we have experience. This makes us long for what we have formerly enjoyed, and strengthens faith, as to what we pray for and expect.

In every darkness, in every damp of spirit, under every apprehension of deadness, or the withdrawing of the sense of divine love, the soul knoweth what it wants, and what it doth desire. O! saith such an one, that it were now with me as in former days! I know he who then gave me such refreshing tastes of his own goodness, who made every thing of himself sweet and pleasant to me, can renew this work of his grace towards me; he can give me a new spiritual appetite and relish, and he can make all spiritual things savory to me again.

As a man under a languishing sickness, or when he is chastened with strong pain, so as that his soul abhorreth bread, and his daily meat, can remember what appetite he had, with what gust and relish he was wont to take his food in the days of his health, which makes him to know that there is such a condition, and to desire a return to it. So it is with a sin-sick soul; it can find no relish, no gust, no sweetness in spiritual things: he finds no savor in the bread of the word, nor any refreshment in the ordinances of the gospel, which yet in themselves are daily meat, a 'feast of fat things, and of wine well refined;' yet doth he remember former days, when all these things were sweet to him, and if he have any spark of spiritual life yet remaining, it will stir him up to seek with all diligence after a recovery. How is it with you, who are now under spiritual decays; who find no taste nor relish in spiritual things? to whom the word is not savory, nor other ordinances powerful? Call to mind how it hath been with you in former days, and what ye found in these things; if so be, saith the apostle, that you have tasted that the Lord is gracious. If you have not, it is to be feared that you have never yet had the least sincere love to spiritual things; for where that is, it will give a spiritual relish of them. If you have, how is it you can give yourselves rest one moment, without an endeavor after the healing of your backsliding?

(3.) It is required that our affections be so set on spiritual things, so as to be a continual spring of spiritual thoughts and meditations. No man can be so forsaken of reason, as to suppose that he hath any sincere affections for what he thinks little on, or not at all; or that he can have a true affection for any thing which will not stir up, and ingenerate in him continual thoughts about it. Let men try themselves as to their relations, or their employments, or the objects of their predominant lusts, and they will find how things are stated in their own minds. And, therefore, whereas all men pretend to love God and Christ, and the ways of God, and yet know in their own hearts that they little think of them, or meditate upon them, both their pretence and religion is vain. Where our affections are duly placed on heavenly things, so as that we are indeed spiritually minded, they will be a constant spring of spiritual thoughts and meditations. But this also hath been before spoken to.

Fourthly. When our affections are thus applied to spiritual things, they will be prevalent and victorious against solicitations to the contrary, or allurements to draw them off to any other objects. The work of all our spiritual adversaries, is to solicit and tempt our affections, to divert them from their proper object. There are some temptations of Satan that make an immediate impression on the mind and conscience. Such are his injection of diabolical blasphemous thoughts concerning God, his being, nature, and will; and the distresses which he reduceth men to in their consciences, through darkness, and misrepresentations of God and his goodness. But the high road and constant practice of all our spiritual adversaries, is by the solicitation of our affections to objects that are in themselves, or in the degree of our affections towards them, evil and sinful. Of the first, are all sensual pleasures of the flesh, in drunkenness, uncleanness, gluttony, chambering, and wantonness, with all sorts of sensual pleasures. Of the latter, is all our inordinate love to self, our families, and the whole world, or the things of it. To this end, every thing in the whole world that may make provision for lust is made use of. Herein consists the nature and efficacy of most of those temptations which we have to conflict with. Solicitations they are of our affections, to draw them off from things spiritual and heavenly, and to divert them to other things. Hereby do our enemies endeavor to beguile us, as the serpent beguiled Eve, with fair and false representations of other beloveds, that our hearts be not preserved, as a chaste virgin, in all their affections for Christ.

And it is almost incredible how apt we are to be beguiled by the specious pretences wherewith we are solicited.

That our affections in the degree treated about, suppose of love to the world and the things of it, are lawful and allowable, is one of the sophisms and artifices wherewith many are deluded. Hereon, provided they run not out into scandalous excesses, they approve of themselves in such a worldly frame of mind, and acting according to it, as renders them fruitless, useless, senseless, and is inconsistent with that prevailing adherence of affections to spiritual things, that ought to be in us. Others are deluded by a pretence, that it is in one instance only they would be spared; it is but this or that object they would give out the embraces of their affections to; in all other things they will be entire for God: the vanity of which pretence we have spoken to before. Others are ruined by giving place to their solicitations, with respect to any one affection whatever. As suppose it be that of fear. In times of danger for profession, multitudes have lost all their affections to spiritual things, through a fear of losing that which is temporal, as their lives, their liberties, their goods, and the like. When once Satan or the world have gotten, as it were, the mastery of this affection, or a prevalent interest in it, they will not fail to draw all others into a defection from Christ and the gospel. He that loves his life shall lose it.

Wherefore it is no ordinary nor easy thing to preserve our affections pure, entire, and steady in their vigorous adherence to spiritual things, against all these solicitations. Watchfulness, prayer, faith in exercise, and a daily examination of ourselves are required hereto. For want of a due attendance to these things, and that with respect to this end, namely, the preservation of our spiritual affections in their integrity, many, even before they are aware, die away as to all power and vigor of spiritual life.

Fifthly. Affections thus fixed upon things spiritual and heavenly, will give great relief against the remainders of that vanity of mind which believers themselves are ofttimes perplexed with. Yea, I do not know any thing that is a greater burden to them, nor which they more groan for deliverance from. The instability of the mind, its readiness to receive impressions from things vain and useless, the irregularity of their thoughts, are a continual burden to many. Nothing can give the soul any relief herein, nothing can give bounds to the endless vanity of foolish imaginations, nothing can dry up the springs from whence they arise, or render the soil wherein they grow barren, as to their production and maintenance, but only the growth of spiritual affections, with their continual vigorous actings on heavenly things: for hereby the heart and mind will be so united to them, (that which the Psalmist prays for, Psal. lxxxvi. 11,) as that they will not be ready to depart from them, and give entertainment to vain, empty, foolish imaginations. Thoughts of other things, greater and better than what this world can contain, will be continually arising in the mind, not to be laid aside by any solicitations of vanity. For he that is wise cannot but know and consider, that the spiritual things which it exerciseth its thoughts about have substance in them, are durable, profitable, always the same; that the advantage, peace, rest, riches and reward of the soul lieth in them; but other imaginations, which the foolish mind is apt to give entertainment to, are vain, empty, fruitless, and such as end in shame and trouble.

Again, the vanity of the mind, as an indulgence to foolish imaginations, ariseth from, or is animated and increased by, that gust and relish which it finds in earthly things, and enjoyments of them, whether lawful or unlawful. Hence on all occasions, yea, in holy duties, it will be ready to turn aside, and take a taste of them, and sometimes to take up with them; like a tippling traveler, who, though he be engaged in a journey on the most earnest occasion, yet he cannot but be bibbing here and there as he passes by, and it may be, at length, before he comes to his journey's end, lodgeth himself in a nasty ale house. When men are engaged in important duties, yet if they always carry about them a strong gust and relish of earthly things, they will ever and anon in their thoughts divert to them, either as to such real objects as they are accustomed to, or as to what present circumstances administer to corrupt affections, or as to what they fancy and create in their own minds. And sometimes, it may be, after they have made them a few shorter visits, they take up with them, and lose wholly the work they were engaged in. Nothing, as was said, will give relief herein, but the vigorous and constant exercise of our affections on heavenly things: for this will insensibly take off that gust and relish which the mind hath found in things present, earthly, and sensual, and make them as a sapless thing to the whole soul. They will so place the cross of Christ in particular on the heart, as that the world shall be crucified to it, losing all that brightness, beauty, and savor, which it made use of to solicit our minds to thoughts and desires about it.

Moreover, this frame of spirit alone will keep us on our watch against all those ways and means whereby the vanity of the mind is excited and maintained. Such are the wandering and roving of the outward senses. The senses, especially that of the eye, are ready to become purveyors to make provision for the vanity and lusts of the mind. Hence the Psalmist prays, Turn away mine eyes from beholding vanity. If the eyes rove after vain objects, the mind will ruminate upon them; and another affirms, that he had made a covenant with his eyes, to preserve them from fixing on such objects as might solicit lust or corrupt affections. And it were an useful labor, would this place admit of it, to discover the ready serviceableness of the outward senses and members of the body to sin and folly, if not watched against, Rom. vi. 13, 19. Of the same nature is the incessant working of the fancy and imagination, which of itself is evil continually, and all the day long. This is the food of a vain mind, and the vehicle or means of conveyance for all temptations from Satan and the world. Besides, sundry occasions of life and conversation are usually turned or abused to the same end, exciting and exercising of the vanity of the mind. Wherever our affections are fixed on spiritual things, our minds will constantly be under a warning or charge to keep diligent watch against all these things, whereby that vanity which it so abhorreth, which it is so burdened with, is maintained and excited. Nor without this prevalency in the mind, will ever a work of mortification be carried on in the soul. Col. iii. 2—5.

CHAPTER XXI.

Having declared wherein this duty of being spiritually minded doth consist, that which remains in compliance with the text, from whence the whole is educed, is to manifest how it is life and peace, which is affirmed by the apostle. This shall be done with all brevity, as having passed through that which was principally designed

And two things are we to inquire into.

(1.) What is meant by life and peace?

(2.) In what sense, to be spiritually minded is both of them?

(1.) That spiritual life whereof we are made partakers in this world, is three fold, or there are three gospel privileges, or graces so expressed.

(1.) There is the live of justification. Therein the just by faith do life, as freed from the condemnatory sentence of the law. So the 'righteousness of one comes on all that believe unto the justification of life.' Rom. v. 18. It gives to believers a right and title to life: for they that 'receive the abundance of grace, and the gift of righteousness, shall reign in life by one,

Christ Jesus.' v. 17. This is not the life here intended, for this life depends solely on the sovereign grace of God by Jesus Christ, and the imputation of his righteousness to us, unto pardon, right to life and salvation.

(2.) There is a life of sanctification. As life, in the foregoing sense, is opposed to death spiritual, as to the guilt of it, and the condemnatory sentence of death wherewith it was accompanied; so in this it is opposed to it, as to its internal power on, and efficacy in, the soul, to keep it under an impotency to all acts of spiritual life, yea, an enmity against them. This is that life wherewith we are quickened by Christ Jesus, when before we were dead in trespasses and sins, Eph. ii. 1, 5. Of this life the apostle treats directly in this place; for having, in the first four verses of the chapter, declared the life of justification, in the nature and causes of it; in the following he treats of death spiritual in sin, with the life of sanctification, whereby we are freed from it.

And to be spiritually minded in this life in a double sense.

(1.) In that it is the principal effect and fruit of that life. The life itself consists in the infusion and communication of a principle; that is, of faith and obedience to all the faculties and powers of our soul, enabling us to live to God. To be spiritually minded, which is a grace whereto many duties concur, and that not only as to the actings of all grace in them, but as to the degrees of their exercise, cannot be this life formally; but it is that wherein the power of this principle of life, in the first and chiefest place, puts forth itself. All actings of grace, all duties of obedience, internal and external, proceed from this spring and fountain. Nothing of that kind is acceptable to God, but what is influenced by it, and is an effect of it; but it principally puts forth its virtue and efficacy in rendering our minds spiritual, which, if it effect not, it works not at all; that is, we are utterly destitute of it. The next, and immediate work, of the principle of life in our sanctification, is to renew the mind, to make it spiritual, and thereon gradually carry it on to that degree which is here called being spiritually minded.

(2.) It is the proper adjunct and evidence of it. Would any one know whether he be spiritually alive unto God, with the life of sanctification and holiness; the communication of it to him being by an almighty act of creating power, (Eph. ii. 10,) it is not easily discernible, so as to help us to make a right judgment of it, from its essence or form; but where things are in themselves indiscernible, we may know them from their proper and inseparable adjuncts, which are therefore called by the names of the essence, or the form itself. Such is this being spiritually minded, with respect to the life of sanctification; it is an inseparable property and adjunct of it, whereby it infallibly evidenceth itself to them in whom it is. In these two respects it is the life of sanctification.

(3.) Life is taken for the comforts and refreshments of life; so speaks the apostle, 1 Thess. iii. 8. 'Now we live, if you stand fast in the Lord;' now our life will do us good; we have the comforts, the refreshments, and the joys of it. *Non est vivere, sed valere vita.* The comforts and satisfactions of life, are more life than life itself. It is life, that is, that which makes life to be so, bringing in that satisfaction those refreshments to it which make it pleasant and desirable. And I suppose this is that which is principally intended in the words of the apostle; it is life, a cheerful, joyous life; a life worth the living. In explication and confirmation whereof, it is added, that it is peace also.

Peace is twofold; (1.) general and absolute; that is, peace with God, through Jesus Christ, which is celebrated in the scripture, and which is the only original spring and fountain of all consolation to believers, that which virtually contains in it every thing that is good, useful, or desirable to them: but it is not here precisely intended. It is not so,

(1.) As to the immediate ground and cause of it, which is our justification, not our sanctification, Rom. v. 1. Being justified by faith, we have peace with God. So Christ alone is our peace, as he who hath made peace for us by the blood of the cross, Ephes. ii. 14, 15. Hereof our being spiritually minded is no way the cause or reason, only it is an evidence or pledge of it, as we shall see.

(2.) Not as to the formal nature of it. Peace with God, through the blood of Christ, is one thing, and peace in our minds, through a holy frame in them, is another. The former is communicated to us by an immediate act of the Holy Spirit dwelling in us. Rom. v. 5. The latter is an effect on our minds, begun and gradually carried on, by the duties we have before at large declared. The immediate actings of the Holy Spirit, in sealing us, witnessing to our adoption, and being an earnest of glory, are required to the former: our own sedulousness and diligence in duties, and the exercise of all grace, are required to the latter

(2.) Peace is taken for a peculiar fruit of the Spirit, consisting in a gracious quietness and composure of mind, in the midst of difficulties, temptations, troubles, and such other things as are apt to fill us with fears, despondencies, and disquietments. This is that which keeps the soul in its own power, free from transports by fears or passions, on all the abiding grounds of gospel consolation. For although this be a peculiar especial grace, yet it is that which is influenced and kept alive by the consideration of all the love of God in Christ, and all the fruits of it.

And whereas peace includes in the first notion of it, an inward freedom from oppositions and troubles, which those in whom it is are outwardly exposed to, there are two things from which we are secured by this peace, which is an effect of being spiritually minded.

The first is offences. There is nothing of whose danger we are more warned in the gospel than of offences. Wo to the world, saith our Saviour, because of offences. All ages, all times and seasons, are filled with them, and they prove pernicious and destructive to the souls of many. Such are the scandalous divisions that are among Christians; the endless differences of opinions, and diversity of practices in religion and the worship of God; the falls and sins of professors; the fearful ends of some of them; the reproaches that are cast on all that engage into any peculiar way of holiness and strictness of life, with other things of the like nature, whereby the souls of innumerable persons are disquieted, subverted, or infected, are to be reckoned to this head. Against any hurtful or noxious influence on our minds from these things, against disquietments, dejections of spirit, and disconsolations, are we secured by this peace. So the Psalmist assures us, Psal. cxix. 165. Great peace have they that love thy law, and nothing shall offend them. The law, or the word of God, is the only way of the revelation of God, and his will to us, and the only outward way and rule of our converse and communion with him. Wherefore, to love the law, is the principal part of our being heavenly minded, yea, virtually that which comprehends the whole: for to such as do so, nothing, none of the things before mentioned, nor any other of the like nature, shall be an offence, a stumbling block, or cause of falling into sin. And the reason is, because they have such an experience in themselves of the truth, power, efficacy, and holiness of the gospel, as that the miscarriages of men, under a profession of it, shall never be to them an occasion of falling, or being offended at Christ. And I look upon it as a sign of a very evil frame of heart, when men are concerned in the miscarriages of some that have made profession, whereby they are, it may be, damaged in their outward concerns, so as that they are surprised into reflections on that religion which they profess, professing the same themselves.

(2.) The second is afflictions, persecutions, and sufferings of all sorts. It is known by all, (it were well if it were not so well known,) what disquietments, dejections, and disconsolations, these things are apt to fill the minds of men with; what fears, troubles, sorrows, they reflect upon them. Against all these effects of them, this peace intended gives us security. It makes us preserve a peaceable, yea, a joyous life in our conflict with them. See Job xvi. 33.

Both these, as here joined together, life and peace, comprise a holy frame of heart and mind, wherein the souls of believers find rest, quietness, refreshment, and satisfaction in God, in the midst of temptations, afflictions, offences, and sufferings. It is the soul's composure of itself in God, in his love in Christ Jesus, so as not greatly to be put out of order, to be cast down with any thing that may befall it, but affords men cheerfulness and satisfaction in themselves, though they walk sometimes in the valley of the shadow of death. Such persons have that in them, abiding with them, as will give them life and peace under all occurrences.

(2.) Our next inquiry is, how this spiritual mindedness is life and peace, or what it contributes to them; how it produceth the frame of heart and mind so expressed; and this it doth several ways.

(1.) It is the only means on our part of retaining a sense of divine love. The love of God, in a gracious sense of it, as shed abroad in our hearts by the Holy Ghost, is the first and only foundation of all durable comforts; such as will support and refresh us under all oppositions and distresses; that is, of life and peace in our souls in any condition. This God communicates by an act of sovereign grace, for the most part without any preparation for it in ourselves. He creates the fruit of the lips, peace, peace. But although divine love be in itself unchangeable, and always the same, yet this sense of it may be lost, as it was with David, when he prayed that God would restore unto him the joys of his salvation, Ps. li. 12; and so many others have found it by woful experience. To insist upon all that is required on our parts, that we may retain a gracious refreshing sense of divine love, after it is once granted to us, belongs not to my present purpose. But this I say, there is not any thing wherein we are more concerned to be careful and diligent in, than what belongs to that end: for men who, by a mere act of sovereign grace, have tasted herein of the goodness of God, who have had the consolation and joys of it, to be negligent in the keeping and preserving it in their souls, is a provocation that they will at one time or other be sensible of. There is nothing doth more grieve the Holy Spirit, than to have his especial work, whereby he seals us unto the day of redemption, neglected or despised. And it argues a mighty prevalency of some corruption or temptation, that shall cause men willingly, and by their own sloth, to forfeit so inestimable a grace, mercy, and privilege. And it is that which there are but few of us who have not reason to bewail our folly in. Every intimation of divine love is an inestimable jewel, which, if safely treasured up in our hearts, adds to our spiritual riches, and being lost, will at one time or another affect us with sorrow.

And I am afraid that many of us are very negligent herein, to the great prejudice of our souls and spiritual state. Many such intimations are given us by the Holy Ghost through the word, which we take little notice of; either we know not the voice of Christ in them, or do not hearken to him in a due manner, or refuse a compliance with him, when we cannot but know he speaks to us. See Cant. v. 2, 3. Or if we receive any impressions of a gracious sense of divine love in them, we quickly lose them, not knowing how much the life of our souls is concerned therein; and what use of them we may have in our following temptations, trials, and duties.

Now, a great means of retaining a sense of the love of God, which is the only spring of life and peace to our souls, is this grace and duty of being spiritually minded. This is evident from the very nature of the duty: for,

(1.) It is the soul's preserving itself in a frame meet to receive and retain this sense of God's love. What other way can there be on our part, but that our minds, which are so to receive and retain it, are spiritual and heavenly, always prepared for that holy converse and communion with himself, which he is pleased to grant to us through Jesus Christ? And,

(2.) It will fix our thoughts and affections upon the grace and love of God, communicating such an inestimable mercy to us as is a sense of his love, which is the only means for the preservation of a relish of it in our hearts. He who is in this frame of mind, will remember, call over, and ruminate upon, all such gracious pledges of divine favor; as David is often remembering and calling over what he received in such places as in the land of the Hermonites, and at the hill Mizar, Psal. xlii. This is the great way whereby this treasure may be preserved.

(3.) A person so minded, and he alone, will have a due valuation of such intimations and pledges of divine love. Those who are full of other things, whose affections cleave to them, never esteem heavenly mercies and privileges as they ought. The full soul loatheth the honey comb. And God is well pleased, when an high valuation is put upon his kindness, as he is greatly provoked by the contrary frame; which, indeed, nothing but infinite patience could bear with. It is an high provocation of God, when men are regardless of, and unthankful for, outward temporal mercies; when they receive them and use them as if they were their own, that they were lords of them, at least, that they are due to them. Much more is he provoked with our regardlessness of the least of those mercies which are the peculiar purchase of the blood of his Son, and the effects of his eternal love and grace. He alone who is spiritually minded, values, prizes, and lays up these inestimable jewels in a due manner.

(4.) Such persons only know how to use and improve all communications of a sense of divine love. These things are not granted to us to lie by us, without any use of them; they are gracious provisions, wherewith we are furnished to enable us to all other duties, conflicts, and trials. On all occasions are they to be called over for our spiritual relief and encouragement.— Hereby are they safely retained: for in the due improvement of them they grow more bright in our minds every day, and are ready for use, in which posture they are safely preserved. But these things will yet be further manifest in the instances that ensue.

(2.) This frame of mind casts out all principles, and causes of trouble and disquietment, which are inconsistent with life and peace. There are in us, by nature, principles of contrariety and opposition to spiritual life and peace, with sundry things, whose abode and prevalency in us is inconsistent with them. I shall give only one or two instances hereof.

(1.) It will cast out all filthiness and superfluity of naughtiness from our minds. Without this we can receive no benefit by means of grace, nor perform any duty in a right manner. Jam. i. 27. This is that which stands in direct immediate opposition and contrariety to our being spiritually minded, so as they can have no consistency in the same person, and they expel one another like heat and cold. And where there is this filthiness and superfluity of naughtiness, there is neither life nor peace. Unclean lusts of the flesh, or of the spirit, working, tumultuating, acting themselves in the minds of men, will not suffer either the life of holiness to flourish in them, or any solid peace to abide with them. The soul is weakened by them as to all spiritual actings, and made like a troubled sea that cannot rest, whose waters cast up mire and dirt. Where they are absolutely predominant, there is an hell within, of darkness, confusion, and enmity against God, preparing men for an hell of punishment without to eternity: and according as they remain, or have any prevalency in us, so are spiritual life and peace impaired and obstructed by them. Now the very nature of this grace, and its universal exercise, is suited to the casting out of all the relics of this filthiness and superfluity of naughtiness. It brings a principle into the mind directly contrary to that from whence they proceed. All the actings of it which we have described, lie in direct tendency to the extirpation of these causes of filthiness, which ruin life and peace; nor will they by any other way be cast out. If the mind be not spiritual, it will be carnal; if it mind not things above, it will fix itself inordinately on things below.

(2.) That disorder which is by nature in the affections and passions of the mind, which is directly opposite to spiritual life and peace, is cast out or cured hereby. It is a blessed promise of the times of the New Testament, of the kingdom and rule of Christ, that, through the efficacy of gospel grace, the lion shall lie down with the lamb and the leopard with the kid, Isa. xi. 6. Persons of the most intemperate and outrageous passions, shall be made meek and lovely. Where this is not in some measure effected, according to the degrees of the prevalency of such passions in us, we have not been made partakers of evangelical grace. It were an easy task to demonstrate how the disorder of our affections and passions is destructive of spiritual life and peace. The contrariety that is in them, and the contradiction one of another, their violence, impetuousness, and restlessness; their readiness to receive and take in provocations on all occasions, and frequently on none at all but what imagination presents to them, are sufficient evidences hereof. Can we think that life and peace inhabit that soul, wherein anger, wrath, envy, excess in love to earthly things, dwell, and on all occasions exert themselves? there, where there is a continual tumult, fighting, and rebellion, as there is where the passions of the mind are not under the conduct of reason nor of grace?

The nature and principal effect of this spiritual mindedness, is to bring all the affections and passions of our minds into that holy order wherein they were created. This was that uprightness wherein God made us, namely, the whole blessed order of all the powers, faculties, and affections of our souls, in all their operations, in order to our living to God: and this is restored to us by this grace, this duty of being spiritually minded. And wherein it falls short of that perfection which we had originally, (for the remainders of that disorder which befel us by sin will still in part continue,) it is recompensed by the actings of that new principle of gospel grace which is exercised in it: for every act of our affections towards God, in the power of grace, exceeds, and is of another nature, above that we could do, or attain to, in the state of nature uncorrupted. Hereby are life and peace brought into our souls, and preserved in them.

(3.) It is that whereby our hearts and minds are taken off from the world, and all inordinate love thereto. Where this is in prevalent degree, there is neither life nor peace; and every excess in it both weakens spiritual life and disturbs, yea, destroys, all solid spiritual peace. I have occasionally spoken to it before, as also the way whereby our minding of the things that are above in a due manner, doth deliver and preserve our souls from the snares of it; and if we diligently examine ourselves, we shall find, that in our inordinate affections, and cleaving to these things, the principal causes why we thrive no more in the power of spiritual life, and whence we meet with so many disquietments and dejections of spirit, to the disturbance of our praise and rest in God, is from hence: for there is no grace which is not impaired by it in its nature, or not obstructed by it in its exercise. Wherefore, to be spiritually minded is life and peace, because it subdues and expels that inordinate love to present things, which is destructive of them both, and inconsistent with them.

(4.) It preserves the mind in a due and holy frame in the performance of all other duties. This also is indispensably required to the preservation of life and peace, especially to the improvement of them. They will not abide, much less thrive and flourish, in any persons who are negligent in holy duties, or do not perform them in a due manner. And there are four things which impede or hinder us from such an attendance to holy duties, as may be advantageous to our souls; against all which we have relief by being spiritually minded.

(1.) Distractions. (2.) Despondencies. (3.) Weariness. (4.) Unreadiness of grace for exercise.

(1.) Distraction of mind and thoughts, hath this evil effect, which many complain of, few take the right way of deliverance from. For this evil will not be cured by attendance to any particular directions, without a change of the whole frame of our minds. Nothing can give us relief herein, but a prevalent delight in being exercised about things spiritual and heavenly. For hence arise all our distractions; the want of fixing our minds on spiritual things with delight, makes them obnoxious to be diverted from them on all occasions, yea, to seek occasions for such diversions. It is this frame alone, namely, of spiritual mindedness, that will give us this delight: for thereby the soul is transformed to the likeness of spiritual things; so as that they are suited to it, and pleasant to our affections. The mind and the things themselves, are thereby so fitted to each other, that on every occasion they are ready for mutual embraces, and not easily drawn off by any cause or means of the distractions so complained of; yea, they will all be prevented hereby.

(2.) Despondencies in duties arise from the frequent incursions of the guilt of sin. The remembrance hereof frequently solicits the minds of persons in their first entrances to duty, unless they are under especial actings of grace, stirring them up to earnestness and fervency, in what they undertake. At other seasons it renders men lifeless and heartless, so as that they know not whether they had best pray or not, when duty and opportunity call them thereunto. To be spiritually minded, we have manifested in many instances, is the great preservative against these disheartening incursions of sin. It is the soul's watch and guard against them, whence ever they arise or proceed. No lust or corruption can be prevalent in a spiritual mind. And this is the principal cause of such incursions of sin, as affect the soul with a disheartening sense of guilt. No affections can abide in any sinful disorder, where the mind is so affected. This also gives sin an entrance to a distracting sense of guilt. But the sole cure hereof lies in this grace and duty. The like may be said of all other ways, means, and occasions of such incursions of sin.

(3.) Weariness in and of spiritual duties, abates their tendency to the improvement of life and peace in us. This evil ariseth from the same cause with that of distraction before mentioned. And it is ofttimes increased by the weakness and indispositions of the flesh, or of the outward man. Sometimes the spirit is willing, but, through the weakness of the flesh, it is disappointed. The principal cure hereof lies in that delight which spiritual mindedness gives to the soul in spiritual things. For where there is a constant delight in any thing, there will be no weariness; at least, not such as shall hinder any from cleaving firmly to the things wherein he doth. Whilst therefore we are exercised in a delight in spiritual things, weariness cannot prevalently assault the mind. And it is the only relief against that weariness which proceeds from the indispositions of the outward man: for, as it will preserve the mind from attending too much to their solicitations, crying, spare thyself, by filling and possessing the thoughts with other things; so it will offer an holy violence to the complaints of the flesh, silencing them with a sense of, and delight in, holy duties.

(4.) The unreadiness of grace for its due and proper exercise, is another thing which defeats us of the benefit of holy duties. The seasons of them are come; sense of duty carries men to an attendance to them, and the performance of them. But when they should enter upon them, those graces of faith, love, fear, and delight, wherein the soul and being of them do consist, are out of the way, unready for a due exercise; so as that men take up and satisfy themselves with the mere outward performance of them. The heart and mind have been taken up with other things; due preparation hath been wanting; men come to them with reeking thoughts of earthly occasions; and it is no easy matter in, or immediately out of, such a frame, to stir up grace to a due exercise. But herein lieth the very life of being spiritually minded. The nature of it consists in the keeping and preserving all grace in a readiness for its exercise as our occasions require. And this is an effectual way, whereby this grace comes to be life and peace. For they cannot be attained, they cannot be preserved, without such a constancy and spirituality in all holy duties, as we shall never arrive at, unless we are spiritually minded.

Lastly; this frame of mind brings the soul to, and keeps it at, its nearest approaches to heaven and blessedness, wherein lie the eternal springs of life and peace. According to the degrees of this grace in us, such are those of our approaches to God. Nearness to him will give us our initial conformity to him, by the renovation of his image in us, as our presence with him will give us perfection therein; for when we see him we shall be like unto him. God therefore alone, as he is in Christ, being the fountain of life and peace, by our drawing nigh to him, and by our likeness of him, will they thrive and flourish in our souls.

THE END.